THE STORE
COOKBOOK

THE STORE COOKBOOK

Recipes and Recollection from "The Store in Amagansett"

Bert Greene and Denis Vaughan

Henry Regnery Company · Chicago

Library of Congress Cataloging in Publication Data

Greene, Bert.
   The Store cookbook.

   1. Cookery, American. I.   Vaughan, Denis.
II.   Title.
TX715.G8117   641.5   74-6894
ISBN 0-8092-8885-0

Acknowledgments

The authors wish to extend their thanks to Phillip Schultz
for his tireless efforts and cooperation
in cataloging the material, typing the text, and last,
but by far not least, in testing the recipes.

Contents

Introduction

BERT GREENE

This is the kind of cookbook that began as cocktail small talk in somebody's conversation pit-cum-deck, overlooking somebody else's greensward, on an Indian summer afternoon.

If it had rained, there might never have been a "Store in Amagansett," nor a collection of recipes bearing its imprimatur. But the sky held still. And if imperfect memory serves, it was a rather pleasant way for some rather pleasant strangers to while away the dreaded void between dip and dinner.

Consider the usual covey of city refugees, spacing their martinis and comparing their compost heaps—and one turns tail at first sight. But this afternoon was rather special.

Five little Indian summer people met at a cocktail party.

What they had in common that afternoon may have only been an ability to listen for the heartbeat of the sea that punctuated the end of any conversation in those dear, dead days before beach traffic made hearing a lost art.

For one thing, they ate long and drank well. For another, they were all weekenders, single-minded with one preoccupation: to plan an escape from Manhattan for longer than the weekend.

Winter conversation in a summer resort becomes something strictly parochial.

"Wouldn't it be wonderful to stay here all year round?" someone would say as the inevitable Sunday night packup began.

"Wonderful. But doing what?"

"I don't know. But there must be something to do. . ."

Thoughts to mull over while thermostats are being turned down to fifty-five degrees; while locks are checked and trash cans are lashed together against the fancies of roaming gourmet, country dogs.

"Ever think of an antique shop?"

As engines refuse to turn over in February.

"Often, But we'd never sell anything. You'd take it all home.

Avid collectors make piss-poor entrepreneurs."

"Well. There must be something. . ."

Something.

Even after the return to the city, five little Indians continued to give out ideas.

"Bert, you know, you *really* should run a restaurant." The last, said loyally by one of my friends as the plates are passed, heaped impossibly high with cheese-drenched, bacon-spattered linguini Carbineri.

"But I don't want to run a restaurant. I'd rather have a shop."

"I know . . . a place that only sells dessert."

"Or a cheese store. You really can't get good cheese out here."

"Or a beer store."

"Or a . . ."

Or an amalgam of them all. A shop that would be a literal superabundance of all that our combined imaginations could conceive. Antiques and artifacts. Cookbooks and *cuillieures.* Rare prints and potholders. And a little cooking on the side.

"Like what?"

"Like anything Bert and Denis feel like cooking that day."

"Like your baked ham. Nobody ever made ham like that."

"And your Ziti salad."

"And . . . and . . . and . . . "

Listening to a litany of your own culinary delights can be a positive bore.

The ardor of the two Indian chefs is something less than enthusiastic.

"That—is what we'll be selling?"

"Damn right. What's wrong with selling all that?"

"It will take time."

Cooking is still thought of as a gentleman's leisure activity.

"Well. You won't have to cook *that* much. We'll fill in with some superior brand of canned goods."

A farm in Pennsylvania makes nut butters, and a Mexican in lower Manhattan packs honest-to-God enchiladas and tortillas that are better than those someone found in Tijuana, the last time they were looking in Tijuana. So inventories are made. Breathless appetites demand and we supply.

A garden of unearthly delights. Costly comestibles.

It sounded like lots of work to Bert, who had always thought work meant writing the kind of plays that inevitably lost money or laboring at some advertising agency to regain a little bit of the lost back again.

Perhaps the idea of a store seemed like escape to the rest of the tribe: one unsatisfied art director, needing something more than a new account to slake his creative urge, and one fashion illustrator, sitting out her latest divorce. It certainly had to promise something better for Denis, sometime theatrical director, than the series of nothing jobs at which he had been playing. It most definitely seemed like a chore to the ex-actress turned housewife. She did not like housekeeping much and she liked cooking even less, but it did seem exciting; and life had not been all that exciting for some time now anyway.

But, what to call it?

"The Amagansett Emporium. What else?"

"Or The Old Country Place? Or a combination of our five first names?"

Denis finally named it. "If we have to do this at all, let's call it The Store in Amagansett."

And for once, five little Indians, five disparate friends, agreed.

So it began. On a sunny July Fourth weekend, doors opened. Without money, without equipment (the kitchen was a sinkless cinder block tomb), produced by willing, calloused hands, it began. Our antique French bread rack was filled with Long Island's best, our marble butcher's table crammed with home-made cookies, and, stacked high, were the row upon row of gleaming cans: a tin paradise of exotic fruits and vegetables.

And, oh yes, there was a little food we had made, displayed in a second-hand deli-case (fragile as to working cold, but stylish in its presentation). Green leaves garlanded the white porcelain salad bowls. And salads there were: lobster in herbed mayonnaise and salad Niçoise . . . cooked Ziti jeweled with brilliants of green pepper and tomato, all but drowned in a sea of sour cream and dill.

The Store opened—and it became an instant success.

Instantly the salads disappeared and were replenished. In no time at all the thick glazed hams and standing roasts were hand-carved away, and frantic phone calls to New York butchers were put through to find more. Friends and relatives rallied and car-drops from Manhattan saw us through that first fantastic day.

Instantly the mousse and the cakes, the brownies and the breads all vanished, as if they were to assuage some enormous collective appetite. What remained at day's end were only the gleaming rows of elegantly tinned foods.

The Store in Amagansett became an institution. What had started as a kind of Indian summer whim became a fixed establishment. Through its ochre-colored screen door rung with Indian temple bells came the rich and the famous, seeking only the food. And the recipes, culled from memory and yellowed cookbooks, became part of a tradition.

The fame of the name grew year by year.

All the borrowed antiquities were carefully dusted and returned to their rightful owners. The tinned roast chickens gradually are going to charity bazaars; the canned soups and the bright colored vegetables go to poor-baskets Thanksgiving after Thanksgiving.

And the five little Indians? The friends and the partners— the bright eager-to-be city refugees? Most of them went too.

The art director left first. He bought the firm he worked for and now he runs it.

His ex-actress wife, who never liked peeling all those cucumbers in the first place, wrote a historical novel and is happy to have "The Store" a mere footnote in her own history.

The fashion illustrator stayed longer, but hard work (for it has never ceased to be that) and the lack of reward for all that labor eventually defeated her as well. She now runs a charming gift shop for others. (And has Sundays off all summer.)

Denis and Bert, ex-director and sometime playwright, remained. Two little Indians still at the range, battling for supremacy in the kitchen.

When it became apparent that a cookbook of all our assorted knowledge, our tips, and our expanding file of "Store" recipes would be a logical next step, we battled over it as well.

Until it became perfectly obvious—after several small wars—that the way to write a cookbook would be to share it. And so we have.

THE STORE

IN AMAGANSETT

COOK BOOK

The Broached Egg

Chapter One

DENIS VAUGHAN

Here lies a tale of cooks and cookbooks. Start with a handful of (you name the ingredient); a limitless fund of energy, summoned from God knows where; and a desire to do things right. As parents of a generation ago were wont to say, "There are only two ways to do things; the right way and the wrong, but there is only one way to do things right."

This cookbook could end on the next page with the following advice: keep a pot of water constantly at the boil. Be able to count with a beat, have a good nose and a good eye (for odor and color). And remember, never take out your hostilities on food. It needs love—not punishment—and it wants to look nice.

Bert Greene and I are writing this book in tandem, and since most of our lives have been spent in tandem—and at odds—we hope to catch the flavor of the battle-gastronome here. We will tell you an occasional anecdote about the people-beautiful and some receipts, hopefully brief and to the point.

Since we disagree about practically everything, we will likely infringe on each other's recipes, and amend certain points. It may make for a bit of confusion, but you always have the option of choice.

I have never been able to soft-cook an egg. I love them, but they are steadfastly indifferent to me and refuse to conform to what I think they should be. Even in restaurants, where they cannot know I am about, they stubbornly decline to have that firm, pliable white and delicate, golden center. I have encountered such an egg once or twice in my life (never of my own making) and treasure the memory. However distant the soft-cooked egg and I are, I have conquered and subdued the egg, one of my favorite edibles, in another guise: the fried egg sandwich.

Late at night, or in the hours of the morning called wee for the insomniac or the mild lush (a real one would laugh in your face, or worse, at the suggestion of food), there are few things more satisfying than a fried egg sandwich. Never mind the cholesterol—you can always eat fish tomorrow.

If you happen to have homemade bread about, count your-self among the blessed on earth. If not, Pepperidge Farm white will do—and barring that—well, you are in trouble, but if you follow this recipe, there is a lot that is salvageable.

FRIED EGG SANDWICH

Peel and roughly chop a scallion and/or small white onion. Place a dollop of butter in a hot skillet. (A dollop, to me, is a little less than the length of my forefinger.) Melt, then add the onion. Quickly toss till golden. Keeping your light high and your skillet hot, break an egg into the skillet. I am a resolute counter, so count slowly: one beat, two beat, etc. to thirty, then turn egg and onions with a spatula and allow to cook for the same amount of time on the other side. Have your two slices of bread ready on a plate and remove the egg from the skillet. It should look vaguely like a sautéed soft-shell crab. There are some who admire to have the bread lavished with mayonnaise, but this is optional, and I truly prefer to allow the pan butter to be the emollient. If this is used as a sobering-up process, a glass of ice cold milk allows one visions of nirvana. On the other hand, if one is four square, straight-up, and no sheets to the wind, an ice cold can or glass of beer can have a decidedly euphoric effect.

Then there is that admirable, but tiring, method of scram-bling the egg, the Brillat-Savarin, recommended by M. F. K. Fisher. If you are as queer for eggs as I am, this is an unbelievably delectable manner in which to serve them—and any self-respecting egg would give its life to be served in this stylish fashion. First off, the process takes one-half hour. If you are doing it for lunch on Sunday, give yourself this much time and arrange to have Bloody Marys and guests around you. It should only be done for guests—or someone you love very much—never for yourself or casual acquaintances, for if boredom and wan-dering away to the hi-fi, TV, or toilet set in—all is lost. You are locked into a space in time of thirty minutes at your skillet, but the results are worth it.

BRILLAT-SAVARIN

Heat an enameled skillet and melt enough butter to comfortably cover the bottom. Allow 2 eggs per person. Off the heat, break the eggs into a bowl. Do not disturb them, but pour them into the skillet and on their heels follow with a puddle of heavy cream. You will know what a puddle is from the look of it in relation to the eggs. I add a tiny bit of salt and pepper and then begin: stir gently on low heat and the eggs will slowly begin to intermingle, yolks and whites amalgamating into what will be a most sensual and voluptuous gastronomic experience. The consistency of velvet should be arrived at. I think possibly my dream meal might be these eggs served with a small portion of Beluga caviar on a fresh green leaf, or a grilled slice of lean bacon, a fresh, flaky croissant, ice-cold champagne, steaming hot coffee—and I'm yours for life.

As long as I am on the subject of eggs, the hard-boiled, which I can cook but can seldom peel, is an admirable accompaniment to curry, spinach, or gazpacho. A fresh egg cooked by any method and flavored with salt and freshly ground pepper can be a thing of great delicacy, but eggs unadorned can soon jade the tastebuds in reverse with their blandness: the appetite sighs for new zest and tang. I am going to toss a few suggestions in your direction for glamorizing the lovely egg.

Eggs Ninon is a recipe I have used many times and love. It is named for the legendary Ninon d'Lenclos, courtesan extraordinaire, who took her last lover in 1705 and died a year later at the age of 90. The strain of such activity and not this delectable recipe dispatched her, I am sure.

EGGS NINON

Use 6-8 fresh asparagus tips. Employ a count of forty after plunging them into fiercely boiling salted water. Dump out and douse instantly with cold water. Drain and arrange on 2 toast rounds. Poach 2 eggs. To poach an egg, use a large skillet with enough liquid—water with a few drops of vinegar added, broth, stock, gravy, sauce, wine, even butter can poach—to cover the eggs. For this recipe, however, use the French method, water with a few drops of vinegar. It brings the whites to firmness faster and reduces the froth that always rises from eggs as they are poached. The liquid should be simmering gently throughout the poaching. Create two tiny whirlpools in the liquid by stirring with a circular motion. Break the eggs into two small glasses and then drop them into the whirlpools. This step reduces the tendency of the egg to disperse itself.

An egg is poached when the yolk has been delicately covered by the white and is a firm, but pliant, oval. Remove from the skillet with a slotted spoon, drain on absorbent cloth or paper towel and place the eggs on the asparagus tips and cover with Hollandaise sauce (page 5). Serves two. It does not guarantee you all the fringe fun of a d'Lenclos, but it is a most elegant and attractive thing to eat.

If you're as lazy as I am, the shirred egg is the easiest in the world to prepare. It can withstand mild mistreatment such as opening the oven door to watch its progress—even jostling does not disturb it. American shirred eggs is a recipe I have used to success when I have had several people unexpectedly for lunch or breakfast. This recipe is based on a single portion. You are not likely to do it for yourself so multiply the quantities accordingly.

AMERICAN SHIRRED EGGS

Preheat oven to 375°. Take a baking dish, allowing the amount of people to determine the size, throw in a dollop of butter (you remember the dollop) per person, a slice of pre-cooked ham, halved, or 2 slices of bacon per person. Put the dish in the oven till the butter melts, then slide in 1 raw egg per person, arrange ham or bacon around the edge, and bake six to ten minutes. If you remember to look at the dish after six minutes, you will be able to pretty much gauge your cooking time. If you don't remember, you are in trouble. If it comes out fine, decorate with a bit of freshly chopped parsley and accompany with a piping hot, meltingly buttered English muffin, good strong coffee, and you have a hearty little meal.

Eggs Benedict, a classic egg dish, is said to have been created in the kitchen of the Vatican around 1760 for Pope Benedict XIII. You can make any day a holiday with this simple, lovely dish.

EGGS BENEDICT

Toast 1 English muffin, lightly sauté 2 slices of ham in sweet butter, and poach 2 eggs. Then place ham on muffin, egg on ham, and cover with Hollandaise sauce (recipe follows). If you are feeling affluent, a truffle is wanted to adorn; if not, a slice of pitted black olive will do. It depends on the circumstance and the company. Serves 2.

HOLLANDAISE SAUCE

1½ sticks sweet butter, at room temperature
2 egg yolks
pinch of salt
3 tablespoons lemon juice
1 tablespoon cold water
dash of cayenne pepper
½ packet of G. Washington golden bouillon powder
  (optional)
white pepper to taste

I.   Cut 1 stick of butter into small bits in a heavy enamel saucepan. With a wire whisk, beat the egg yolks into the butter for about a minute. Put over low heat and continue to whisk until they become sticky and slightly thick. Remove from heat. Add salt, lemon juice, water, a dash of cayenne, and bouillon powder—if you have a preference for a heightened flavor.

II.   Return to the heat and continue to whisk over low heat until the mixture forms a smooth cream. This will take about 2 minutes or so. Immediately beat in the extra half stick of butter, and whisk until the sauce sets. Add white pepper to taste.

III. If sauce becomes too thick, add 1 tablespoon of butter, slightly softened. If the heat is too high and the sauce curdles, quickly add cold water by tablespoons and you can usually beat it smooth. Before you serve the sauce, taste it. If it is too tart, add a little melted butter. If too bland, add more white pepper and salt. Makes 1½ cups. Serves 4-6 people.

George Villiers, the first Duke of Buckingham and a favorite of King James I of England, was as legendary in his way as was Ninon d'Lenclos. He brought his own brio to the egg in this recipe created for him on a visit to Italy in 1630. He transplanted it to England and it is a constant delight anywhere.

EGGS BUCKINGHAM

Take 8 slices of bacon; cook till very crisp, and drain on a paper towel. Sauté 4 chicken livers in bacon fat and drain. Pour all but the thinnest film of fat from the pan and place what remains on very low heat. Mix 5 eggs with 4 teaspoons of tomato paste lightly thinned with water, salt, and pepper, and lightly scramble. For each serving place some egg on a toast triangle with a chicken liver and 2 slices of bacon. Hopefully it will do for you what it did for George. If not, you have still got a nicely succulent morsel to savor. Serves 4.

If you have any smoked salmon lying about, or even if you don't, go out and buy some and try this delicious dish for yourself. You are sure to like it, and then spring it on your friends. It makes for a fast and simple light meal, accompanied by a salad.

DANISH SHIRRED EGGS

Spread ¾ cup of cooked salmon, which you will flake slightly, in a buttered baking dish. Make a dent in the middle of the salmon to hold the egg. Break 1 egg into the dent and dust with pepper. If you use smoked salmon, do not add salt; if you use fresh, or canned, and you may, then add a pinch of salt. Pour 1 tablespoon of heavy cream over the egg and bake in a preheated 350° oven 10-12 minutes. Makes 1 portion.

If you have been drinking Scotch and it has gone and you have a little club soda left over, do not throw it out—scramble some eggs with it. Here is a recipe I came across several years ago.

EGGS SCRAMBLED WITH CLUB SODA

Break 5 eggs into a bowl; add a dash of salt and pepper and 1 cup of club soda. Beat together and softly scramble in a lightly buttered pan. Constantly scrape the cooked portions from the pan's bottom and sides as the eggs cook. A rubber spatula is pretty effective for this kind of operation. Serve over 4 slices of thin toast for 4. These are the airiest scrambled eggs you will ever eat.

From the British buffet breakfast—a marvelous tradition—comes this dependable standby.

SCOTCH WOODCOCK

Hard-boil 4 eggs and then chop them coarsely. Melt 4 tablespoons of butter in a saucepan. When melted, reserve 2 tablespoons. Add 1½ cups heavy cream and the chopped eggs to the butter in the saucepan. Simmer until the eggs are warmed. Chop 4 anchovy fillets and blend with the remaining 2 tablespoons of butter. Spread this on 4 slices of toast. Pour the egg mixture over the toast, and dust the tops of each serving with a dash of cayenne pepper. Serves 4.

Let us stay a moment longer in the Highlands and savor a recipe that is a succulent, mouth-watering variation on the egg. It can be served as a first course or as an impressive breakfast dish. Do everything beforehand and avoid smoky kitchens.

SCOTCH EGG

Shell 4 hard-cooked eggs. Beat 1 uncooked egg lightly and dip the hard-cooked eggs in it, then roll them in 1 tablespoon of flour. Roll out ½-pound of the best-grade sausage meat you can find with a well-greased rolling pin, or between 2 sheets of waxed paper. If you tend to be erratic, as I am, stick with the waxed paper—an almost fail-proof method. Envelop each egg with a blanket of sausage. Secure the closing as best you can and then roll in more flour to which you have added some cracked peppercorns and a dash of salt. For this recipe you need a deep pan, a wire basket, and a quantity of oil or vegetable shortening for deep frying. Bring the liquid to a boil; lower the covered eggs into it, and fry until the outsides have formed crusts and are crisp. It is a tasty treat that serves 4.

Try an egg for dessert. This dish was created in 1750 for Frederick II of Prussia.

APPLES FREDERICK

Beat 2 whole eggs with 2 egg yolks. Add 2 tablespoons of flour, 1 cup of milk, 1 tablespoon of sugar, a dash of salt, and nutmeg, and continue beating. When the mixture is smooth and creamy, set it aside to rest for about 10 minutes. Do your nails, shave, or watch your favorite "soap." Then heat 2 tablespoons of butter in a skillet. Add 6 green apples that have been peeled, cored, and sliced. When they become translucent, add the egg mixture. Lift the edges of the mess with a spatula and tilt the pan to allow all the liquid to reach the hot metal. When the top begins to set, turn the omelet—a tricky business that will set you to cursing—and cook 2 — 3 more minutes, not more than a fairly rapid count of 120. Slide it then onto a warm plate and sprinkle with brown sugar mixed with cinnamon, to taste. Glaze under the broiler for 1 — 2 minutes to soften the sugar, and you have a dish guaranteed to melt the heart of the coldest man alive.

Before I leave the egg and you alone, if you live alone and are as fond of the egg as I, you will make a small investment in what is called a poacher. We now know it is not, but so what? This is a very small pan with a shallow cup and cover. To use it, put a slight amount of water in the pan, an equally slight amount of butter in the cup, and swirl it about until all is laved. Break in an egg, cover, and allow it a count of sixty. If you lived with me you would be counting all the time. It is not a poached egg, but it is as close to soft-boiled as I've been able to come. Served on or with crisp hot toast with steaming tea or coffee, it is very good—and leaves you liking the world a bit more than you might have before.

I will now leave the egg. And you I leave in the hands of Bert Greene, formidable and capable.

Everything from the Garden

Chapter Two

BERT GREENE

It has occurred to me that this collection of recipes might reasonably be subtitled "Any and Everything from The Garden," since that is the mainstay of the cuisine at The Store in Amagansett.

During the three short months from Decoration Day through Labor Day, the white-washed kitchen at The Store produces ten or twelve different vegetable dishes daily. (They are usually, but not exclusively, cold.) The rest of our year is spent in a diligent quest for fresh and yet even fresher ways to produce variations on that theme, a search for variety that has literally taken us through some of the world's great kitchens, and some of the world's great gardens as well.

A great, dead chef pronounced that the ultimate test of any cookery was the immediacy of the ingredients involved. Satisfied am I with that thought. Great cooking certainly takes place where the pickings are good.

The almost end of Long Island in August is a landscape of tall corn ringed by potato and cauliflower as far as the avarice in the developer's eye allows.

Our summer airs are perhaps more redolent of suntan oil and high octane than they were once, but still, beneath the skin, there is always the slightly bittersweet scent of tomatoes ripening on the vine, mixed with a rich, fresh soil smell that one can never disassociate from fresh-dug new potatoes.

Cooking with what one finds in a South Fork vegetable patch is a mandate one simply cannot ignore. Even our bees and gypsy moths keep well fed. The very sight of some young and tender green zucchini dawn-picked and still slightly fuzzy to the touch sets my mouth to water and my hand reflexively reaching for the onion basket.

I like to cut fresh squash into fine, slim coins, and then toss them raw with whole cherry tomatoes and slivers of purpley shallots. Seasoned with a scant handful of fresh, scissored basil and just lightly drenched in a vinaigrette that is tart and lemony,

11

they are a wonderful way to start a lunch, particularly when the next course is merely a platter of leftover cold meats and cheese.

Nothing in the kitchen elicits more response from me than a cornucopia of eggplant, onions, and pepper tossed together in the bottom of a brown paper bag; thoughts of ratatouille unsettle any other culinary concoction I might have had on the fire.

I admit the passion: I love the vegetable extravagantly. Have even thought of naming dogs and children for them. And I have a high and moral regard for those recipes that savor a vegetable's individuality. Perhaps that explains my predilection for hardly cooking them at all. Even the dreaded plastic-domed stepchild, long removed from the hot house and super-marketed beyond belief, can be skillfully resuscitated if enough loving care and treatment is expelled.

Dressing: the correct one for any individual viand plays an enormous part in the design of a salad, and I will tell the secrets of mine presently. But first, let me go through my garden variety of stored treasures, just looking at random.

The first two salads (or hors d'oeuvres, as you will) are French in origin, and their secret was cajoled from a sharp-eyed *charcuterie ménager* who ran a shop practically facing the blue, blue Mediterranean. Partly American persistence (we kept coming back for more day after day) and partly pure Provençal good nature produced these two gifts from the kitchen garden.

SALADE CARROTS VICHY

2 bunches of carrots, scraped and tops removed
2 shallots and 1 small red onion, finely minced
1 cup mayonnaise
½ cup sour cream
½ cup Chinese Duck sauce
½ cup roughly chopped ham
1 packet beef bouillon powder
salt and fresh ground pepper to taste
rind of 1 lemon, finely shredded
fresh chopped parsley

I.   Shred the carrots until they are thin, thin shoestrings. To the raw carrots add the minced onion, shallot mixture, and the chopped ham.

II.　　Combine the sour cream and Duck sauce and add to the mayonnaise.

III.　　Add the bouillon powder and season with salt and pepper. Whisk the sauce until it is light and runny enough to be poured over the carrots. If too thick, thin with ½ cup of milk and a tablespoon of wine vinegar.

IV.　　Garnish with shredded lemon peel and chopped parsley. Serve cold. Makes about enough for 4–6 persons.

COLD CAULIFLOWER NIVERNAIS

3–4 heads of cauliflower
2½ cups mayonnaise
½ cup sour cream
1 whole jar Dijon mustard
salt and fresh ground pepper to taste
fresh chopped parsley

I.　　Break cauliflower into small flowerets. Cook in boiling water for 7 minutes *only*. Do not overcook. Blanch in in cold water. Drain. The vegetable will be crisp and crunchy.

II.　　Combine sour cream, mayonnaise, and mustard. Whisk till light and creamy. If too thick, thin with a little light cream.

III.　　Pour dressing over cauliflower till all the pieces are well coated. Season with salt and a grating of fresh black pepper.

IV.　　Garnish with chopped parsley. Serve chilled. Makes enough to serve about 10–12 persons.

One's very own cookbook is an intensely personal business, akin only to a diary in the degree of honesty the writer permits posterity. Hence, a few truths:

I have always hated the concept that great cooks flaw their recipes so that *the* secret ingredient that makes the difference between a dish and a "plat" must always be surmised or ap-

proximated when the second stringer takes a turn at its reproduction. No great chef ever withheld a pinch of this or a peck of
that — if he had any real greatness in him.

Some do admit to the prejudices of cupboard secrets.
And why not? Think, before you castigate, of the years Escoffier
must have spent tracking down the right way to stew an artichoke inside a rack of lamb for something as subtle as carré d'
agneau Beaucaire. For want of a zest of lemon, who knows?
Immortality might well have been lost.

There are certain recipes I husband to my breast, miserlike,
covering my reluctance to share with the rationalization that it
is each cook for himself in this world. But in the end when I
am inevitably asked, "How do you make this? It's *so* delicious,"
the aggregate pleasure of culinary pride and super-ego overcomes
niggardliness, and I acquiesce in the extreme and tell in fact so
many things about a dish that my questioner goes abroad dazed
with marginalia.

Let me recite a few at random.

On dressings: most cold vegetable salads take a bath in
either vinaigrette sauce or a light mayonnaise before they are
served. A few require the subtle combination of both, or the
addition of some creamy emollient like sour cream or yoghurt
to pacify the ratio.

A good vinaigrette is at its best freshly made and composed
of prime ingredients. When wine vinegar is demanded, never
stint. Unless you have at hand a batch of your own acetous
fermentation as we often do at The Store, fresh-import *Dessaux
Fils* is an absolutely unbeatable condiment.

There are purists who never permit a trace of garlic or
shallot in a vinaigrette; they take their oil and vinegar neat.
And there are others who abjure the mere suggestion of vinegar;
they are lemon freaks all the way. Needless to say, the lemon
juice must always be fresh. There is no such thing as a reconstituted lemon, merely reconstituted taste buds.

I have said that my rule is to use all prime ingredients,
but my exception to that rule is oil. It will seem idiosyncratic to
some, but I prefer a lightened oil for cooking to the best unadulterated oils you can buy. So I mix my own.

In France and Italy the olive and walnut harvest produces
a fresh tasting oil that I simply cannot find at home. Perhaps
the sea change affects its flavor, but whatever the cause, I am

decidedly put off by its pungency and never use it straight. I usually dilute pure Plagniol oil from Marseille with Wesson or Hain polyunsaturated oil. I divide the mixture into one-third imported to two-thirds domestic.

When it comes to salty talk, I insist on the rough stuff because it is saltier. A good kosher salt is fairly inexpensive, and a box lasts a long time; French sea salt costs a bit more, but it has a marvelous briny taste. I recommend that you look into a salt grinder as a salad adjunct because it is a healthy investment and will last your lifetime.

Never use a commercially ground pepper in a salad. Black Malabar peppercorns, freshly ground, do more for a lacking vinaigrette than any single ingredient I know.

For a hearty dressing that brings out the mint taste of freshly cooked vegetables, we concocted the following vinaigrette sauce. Liberal in its dependence on both onion cousins, its bite is derived from both vinegar and lemon and a mite of bouillon powder as well. *Vive le difference,* I say!

THE STORE SAUCE VINAIGRETTE I

1 lemon
1 packet G. Washington brown bouillon powder
1 teaspoon Dijon mustard
1 small clove garlic, mashed
1 large shallot, crushed
2½ — 3 cups salad oil
⅓ cup good wine vinegar
dash of coarse salt
2 grinds fresh pepper

I. Squeeze the juice of a lemon into a large mixing bowl. Add the bouillon powder.

II. Stir in the mustard, mashed garlic, and the crushed shallot.

III. Whisk this mixture slightly and pour in the oil, slowly at first, until you have beaten in about 2½ cups and the dressing becomes the consistency of very thick cream.

IV.   Add wine vinegar to thin slightly, plus 2 grinds of your
pepper shaker and a dash of coarse salt. If too vinegary,
add more oil. Makes about 1 quart. Recipe may be
cut in half.

I know that I told you it is best fresh, but if you are a
thrifty cook and have a quantity of dressing left over, it may
be stored in your refrigerator in a covered jar or a well-corked
bottle for a day or so. But never keep this sauce too long
because the onion flavor tarnishes. Do let it stand at room
temperature and shake well before reusing if the oil has
solidified.

A slightly simpler vinaigrette is one that I always make
for a green salad. It has an equal affinity for freshly cooked
vegetables and can be put together in ten minutes flat.

SAUCE VINAIGRETTE II

large pinch of kosher salt
1 small clove garlic
½ teaspoon Dijon mustard
juice of ½ lemon
1 teaspoon wine vinegar
⅓-½ cup good oil
good grind of fresh pepper

I.   Place a large pinch of kosher salt in a small bowl. Press
the garlic over the bowl, and mash the two together
with the back of a spoon. Add the mustard and lemon
juice. Whisk well with a wire whip. Add vinegar, oil,
and pepper. Adjust to taste and serve. Makes enough
for 2 days or 1 large salad.

The green snap bean loves fresh herbs as much as any
vegetable I know. And the following recipe marries them off
indestructibly. Since fresh herbs are not always readily available,
may I suggest a few tips for reviving the taste of dried herbs.

If you have grown your own basil (either in a garden or
on a window sill) remove the leaves in the fall. Loosely pack
them in a large glass jar and cover them completely with salad
oil. If the jar is well sealed, the oil becomes richly basil-

flavored, greenish in hue, and the leaves retain their true taste for an unconscionably long while.

I always store commercially dried basil leaves in a slightly larger container than the one they come packaged in. I pour an ounce or so of Galliano liqueur over them until they are well steeped and let them stand covered and unrefrigerated until I have a use for them. The liqueur gives them a pungent bouquet and flavor, and a drop or two of the liquid is usually enough to conjure the loss of innocence in a cooked dish. If a recipe calls for freshly chopped basil, I cut the amount required in half, spoon my dampened herbs on a like amount of fresh parsley, and chop them together to make up the difference. I promise you will be amazed at how fresh your vegetable salad will taste after that addition.

COLD STRING BEANS IN VINAIGRETTE

1½ pounds fresh string beans
1 red onion, finely minced
1 clove garlic, mashed
¼ cup chopped fresh basil or 4 tablespoons dried basil
½ teaspoon fresh thyme or ¼ teaspoon dried thyme
¼ cup finely-chopped fresh parsley
1 cup vinaigrette dressing
1 teaspoon coarse salt
several grinds of fresh pepper

I. String and trim beans. Cut into bite-size pieces.

II. Fill a three-quart saucepan with water and bring to a boil. Throw in beans, let water come back to the boil, and count to 20. Drain immediately. Do not let beans overcook. They will be a beautiful bright green color and very crisp. Douse in cold running water to retard cooking. Drain when beans are no longer warm.

III. Mix the onion, garlic, and herbs together. Toss in vinaigrette dressing. Salt and pepper to taste. Pour over beans and toss. Serve chilled. Beans taste best when they marinate for about an hour before serving. Serves 6.

If you are not using fresh herbs, place a quantity of the dried herbs over the fresh parsley and chop them together. It will revive the taste of the dry ingredients.

TOMATOES NIÇOISE

2 pounds small ripe tomatoes, quartered
6 shallots, finely chopped
½ cup roughly chopped fresh basil
       or ¼ cup dried basil chopped in with ¼ cup fresh
       parsley
dash of salt
good grind of fresh pepper
¼ cup roughly chopped parsley
1 can of anchovies, drained
1 clove garlic, mashed
1 cup vinaigrette dressing
1 cup pitted black olives

I.   Mix the following in a bowl: tomatoes, shallots, salt, pepper, and half the herbs.

II.   Mash the anchovies and garlic. Add to the vinaigrette dressing. Pour over tomatoes.

III.   Slice the olives in half. Add to the tomatoes and lightly toss. Garnish with the remaining herbs or with parsley. Serve well chilled. Serves 8.

SALADE BERNOISE

1 cup slivered white cabbage, green cabbage, or celery
1 cup Swiss cheese cut into small sticks
¼ teaspoon caraway seeds
⅓ cup vinaigrette dressing
crisp lettuce leaves
2 hard-cooked eggs, quartered

I.   Mix the vegetables and cheese together.

II.   Mash the caraway seeds into the vinaigrette dressing and pour over the vegetable and cheese mixture.

III.   Let the salad macerate for a couple of hours and serve on crisp lettuce leaves with quartered hard-cooked eggs or crumbled egg yolk. Serves 2 — 4.

POTATO SALADE PROVENÇALE

2 pounds boiling potatoes (8-10 medium-sized)
4 tablespoons dry white wine or vermouth
½ cup vinaigrette dressing
3 tablespoons chopped mixed herbs or parsley
2 tablespoons minced shallots
½ cup pitted black olives, halved
freshly chopped parsley

I.   Scrub the potatoes. Drop in boiling salted water and boil until just barely tender. Drain and douse with cold water to retard cooking. Drain again.

II.   When cool enough to handle, peel and cut into slices about ⅛ inch thick. Place in a large mixing bowl. Pour the wine or vermouth over the warm potatoes. Toss gently and then set aside for a few minutes until the liquid has all been absorbed.

III.   Pour the vinaigrette sauce over the potatoes. Add the herbs, shallots, ½ of the olives and toss gently to blend. Season to taste.

IV.   Garnish with the remaining olives and chopped parsley. May be served warm or chilled. Serves 8.

EGGPLANT ORIENTAL

3 medium-sized eggplants
2 large yellow onions, finely sliced
2 cloves garlic
⅓ cup salad oil or a mixture of ⅔ salad oil and ⅓ olive oil
1 teaspoon coarse salt
2 grinds fresh pepper
dash of Dessaux wine vinegar
¼ cup roughly chopped fresh dill

I.   Preheat oven to 450°. Cut eggplant into ½-inch slices.

II.   Place a layer of eggplant on a generously buttered cookie sheet or in the bottom of a shallow baking pan.

Cover with a layer of onions. (If necessary, continue the process on another cookie sheet or in another pan). Press mashed garlic on top. Drizzle oil over the whole thing. Salt and pepper well.

III.   Bake in the oven for about 45 minutes or until the eggplant looks roasted.

IV.   Let cool slightly. Place in a wooden bowl and coarsely chop. Add the vinegar and correct seasoning if necessary.

V.   Place in a serving bowl. Garnish lavishly with fresh dill. Chill thoroughly before serving. Serves 8-10.

DANISH CUCUMBERS IN SOUR CREAM

4 large cucumbers
1 tablespoon salt (for preparation of cucumbers) plus 2 teaspoons salt (for sour cream mixture)
2 cups sour cream
¼ cup cider vinegar
1½ teaspoons sugar
1 teaspoon celery seed
4 tablespoons chopped chives
½ cup roughly chopped fresh dill
several grinds of fresh pepper

I.   Peel the cucumbers and slice very thin. Arrange in a shallow bowl. Salt and place a heavy plate over all to press out the moisture. Cover and refrigerate for several hours.

II.   Meanwhile, combine the following in a sauce: sour cream, vinegar, salt (2 teaspoons only), sugar, celery seed, and chives.

III.   Drain the cucumbers and layer in the bottom of a serving bowl. Spoon some of the sauce over the cucumbers to barely cover. Sprinkle with a handful of dill and continue to layer until the cucumbers and sauce are used up (ending up with a covering of the sour cream mixture). Garnish lavishly with pepper and the remaining dill. Serve chilled. Serves 8-10.

Another word or two about herbs: there is no excuse in this wide world for ever using dried dill or dill seeds in a recipe such as cucumber in sour cream—it doesn't taste as good for one thing and the eminently fresh ingredient is available year-round, for another. You may have to march round a few vegetable counters demanding, but it will appear, I promise you.

Fresh parsley is something else that you can depend on winter and summer. And it keeps for weeks in your refrigerator if you wash it well and store it slightly damp in a covered glass jar.

Fresh tarragon is sometimes available (at Tiffany prices in Tiffany-type vegetable marts). We buy it during the winter because commercially dried tarragon is a disaster, tasty as a bit of moldy hay. Cooking revives the memory of the taste somewhat, but it is an absolute zero in a salad. I suggest you try the same trick with dried tarragon as with basil, but in this case, cover it with Pernod. And be generous with your pouring arm. While the results are not exactly fresh, the effect is certainly worth the extravagance.

Dried thyme is always stronger than fresh thyme, and a speck goes a long, long way. The addition of a dram of vodka produces a slightly redolent herbal essence that acts as a palliative to most dishes that shied away from the herb before.

Nothing, I am sorry to say, works wonders with chervil or savory, but dried fennel seeds do capture the intrinsic taste of their freshest forebears when sprinkled on celery as it is being chopped.

In a time of such conspicuous consumption, a bouquet of fresh herbs in January no longer presents an insurmountable problem. Most florist and gourmet shops sell pre-seeded herb planters that are meant to thrive indoors so you can keep a garden in your kitchen all through the year.

A lovely Eastern recipe I like depends on fresh mint as its essential ingredient. I have tried using dried mint leaves soaked in an essence of white creme de menthe with a drop or two of white vinegar to cut the sweetness. The results were nourishing but hardly inspired. I infinitely prefer to grow the real thing.

PERSIAN BEETS IN YOGHURT

2 cans small baby beets
1 large shallot
1 cup plain yoghurt
¼ cup heavy cream
1 packet G. Washington brown bouillon powder
½ cup of fresh mint leaves

I. Drain the beets and place in a bowl. Mince the shallots and sprinkle them over the beets.

II. Thin the yoghurt with the cream and add the bouillon powder. Beat until it is the texture of very heavy cream.

III. Pour this mixture over the beets and decorate with the mint leaves. Serve chilled. Serves 4-6.

NEWLY MINTED PEAS

2 packages frozen peas
½ cup mayonnaise (preferably homemade)
½ cup sour cream
a dash of salt
several grinds of fresh pepper
¼ teaspoon Dijon mustard
½ cup roughly chopped fresh mint
pimiento strips for garnish

I. Throw the peas into a saucepan full of boiling water for approximately 4 minutes. Immediately douse in ice cold water to retard cooking. Drain when peas are no longer warm.

II. Combine the mayonnaise, sour cream, salt, pepper, and Dijon mustard. Whisk till creamy. Pour over the peas. Combine with the mint and gently toss until all the peas are well coated with dressing.

III. Garnish with whole mint leaves and pimiento strips. Serve chilled. Serves 8.

Courtesy of a Norwegian traveler is the appetizing classic cold roasted peppers in mustard sauce. The receipt is simple in the extreme. To blanch, as required in the recipe, you simply throw a peck of peppers into boiling water for a minute, and then slosh them under a cold running faucet to retard the cooking action before you drain them. This dish is a sumptuous visual experience when the red peppers are in bloom, I can tell you.

COLD NORWEGIAN ROASTED PEPPERS

5 green peppers
5 red peppers
⅓ cup olive oil
3 tablespoons Dessaux wine vinegar
coarse salt to taste
fresh pepper to taste
big pinch of dry mustard
¼ cup chopped parsley

I.   Preheat oven to 350°. In a saucepan of boiling water, blanch the whole peppers for one minute. Drain.

II.   Place them in a shallow baking dish lined with aluminum foil and roast for ½ hour. Remove from the oven and slightly cool.

III.   Peel the peppers, removing the fibrous portions and seeds. Cut into strips and place in a serving dish.

IV.   Combine the oil, vinegar, salt, pepper, and mustard in a bowl and whisk into a sauce. Pour over the peppers.

V.   Refrigerate. Serve well chilled. This dish should be prepared several hours in advance to allow time for complete marination. Before serving, decorate with finely chopped parsley. Serves 8-10.

The French have a saying, *"Les grands sentiments font les bons gueuletons,"* which roughly translates as, "Noble feelings make good meals."

In the kitchen, my own stirrings of nobility are always awakened when I realize a skill hitherto neglected. I came into mayonnaise-making late in life because I erroneously thought that Hellman was God. I misspent my childhood on mayonnaise sandwiches composed entirely of white bread and a thick layer of lubricosity. I was also never taught, as most French baby-cooks are, that it is easy as anything to concoct the golden mean yourself.

There are no curves thrown to the incipient mayonnaise maker in the following recipe, if he or she comprehends one basic precept: *everything must be at room temperature.* Everything! Eggs, oil, lemons, vinegar, *and* whisk. The bowl might even be a bit warmer.

In my emotional lexicon, making mayonnaise at home ranks high with the most satisfying kitchen experiences I have ever had. I love making it plain, green, curried, and tomatoed, as well.

I no longer eat it on white bread. But why not, when the product is so infinitely superior, I cannot tell you.

HOMEMADE MAYONNAISE

3 egg yolks
1 tablespoon Dessaux wine vinegar
juice of 1 lemon
½ teaspoon salt
pinch of white pepper
1 packet G. Washington Brown bouillon powder
½ teaspoon Dijon mustard
2-2½ cups salad oil or a mixture of ⅔ salad oil and ⅓ olive oil
shake of Tabasco sauce
2 tablespoons boiling water

I.   All ingredients must be at room temperature. If eggs have not been left out of the refrigerator for at least 4 hours, let them stand in a pan of very hot tap water for 10 minutes before you begin. Warm a 3-quart pottery bowl in hot water and dry it before you break the egg yolks into it. With a large wire whisk, beat the yolks until they are thick and sticky. Add the vinegar, lemon juice, salt, pepper, bouillon powder, and mustard. Beat a minute longer.

II.   The egg yolks are now ready to receive the oil—and this is the only trick to producing mayonnaise: one must pour it in, droplet by droplet, and *not stop* beating until the sauce has thickened appreciably. A speed of 2 strokes per second is desirable. Add drops of oil until ⅓ to ½ cup of the oil has been incorporated. (Then the mayonnaise base will have thickened into a very heavy cream-like mixture, and the crisis is over. The arm may be rested for a moment!)

III.   Continue beating the oil in by 2 tablespoon droplets, blending thoroughly after each addition. When sauce becomes too thick and stiff, thin it with a few drops of lemon juice or vinegar. Then go back to beating in the oil. Yields 2-2¾ cups.

IV.   When the sauce is of a thick, rich, heavy consistency, add the Tabasco sauce and the boiling water, which is an anti-curdling device. Season the mayonnaise to taste. You may want more lemon juice, white pepper, mustard, or Tabasco. Keep refrigerated.

GREEN MAYONNAISE

Add 3 to 5 tablespoons of minced dill, parsley, tarragon, and chives to 1½ cups of mayonnaise. Chill thoroughly. Serve over chilled fish that has been poached in court bouillon.

CURRY MAYONNAISE

Add 2 tablespoons of curry powder, 1 teaspoon turmeric, and 1 tablespoon of wine vinegar to 1½ cups of mayonnaise. Blend. Add 2 tablespoons capers. Serve over shrimp cooked in court bouillon. Garnish with chives and serve chilled.

TOMATO MAYONNAISE

Blend 2 fresh tomatoes that have been seeded and cooked in a saucepan with a bouillon cube, 2 basil leaves, and ½ teaspoon of sugar until very soft and fresh tomato paste is made. Add 2 tablespoons of sour cream to the blended sauce and combine with 1 cup of mayonnaise. Serve over cold, cooked asparagus, or cauliflower that has been marinated in vinaigrette dressing and then drained.

Cold Ziti Salad is probably The Store's single best-seller. Tons of it are prepared and consumed every summer. I used to love it myself, but success ended the affair. A rough cut bracelet of pickles, peppers, tomatoes, and Italian onion laved with velvety sour-creamed mayonnaise, it is the crowning glory of all our luncheon salads. It is to grown-ups what red hots once were to kids.

THE STORE COLD ZITI SALAD WITH TOMATO AND PEPPERS

1½ tablespoons salt
2 tablespoons oil
1 box Ziti
¼ cup milk
1 red onion
2 tomatoes
6 sweet pickles
2 small green peppers (seeded)
1 large shallot
½ cup sour cream
1½ cups mayonnaise
2 packets G. Washington brown bouillon powder
3 grinds fresh pepper
dash Dessaux wine vinegar
1 tablespoon pickle juice
handful of roughly chopped fresh dill

I.   Bring a 4-quart saucepan of water to a boil. Add 1 tablespoon salt and 2 tablespoons oil (to keep the Ziti from sticking together); then add the Ziti. Boil for 10 minutes or until just tender, stirring occasionally. Drain. Rinse thoroughly in cold water. Drain again.

II.   Place the cooked Ziti in a bowl. Add enough milk (about ¼ cup) to thoroughly moisten the Ziti and toss.

III.   Chop the onion, tomatoes, pickles, and peppers into ¼-inch cubes. Reserve a large tablespoon of each for garnish. Mince the shallot.

IV.   Beat the sour cream and mayonnaise together with a whisk until creamy, and add the bouillon powder, ½ tablespoon salt, and the pepper. (Thin with milk if necessary). Pour over the Ziti. Add the shallots, tomatoes, pickles, green peppers, vinegar, and pickle juice. Mix well.

V.   Garnish with the reserved vegetables. Cut fresh dill over all. Serve chilled. Serves 8-10.

Speaking of childhood, the passion for the taste of fresh corn never abates, I think. But tooth and gum rebel a bit as one grows on. This Mexican corn salad provides a winning compromise to bind the generation gap.

COLD CORN ENSALADA MEXICANA

8 ears of corn or 2 packages frozen corn kernels
1 large green pepper
1 Italian red onion
2 shallots
4 scallions
1 tomato, seeded with inside pulp removed
¼ cup sour cream
½ cup strong beef bouillon
2-3 tablespoons good wine vinegar
½ cup good mayonnaise (home-made is predictably best)
salt
fresh ground pepper to taste
¼ cup pimiento strips

I.   Throw corn ears into a large saucepan of boiling salted water for three or four minutes. Plunge into cold water to retard cooking. When cool, slice the kernels free with a sharp knife. If you are lazy or a busier-than-most cook, throw frozen corn kernels into the same saucepan of boiling water for *two* minutes only. Immediately put them into a colander and wash with icy water until the corn is well chilled. Drain and set aside.

II.   Chop a green pepper until it is finely minced. Chop a red onion until it is finely minced as well. Slice shallots and the white portion of the scallions until they are slivered well. (Save the green stems of the scallions.) Set all of this aside.

III.   Cut a tomato in half horizontally. Gently squeeze to remove seeds, juice, and pulpy insides. Then roughly cut up the flesh into ½-inch cubes.

IV.   Mix the sour cream and bouillon, and beat with a whisk till fluffy. Add vinegar to thin slightly, and finally, add the mayonnaise. Again, whisk till light.

V.   Toss the cream mixture over the cold corn, adding the minced ingredients and mixing well. Salt and pepper to taste. Toss in the tomato cubes, and decorate the salad with strips of pimiento and the finely scissored tops of scallions. Serve well chilled. This salad is a treat with cold fried chicken, or warm baked ham. Serves 8-10.

Something Roman is something noble when the almost-raw potato forms an entente with pungent Fontina cheese and smoky Italian prosciutto as follows:

POTATO AND CHEESE MAYONNAISE ALLA ROMANA

6 medium-sized potatoes
juice of 1 lemon
½ pound Swiss or Fontina cheese
1½ cup homemade mayonnaise
1 teaspoon coarse salt
good grind of fresh pepper
¼ teaspoon cayenne pepper
1 teaspoon finely chopped chives
½ pound prosciutto, roughly chopped
2 raw mushroom caps, peeled
2 tablespoons roughly chopped parsley

I.   Peel the potatoes under cold running water. Slice them wafer thin or put through the blade of an electric grater. Put in cold water with the juice of one lemon to keep them white.

II.   Clean and dry the blade of the grater. Force cheese through machine or cut the cheese into matchlike strips.

III.   Put potato strips in rapidly boiling water and simmer for 2 minutes. Potatoes should be crisp.

IV.   Combine mayonnaise, salt, peppers, and chives with the drained potatoes and cheese. Toss the mixture gently, but thoroughly.

V.   Decorate with prosciutto and sliced, uncooked mushrooms and chopped parsley. Chill and serve. Serves 8-10.

This salad is a marvelous first course or an unusual buffet dish. But it literally cries out for a chilled white wine as an accompaniment. Try Italian Valpolicella or a French Pouilly Fuissé. And make sure that they are well iced.

I have three excuses for making ratatouille. And three recipes to justify them.

The first is human need. I am simply starving for the warm, oily smell of Nice where I first truly found my love for the dish. There had been ratatouilles in my life before, but they were pallid encounters all but swallowed in youthful exegetics about never cooking so many vegetables together and vitamin loss. Truth to tell, I could not know what all the shouting was about, because the ratatouilles I had tasted were remarkably unstimulating.

My first real taste of the true Provencale creation swept all arguments from the tongue. I obviously had not liked it in the past because it had not been well made. This recipe tells you how:

RATATOUILLE I

½ *pound eggplant, sliced*
½ *pound zucchini, sliced*
1 teaspoon salt
4 tablespoons olive oil
1½ cups yellow onions, sliced fine
2 green peppers, seeded and cut in strips
1 pound tomatoes, cut into ½-inch wedges
2 cloves garlic, mashed
freshly ground pepper and more salt to taste
¼ cup freshly chopped parsley

I.   Place the eggplant and the zucchini in a large mixing bowl and toss with 1 teaspoon salt. Let stand for about half an hour. Drain. Dry each slice in a paper towel. Sauté the eggplant and then the zucchini in 4 tablespoons hot oil for about 1 minute on each side to lightly brown. Do a few at a time. When completed, remove and set aside.

II.   In the same skillet, cook the onions and peppers slowly for about 10 minutes, or until tender but not browned. Use more oil if necessary. Add the tomatoes and garlic, season with salt and pepper, cover, and cook over low heat for 5 minutes. Uncover, raise the heat, and boil for several minutes until the juice has been absorbed.

III.   Place a third of the tomato mixture in the bottom of a fireproof casserole and sprinkle 1 tablespoon parsley over it. Arrange half of the eggplant and zucchini on top and continue to layer, finishing with tomatoes and parsley.

IV.   Cover the casserole and simmer over low heat for 10 minutes. Uncover, correct seasoning and raise heat slightly. Cook for about 15 minutes, basting, until all juices have been absorbed. Serve hot or cold, garnished with chopped parsley. Serves 6-8.

The second excuse is because it is so easy. I learned this recipe from the redoubtable M.F.K. Fisher, who probably knows more, cares most, and writes better about food than any in her peer group. And that is a goodly number! Mary Frances' version is probably Franco-Spanish; she has written so much good stuff on the subject that I have forgotten the derivation of this particular exercise. I know that I have eaten one like it in Spain. It sits on the stove all day long, and the entire house is perfumed in marvelous good airs. The moment of partaking is an unequivocal joy.

RATATOUILLE II

1 cup yellow onions, finely sliced
½ pound eggplant, sliced ⅜ inch thick

½ pound zucchini, sliced ⅜ inch thick
2 cloves garlic
2 teaspoons hot crushed peppers
2 green peppers, seeded and cut in strips
1 pound small ripe tomatoes, quartered
1 cup white onions, finely sliced
coarse salt and fresh pepper
¼ cup good oil
¼ cup chopped fresh parsley

I. Preheat oven to 250°. Place a layer of yellow onions in the bottom of a large buttered earthenware pot. Follow this with a layer of eggplant and then a layer of zucchini. Mash the garlic and sprinkle it and the hot peppers over the zucchini. Continue layering with green pepper strips, then tomatoes and white onions. Sprinkle a generous amount of salt and pepper over this. Continue the process until all vegetables are used. Drizzle the oil over the whole. Cover.

II. Bake in a 250° oven for 6 to 7 hours or until the vegetables have cooked together. Cool and coarsely chop.

III. Garnish with parsley. Serve hot or cold. Serves 6-8.

The third excuse is mine own. Searching to find a good, earthy first course when the second would be a roast of lamb, I seized upon this Italian peasant version replete with sausages. I wanted a hot dish that could be made in fifteen minutes flat, and this one fills the bill exactly. You will also not spill your martini one slosh if you slice up the vegetables in advance.

RATATOUILLE III (NIÇOISE)

2 pounds Italian sweet sausage, sliced
½ stick sweet butter
⅓ cup oil
2 cloves garlic, mashed
1 large yellow onion, sliced
5 large shallots, chopped
½ pound string beans, sliced lengthwise
2 green peppers, seeded and cut in strips

salt and freshly ground pepper
5 ripe tomatoes, seeded and roughly cut
½ teaspoon sugar
1 packet G. Washington brown bouillon powder
4 zucchini, finely sliced
dash of dried hot peppers
chopped parsley and/or freshly grated Fontina cheese

I.   Rub a large skillet with oil. Heat until it is very hot. Add the sausage and sauté quickly. Remove sausage and drain on paper towels.

II.   Add butter and oil to skillet, and sauté the garlic, onion and shallots until transparent and golden. Add sliced string beans and pepper strips. Season with salt and pepper and stir-fry.

III.   Add tomato pieces. Correct the seasoning with a sprinkling of sugar and bouillon powder. Cook over moderately high heat for about 8-10 minutes, until tomatoes soften. Replace sausages and stir into the vegetables. Add zucchini and hot peppers and toss well for about 6-7 minutes longer. Serve immediately. Serves 6-8. This is delicious garnished with chopped parsley and/ or freshly grated Fontina cheese.

Some Birds I've Handled

Chapter Three

DENIS VAUGHAN

Have you ever thought of going berserk in the kitchens of the rich? Well, I have!

I once knew a secretary who doubled as a switchboard operator and whose goal in life was to go as she lived—at the post, slumped over the keys, having first announced the name of her firm. I sometimes wonder if she has achieved her goal. To be slumped over the burners with a sauté pan is not my vision of a grand exit, but it may come to that.

Some of the Queens of Love and Beauty we do for, the ladies with the unfocused eyes and Long Island Lockjaw—a seemingly permanent affliction in which the tongue is forced to do battle with firmly clenched teeth—are extremely well versed in the art of shattering one's cool.

"Vite, vite toute de suite," she cried to no one in particular, but if you know your ladies, you know damned well they are shrilling it at you. Standing dead center in the bewilderingly well-equipped stainless steel kitchen where none of the help-in-residence can cook, you turn off and go to work.

These poor hostesses, who are in constant competition with each other, remain in a state of twenty-four hour panic because they do not know how to do anything—or are too indolent to even try. One then focuses on the middle distance and steps to the stove and prepares Chicken Supremes, a delectable and subtle dish that sounds extravagant, but is, in truth, simple enough for a child to make.

CHICKEN SUPREMES

4 supremes (boned breasts from two fryers)
½ teaspoon lemon juice
¼ teaspoon salt
big pinch white pepper
4 tablespoons butter

SAUCE
¼ *cup white or brown stock or canned beef bouillon*
¼ *cup port, Madeira, or dry white vermouth*
1 *cup whipping cream*
salt and fresh pepper to taste
lemon juice as needed
2 *tablespoons fresh minced parsley*

I.   Preheat oven to 400°. Rub the supremes with drops of lemon juice and sprinkle lightly with salt and pepper. Heat the butter in a fireproof casserole until it is foaming. Quickly roll the supremes in the butter, lay buttered waxed paper over them, and place in hot oven. After 6 minutes, press the top of the supremes with your finger. If still soft, return to oven for a moment longer. When the meat is springy to the touch, it is done. Remove the supremes to a warm platter and cover.

II.   To make the sauce, pour the stock or bouillon and wine into the casserole with the cooking butter and boil down quickly over high heat until liquid is syrupy. Stir in the cream and boil down again over high heat until the cream has thickened slightly. Off heat, taste carefully for seasoning, and add drops of lemon juice to taste. Pour the sauce over the supremes, sprinkle with parsley, and serve at once. Serves 4.

There is the other kind of hostess who knows exactly what she wants, but puts one through the perils of hell before the menu is resolved. One such is Mrs. Nathan Halpern, wife to the leader of Theatre National Television. She invariably knows what she wants and what her menu will be, but inevitably one must go through a recital of what can be provided. I may indeed reel off fifteen succulent items that I can provide for her— and my senses are reeling. "And what else?" is the next question. I mutter, stutter, and fumble a bit because there is nothing else to do—when she finally says, "Why don't we have that delicious Chicken Tarragon with the wonderful sauce?" Naturally, I mutter mentally, since that is what she has been having for the last three years.

"Not too lemony, and only breasts, firm, but not too firm, and plump and juicy. And will they be good?" she continues.

How the hell would I know since I'm not the chicken—or the chicken catcher? I mumble something about personally selecting every breast and seeing to it that it is split perfectly in half, hang up the phone, and once again go to work.

CHICKEN TARRAGON HALPERN

3½ pound chicken, cut in pieces
1 clove garlic, sliced
2 lemons
1 packet G. Washington golden bouillon powder
salt and fresh pepper
6 shallots, minced
2 sticks sweet butter
¾ cup dry white wine or vermouth
tarragon leaves
2 medium-sized onions, chopped
1 small green pepper, seeded and cut into strips
4 slices of thick bacon (which has been blanched in boiling water
*   for 5 minutes, drained, and cut into ½-inch strips)*
2 tomatoes, seeded and roughly cut
12 mushroom caps
18 small white onions, peeled
1 teaspoon sugar
2 tablespoons flour
½ cup strong broth
1 egg yolk
¼ cup heavy cream
dash of cognac
tarragon leaves or chopped parsley
6 cups hot rice

I. Preheat oven to 350°. Rub the chicken pieces with garlic and lemon rind. Place in a baking pan and sprinkle with bouillon powder, salt, pepper, shallots, and the juice of 2 lemons. Dot with 5 tablespoons butter. Bake for 30 minutes, basting with ½ cup wine and pan juices every 10 minutes.

II. Add another ½ stick of butter and tarragon and turn

the pieces over. Bake an additional 30 minutes, continuing to baste every 10 minutes.

III.   Place under the broiler to brown (for about 5 minutes) and keep warm while you prepare the vegetables.

IV.   Sauté the onions and peppers in ½ stick butter. When golden, scrape into a dish in which you will serve the chicken.

V.   Add 1 tablespoon of butter to the same pan. Sauté the bacon strips until crisp. Drain on paper towels.

VI.   In the same pan, sauté the tomatoes until slightly cooked. Add to the onion mixture in the dish. Again using the same pan, sauté the mushrooms, adding butter if you need it, until they are golden. Drain well.

VII.   With a sharp knife, cut a small cross in the root end of each small white onion and sauté them in the same pan until they become golden brown. When browned, pour ¼ cup vermouth or wine over them and sprinkle with sugar. Cook the onions over a high flame until all liquid is absorbed.

VIII.   Arrange the chicken pieces on the bed of vegetables. Garnish with bacon bits, mushrooms, and small white onions. Keep warm.

IX.   Pour the strained chicken juices into a pan and whisk 2 tablespoons of flour into it. Add the broth to thin, and whisk until very smooth. Bring to a boil and remove from the heat.

X.   Beat the egg yolk into the heavy cream and slowly add to the juices. Return to the heat and simmer until it thickens slightly. Do not boil. Season with salt, pepper, and cognac. Pour over the chicken and vegetables and return to the oven to warm through. Garnish with tarragon leaves or chopped parsley. Serve over rice. Serves 6.

After an exhausting day in the little shop around the corner, known as The Store in Amagansett, I am sometimes idiotic—

or greedy—enough to set up a date with the six-week señoritas who inhabit this particular spit of land. They are—to a Ms.— invariably late. If I still smoked, I would smoke. I could have a drink, but that would make me snappish, so I settle for an iced coffee and brood about why I am in this business. Suddenly the front doorbell tinkles, signaling *her* arrival—tense, jittery, in immaculate white tennis dress (did she really just come from the courts?), and black glasses so large they envelop half her face. She makes her way across the floor to my side. She can be anywhere from 25 to 60, and she is giving a cocktail party next week or next month or next Friday—two days away.

"And what can you do darling? And can you get me help? And will they be good?"

I know as well as God made little tennis balls that this is the last time I am going to see this baby until some time next year. But I launch as brightly as possible into my monologue.

"Now, darling," she plunges forward, "it must be all finger food!"

That is a loathsome appellation given to hors d'oeuvres; but so be it. Finger food means no plates and no mess—and severely good help. It always works out badly because what started out to be a gathering of thirty mushrooms to eighty or a hundred, and one is rarely apprised of this.

I have now run down a list of perhaps twenty-five things madame can have for her friends, and my throat is parched and I have poignant thoughts about going home and having that drink I denied myself.

I take a deep breath, and as quietly as possible, murmur, "Well, how about chicken bits or perhaps chicken on a stick?"

As I describe them, she shrieks with delight, claps her hands, dashes out into her chic little sports car, and whirls away while visions of daggers swirl through my head. And they will in yours, too, directed at me, if you try the following little buggers.

CHICKEN BITS

For twelve people: use one large chicken, weighing about 5 pounds. Have a butcher debone it; otherwise, you will run mad. When you get it home, cut it into very small pieces no larger than the size of your thumb. A scissors is easiest for this task. In a brown paper bag, place 1½ cups flour, salt and pepper

to taste, a dash of cayenne pepper, and shake up the little
mothers until they are well coated. In an iron skillet, melt ¼-
pound butter. Please use butter—do not fool around with
margarine or oils; there is no comparison. Sauté the chicken
pieces gently until they are golden brown. This may take hours,
but your friends will fall to the floor in delight when you serve
them at cocktail time. When they are finished, drain them on
paper towels and set aside. You may warm them up quickly in
a pre-heated 300° oven for 10 minutes before serving.

CHICKEN ON A STICK

For this cocktail dish use the smallest chicken legs you
can find, allowing 2 to 3 per person. Carefully make an incision
in the skin from the middle of the leg to the bottom and equally
carefully loosen the skin and slide it up to the fleshy part of the
leg. Skewer with a toothpick. Then follow the recipe for Chicken
Bits.

You are giving a small dinner, and you don't want to spend
your life in the kitchen? What is easy and can be done ahead?
And what can you do for me that will not be too expensive or
cause me a nervous breakdown? Questions asked by everyone
from Gwen Verdon to the little lady from Chicago whose
husband is retired and who has two mansions in East Hampton
with a swimming pool half the size of the Atlantic. Well, I
think, Coq au Vin; I can knock that off in a minute.

"Oh, but everyone has that!" she cries, and you feel pretty
much the same way.

That poor chicken, I think, how maligned. Then with the
slight genius of the improvisationalist, my mind rushes to the
French. And with an elaborate bow in their direction, here is a
recipe with which you can't go wrong unless you are a booby.
You can do it as far in advance as the day before.

CHICKEN PARISIENNE

1 chicken, weighing 4 pounds
chicken stock or water
1 carrot, scraped and sliced
2 ribs celery, broken in half

1 onion stuck with two cloves
12 peppercorns
2 large ripe tomatoes
7 tablespoons butter
3 tablespoons finely chopped onions
½ bay leaf
2 sprigs fresh thyme or ½ teaspoon dried
salt and freshly ground black pepper to taste
½ cup flour
¾ cup heavy cream
Tabasco sauce
½ pound broad noodles
3 tablespoons chopped chives
1 egg yolk
¾ cup grated Swiss cheese

I.   Preheat oven to 350°. Place chicken in a large pot, add stock or water to cover and bring to a boil. Add carrot, celery, onion stuck with cloves, peppercorns, and simmer until tender or about 45 minutes.

II.   Meanwhile, prepare the tomato sauce: spear the stem end of the tomatoes, one at a time, with a two-pronged fork. Dip into boiling water for about 10 seconds. Remove and pull away the peel with a paring knife. Pare away stem end. Chop coarsely. Melt 3 tablespoons butter in a saucepan, and add the chopped onion. Cook until wilted and add the tomatoes, ½ bay leaf, thyme, and salt and pepper. Simmer for 5 minutes. Discard the thyme if it is fresh, along with the bay leaf. Set aside.

III. Remove the chicken when done and continue boiling the broth until it is reduced to about 2 cups. Strain and reserve. When the chicken is cool enough to handle, remove and discard the skin and bones. Pull or cut the meat into strips.

IV.   Melt 2 tablespoons butter in a saucepan and add the flour. When blended, add the reserved chicken broth, stirring vigorously with a wire whisk. When smooth, simmer over low heat, stirring occasionally, for about 30 minutes. This is called a velouté.

V.   In a skillet, melt 1 tablespoon butter and add the strips of chicken. Sprinkle with salt and pepper. Blend ½ cup of cream with 1 cup velouté. Add a touch of Tabasco and stir into the chicken. Remove from heat.

VI.   Cook the noodles in boiling, salted water until just tender. Drain and rinse in cold water. Drain again. Heat the remaining butter and toss the noodles in it just long enough to warm them.

VII.   Generously butter a baking dish and add a layer of noodles and a layer of tomato sauce. Sprinkle with chives and spread the chicken in cream sauce over all.

VIII.   Blend the remaining velouté with the remaining ¼ cup cream and the egg yolk. Heat, but do not boil. Spread this over the chicken and sprinkle with cheese. Bake 30 to 45 minutes or until golden brown. Serves 4-6.

An even simpler and more direct approach to the poor little bird is to go to a chicken farm. Not many of them abound anymore, but out here in the Hamptons, there is one very reputable institution: Iacono Farms. If you go in person, I would suggest that you do not look the little creature in the eye, lest it break your heart knowing that in several hours time you will be plunging a knife into that trusting little breast. If you can overlook all this, here are two recipes that will delight you and your guests.

ROAST CHICKEN STUFFED WITH HERBS

4-pound roasting chicken
½ lemon
salt and freshly ground black pepper
1 small peeled onion
1 sprig of fresh thyme or ½ teaspoon dried thyme
1 bay leaf
1 sprig of tarragon
1 sprig of parsley
½ cup melted butter

I.   Preheat oven to 350°. Rub the inside of the chicken with half a lemon and sprinkle with salt and pepper.

Add a small onion to the cavity with the herbs. Truss and place the chicken in a roasting pan.

II.   Pour the melted butter over the chicken (add a drop or two of vermouth, if you wish) and roast in the oven for about 1 hour, 15 minutes, or until done, basting every 15 minutes. The chicken is done when the leg moves back and forth freely and the juices run yellow.

ROAST CHICKEN STUFFED WITH VEGETABLES

1 large clove garlic
2 small roasting chickens
2 medium-sized potatoes
1 large white onion
2 medium-sized carrots
1 medium-sized zucchini
8 tablespoons butter
1 packet G. Washington golden bouillon powder
¼ cup chopped parsley
salt and freshly ground black pepper
4 strips of thick bacon
½ cup dry white wine or vermouth
1 teaspoon flour (approximately)
½ cup heavy cream
1 egg yolk
chopped parsley for garnish

I.   Preheat oven to 375°. Peel the garlic and make a slash in one end. Rub both chickens very well with the slashed end.

II.   Clean and peel the potatoes, onion, and carrots and chop into small cubes. Chop the zucchini, unpeeled.

III.   In an enameled skillet, melt 4 tablespoons butter and add the bouillon powder. Add the vegetables and cook over low heat for 10 minutes, stirring occasionally. Remove from the heat and stir in the chopped parsley. Season with salt and pepper.

IV.   Fill each cavity with the stuffing and truss securely. Dot each chicken with a tablespoon of butter, cover each with 2 strips of raw bacon, and pour ¼ cup wine or vermouth over each.

V.   Bake in the oven for about 1 hour or until done, basting often, about every 10 minutes. Remove from the oven, transfer the chicken to an ovenproof serving platter, and return the chicken to a low oven to keep warm.

VI.   Pour the roasting juices into a small skillet over low heat, add 2 tablespoons butter, and when it melts, vigorously beat in the flour to make a roux. Add the cream and cook for a moment. Mix a tablespoon of sauce into the beaten yolk, then add this to the hot mixture. If the sauce becomes too thick, add a little water.

VII.   Remove the trussing cords from the chickens and pour the sauce over both birds. Sprinkle with parsley. If you are a skilled carver, carve the chickens at the table and scoop out the vegetable stuffing with a long-handled spoon. If you prefer, cut each chicken in half with a sharp shears or knife and serve a half to each person. Elegant and delicious either way. Serves 4-6.

This recipe has a fondness for leftovers. If there is no zucchini, use string beans cooked or raw. Mushrooms and peas make a nice variation. If you have leftover cooked rice, substitute it for the potatoes and you still dine extravagantly well.

My dear, dead mother who came from Ireland, which is about as far from the Mason-Dixon line as you can get, evolved a way with fried chicken that had Southerners beating at her door. As a dutiful son at her knee, along with my prayers I learned the art of this time-consuming but rewarding manner of dispatching the fowl.

FRIED CHICKEN

1 whole chicken
1½ sticks butter
1 cup flour
salt and pepper

Preheat oven to 300°. Cut up one chicken: separate wings from breasts; separate legs from thighs, and split the breasts in half. Melt butter in a large skillet, taking care not to burn. Dredge chicken in a brown paper bag filled with flour, salt, and pepper. Sauté the chicken until golden brown. Remove chicken from pan and drain on paper towels. Place chicken in a baking dish and put it into the oven for about ½ hour. Reduce heat to 200° and cook for 1 more hour.

"I'm having a teeny-tiny dinner for eight," cooed the once and fabled Princess Lee Radziwill. "What can you do for me? Right?"

I should never have become a shopkeeper, because the phone goes dead in my ear and my throat becomes acutely paralyzed. I always wish to hell that Mr. Bell had given up the idea in the first place.

"Right?" the voice comes bright and Bryn Mawrishly through the instrument.

Clearing my throat ostentatiously in order to give myself time to think, "What can I give this broad that will be new, exciting, and inexpensive? Peanut butter sandwiches with sardines? Right?" No, wrong. She ran down her list of guests and the only one missing was the Duchess of Windsor. As I was still rattling around in my head what to give the lady, she said, "And dessert, too. Right?"

A sullen "Yes, do you have anything in mind " came from me.

"Oh that divine blueberry pie, or is it cake, that you make, right?"

"We make both."

"Right."

We establish that she would admire the pie. So much for that. Will she pick up or shall I deliver? No, she and the lady Caroline will come fetch. The heiress to the Kennedy fortune is a rather big girl for her years, and she also speaks through firmly clenched teeth.

"What kind of store is this?" she asked grandly.

"A barber shop," I replied with the straightest face I could summon. No response.

"And is that cash register old?" she said, referring to our antique that is capable only of ringing up "No sale," and "Coats, suits, and dresses."

"Not so old as you, my dear," was my less than salty comeback. The princess smiled. And here is what she had for dinner:

CHICKEN LOUISETTE

2 chickens, 2½ pounds each, cut up for frying
6-7 tablespoons butter
1 small onion, thinly sliced
salt and freshly ground black pepper
¼ pound mushrooms, thinly sliced
1 package G. Washington golden bouillon powder
3 tablespoons flour
½ cup dry white wine
1 cup chicken stock
¼ pound cooked ham, chopped
4 slices white bread, crusts trimmed
chopped parsley

I. Place the chickens in a Dutch oven and brown slowly in 4 tablespoons butter. Put 1 onion on top of chickens, season with salt and pepper, cover and cook slowly for 30 to 40 minutes or until tender. Remove the chickens. Add more butter to the pan and sauté the mushrooms until lightly browned, about 5 minutes.

II. Off the fire, blend in the bouillon powder and flour. Pour in the wine and stock and stir over fire until the mixture comes to a boil. Add the ham to the sauce and simmer for 5 minutes. Return the chickens and simmer for 10 more minutes or until they are heated through.

III. Cut the slices of trimmed bread into triangles and sauté in 1-2 tablespoons butter until golden brown. Arrange the chickens on a hot serving dish. Spoon the sauce over, arrange the bread around the chickens and sprinkle with parsley. Serves 4.

"Darling . . ." the voice of a once famous radio actress ("The Romance of Helen Trent," "Heartbreak—or Hill Top—House," I can't remember which) and a sometime Broadway performer—in both cases, always as the "other" woman—

breathed huskily over the phone. In this business one is expected to know and identify the caller, especially those who are female, wealthy, and of a certain age. This one qualifies in all respects. Living in an elegant mansion where one has to remove one's shoes to enter a drawing room that gives out on an aspect of the gardens of Versailles, she, poor thing, was under the thumb of a ruthless Viennese cook.

"Darling, she's ghastly—won't do a thing, but perfectly divine—and now she's threatened to leave because Arthur is bringing four people from the city . . . terribly important . . . and I'm at a loss. A loss. I know it's terribly short notice, but can you do something for me—anything?"

Well, the poor old fowl flies into my mind again. "How do you feel about Chicken Bonne Femme?" I ask as ingenuously as possible. "Bonne Femme, Bonne Femme—how divine, darling! Helga (or Hilda, or whoever), makes it superbly, you know."

OK, OK, so do I, comes the silent comment.

"Give me two hours and that poor little bird will be on your table"—and can be on yours as well. And here is how:

CHICKEN BONNE FEMME

½-pound chunk bacon
8 tablespoons butter
roasting chicken, 3-pound size, trussed and buttered
15 to 25 peeled white onions, each about 1 inch in diameter
1 to 1½ pounds small new potatoes
¼ teaspoon salt
bouquet garni: 4 parsley sprigs, ½ bay leaf, and ¼ teaspoon
thyme tied in washed cheesecloth

I.   Preheat oven to 325°. Remove the rind and cut the bacon into lardons (rectangular strips, ½ inch wide and 1½ inches long). Simmer for 10 minutes in 2 quarts of water. Rinse in cold water, and dry. In a fireproof casserole, sauté the bacon for 2 to 3 minutes in butter until very lightly browned. Remove to a side dish, leaving the fat in the casserole.

II.   Brown the chicken on all sides in the hot fat. Remove it to a side dish and pour the fat out of the casserole.

III.   Drop the onions in boiling, salted water and boil slowly for 5 minutes. Drain and set aside. Peel the potatoes and trim them into uniform ovals about 2 inches long and 1 inch in diameter. Cover with cold water and bring to a boil. Drain immediately.

IV.   Heat 4 tablespoons butter in the casserole until it is foaming. Add the drained potatoes and roll them around over moderate heat for 2 minutes to evaporate their moisture; this will prevent their sticking to the casserole. Spread them to the sides of the pan, salt the chicken, and place it breast up in the casserole. Place the bacon and onions over the potatoes; add the herb bouquet. Baste all ingredients with the butter in the casserole, lay aluminum foil over the chicken, and cover the casserole.

V.   Heat the casserole on top of the stove until the contents are sizzling, then place in the middle level of the preheated oven and roast for 1 hour and 10 to 20 minutes or until the chicken is done. Baste once or twice with the butter and juices in the pan. No sauce is necessary. Serves 4.

Or try one of the following:

CHICKEN SALAD WITH ALMONDS

chicken, 4-pound size, poached whole (see instructions for
  for chicken curry, page 75)
4 stalks of celery, finely minced
2 small shallots, crushed in a garlic press
¼ cup toasted, slivered almonds
salt and fresh ground pepper to taste
1 tablespoon grated lemon rind
1½ cups mayonnaise, preferably homemade
pimiento strips and chopped parsley for garnish

I.   Remove the skin and bones from a cooked chicken after it has cooled, and cut into thin slices.

II.   Wash the celery well and mince finely. Put two small shallots into a garlic press and add the juice to the chopped celery. Chop up the remaining pulp of the shallots.

III. Put the chicken, celery, toasted almond slivers, and the chopped shallot pulp into a large salad bowl. Season with salt and pepper.

IV. Mix 1 tablespoon of grated lemon rind into 1½ cups mayonnaise and combine with the rest of the salad ingredients. Mix well. Serve very cold. Decorate with strips of pimiento and chopped parsley. Serves 6.

CHICKEN COOKED WITH ORANGE

chicken, 3½-4 pounds, cut into serving pieces
4 tablespoons oil
1 tart apple, chopped
1 stalk celery, chopped
1 onion, chopped
1 carrot, chopped
2 tablespoons curry powder
1 tablespoon flour
½ cup orange juice
¾ cup chicken broth
2 teaspoons grated orange rind
⅓ cup chopped mango chutney
1 bay leaf, crumbled
1 small naval orange, sectioned
salt and pepper

I. Season the chicken pieces with salt and pepper. Heat the oil in a skillet and brown the chicken pieces on all sides. Remove the chicken and keep warm.

II. Add the apple, celery, onion, and carrot to the oil remaining in the skillet and cook, stirring, 4 minutes. Sprinkle with the curry powder and flour, and cook, stirring, 1 minute longer. Gradually stir in the orange juice, chicken broth, rind, chutney, and bay leaf. Bring to a boil, season to taste, and return chicken to the skillet.

III. Reduce heat and simmer, covered, for about 30 minutes or until tender. Garnish with orange segments. Serves 4.

CHICKEN STUFFED WITH SHRIMP

chicken, 4-pound size, with giblets
1 carrot, peeled and chopped
1 onion, peeled and stuck with two cloves
1 leek, chopped
2 stalks of parsley
sprig of fresh thyme or a pinch of dried thyme
½ bay leaf
1 blade of mace or pinch of dried mace
6 peppercorns
1 pound raw shrimp
1 onion, chopped
4 tablespoons good cooking or olive oil
1 cup boiled rice
7 tablespoons butter
salt pork, cut into 10 small squares
1 clove garlic, crushed
1 teaspoon salt and ½ teaspoon pepper
2 tablespoons flour
1 tablespoon tomato paste

I. Preheat oven to 400°. Place the giblets in a saucepan of cold water and place over high flame. When boiling commences, add the carrot, onion stuck with cloves, leek, parsley, thyme, bay leaf, mace, and peppercorns. Cover and boil steadily for 45 minutes. (Add water when necessary).

II. Boil the shrimp until pink. Drain, shell and devein them. Reserve the stock.

III. Brown the chopped onion in 4 tablespoons oil, add the rice, and stir for 5 minutes. Add the liquid that the shrimp was cooked in, adding water if necessary, and boil for 15 minutes. Drain.

IV. Brown the liver in 1 tablespoon butter with the salt pork. When brown, scoop out to a mixing bowl and add the rice and shrimp.

V. Rub the chicken inside and out with crushed garlic and fill the cavity with the rice-shrimp mixture. Place the chicken in a roasting pan and dot with 4 tablespoons butter. Place in the hot oven and roast for 45 minutes. Baste after 20 minutes and then baste every 10 minutes. After 40 minutes, add 1 teaspoon salt and ½ teaspoon pepper.

VI.   Skim the fat off the juice in the pan, place in a saucepan, and lower the oven to 250° to keep the chicken warm.

VII.   Whisk the flour into the juices in the saucepan over high heat; add more flour if necessary. Cook for 2 minutes, stirring constantly. If it becomes too thick, add the stock from the giblets. Add 2 tablespoons butter, tomato paste, and enough stock to make a smooth creamy gravy. Pour over and around the chicken and serve. Serves 6.

CASSEROLE ROASTED CHICKEN IN CHAMPAGNE

1 chicken or capon, 3-pound size
1 lemon, cut in half
½ teaspoon salt
1 stalk tarragon
3 scallions
1½ sticks butter, softened
3 whole shallots, peeled
1½ cups French champagne
1 pound small new potatoes
6 finely chopped shallots
½ pound white mushrooms
juice of ½ lemon
1 egg yolk
2 tablespoons cognac
¼ cup heavy cream
½ cup parsley, chopped fine

I.   Preheat oven to 400°. Rub the chicken or capon on all sides with a half a lemon to keep the flesh white. Then rub salt all over, and place tarragon, scallions, 1 tablespoon butter, and whole shallots into the cavity. Truss the chicken with a needle and string, starting with a big knot through the breast-bone.

II.   Melt 1 stick butter in a large enamel saucepan with a tight cover. When the butter is melted, place the chicken in the pan and brown on all sides. Reduce the heat and cover. After 15 minutes, add the champagne and cook, covered, for 45 minutes.

III.   Meanwhile, peel the potatoes and trim into uniform ovals. Cover with cold water, bring to a boil, and drain immediately. Set aside.

IV.   In an enamel saucepan, place 3 tablespoons of butter and the chopped shallots, and cook slowly until translucent and golden. Scoop out the shallots with a slotted spoon, set aside, and place the mushrooms in the pan. Sauté until brown, squeeze ½ lemon over and turn to brown on all sides. Remove from heat, stir in the shallots, and keep warm.

V.   Remove the chicken from the large saucepan and put in the parboiled potatoes. Brown them until crisp over moderately high heat. Lower heat and continue cooking until tender. When brown, return the chicken and add the mushrooms. Cook for 5-6 minutes to blend the flavors.

VI.   Transfer the chicken to an oven-proof platter and place in a 400° oven to crisp the skin. Allow about 10 minutes for this.

VII.   Strain the sauce into a saucepan and whisk in a well-beaten egg yolk, taking care not to curdle the sauce. Heat gently until the sauce coats a spoon. Add cognac and cream, and correct seasonings.

VIII.   Remove the chicken from the oven and place the vegetables around it. Pour the sauce over, sprinkle with parsley, and serve. Serves 4.

CHICKEN PIE

1 large chicken
1 carrot, peeled and quartered
2 stalks celery, roughly chopped
2 large onions, peeled and halved
3 packets G. Washington golden bouillon powder

bouquet garni: 1 sprig parsley, 1 sprig dill and 1 sprig thyme
butter
2 tablespoons cornstarch
1 teaspoon flour
½ cup milk mixed with ½ pint heavy cream
½ cup vermouth
10 shallots, cut up
8 potatoes, cubed and parboiled
24 small mushrooms, sautéed until golden
1 bunch carrots, cut in small pieces and parboiled
16 white onions, chopped and parboiled
1 bunch celery, chopped fine
1½ cups fennel, minced
pinch of nutmeg
salt and pepper
2 packages frozen peas
¼ cup cognac
parsley and dill, chopped
pie pastry, enough to cover top of pie (or several small pies, if
    made individually)

I.   Preheat oven to 400°. Cover the chicken in a large sauce-pan with water and add the carrot, celery stalks, halved onions, bouillon, and bouquet garni. Bring to a boil and cook until the chicken is tender. Remove the chicken and cool. Reserve the stock.

II.   Melt ¼ pound butter and add 1½ tablespoons stock mixed with 2 tablespoons cornstarch. Stir in the flour. Dilute with the milk mixture and add the vermouth and 1½ cups more stock. Continue beating over moderate heat until sauce thickens and is the consistency of heavy cream. Remove from the heat and set aside.

III. Remove the meat from the chicken in large pieces. Sauté the shallots in butter until golden and stir into the sauce. Add the chicken, potatoes, mushrooms, carrots, onions, celery, and fennel. Season with the nutmeg, salt, pepper, and broth to taste.

IV.   When stew has a full consistency, add the peas. If the stew is too thin, add heavy cream; if too thick, add stock mixed with milk.

V.   Add the cognac and a large lump of butter and sprinkle generously with parsley and dill. Place in pie plates or individual serving units and add pastry covers. (The pie may be frozen at this point and baked later in a 400° oven for about 1 hour). Otherwise, place in a 400° oven, bake for 15 minutes, turn heat down to 350°, and cook about 45 minutes more. Serves 6.

Party of Choice

Chapter Four

BERT GREENE

One's first party is always memorable. The first one that The Store ever catered was a case of the blues. A hydrangea-ringed garden, ultramarine linen, and white wine. Blankets of snowy fresh fish poached over shrimp. Incredibly thin sliced cold veal *parisien,* herbed rice, and limestone lettuce: it was pure Monet. A pastoral scene beside a ferny pool, frosted goblets of iced espresso and blue, blue plums . . . a runny brie and a runnier blackberry mousse. A party never to be forgotten. And, coincidentally, never to be paid for.

The hostess, in some pretty dismay, announced after several weeks of discreetly submitted bills that she and her financier husband were divorcing, and custody of the party bill was up for grabs.

When it was finally settled out of court (several years and two collection agencies later), we were knee-deep in other party fare, and the enchantment of the first, prized event had long since tarnished the brass of our mettle.

Virginity, I am sorely tempted to say, is the last hopeful state left to modern man—in the kitchen or out.

Every party since has unfortunately fallen into one of two categories: nuisance or necessity. The first, due entirely to hostesses' pre-prandial paranoia, and the latter, to a severely shrinking bank balance. We would never attempt another party if we were not compelled to by economic necessity, because, sad to say, parties are no fun for the help.

As a matter of actual fact, the party as a fun form for anyone rates a double zero in my book, with the possible exclusion of those Mafiosi elevator men on upper Park Avenue who practice mild highway robbery on you before they allow entrance to the netherworld of their service area. They and the few indiscriminate lushes who get blotto instantly upon arrival are the sole survivors of that pleasureless pastime.

The caterer, as I can attest from experience, is certainly taking no pleasure. From the state of shock that comes from an initial encounter with the incipient hostess (a consultation, it is roguishly referred to in the trade), to the treachery of enemy kitchens, booby-trapped with self-immolating ovens and deep-freezers in a state of perpetual thaw, he hangs in there: a parsley pimp, giving morticianly touch-ups to an already lifeless meal. As he waits for the desperate dawn hour when he can creep away, bearing the shards of his craft in Reynolds wrap, only one thought abides: "Will there be quibbling about the bill?" *Usually* there is.

The first party we ever attempted in New York (the really big apple for caterers) was for a vastly successful composer of rock music.

He and his wife (of the time) were great admirers of the do-or-die attitude of The Store's eager band of entrepreneurs during our first, fateful summer. With very little coaxing, they persuaded us that cooking on the fabled Garland range in their luxuriously appointed Manhattan kitchen would be essentially no different from cooking on the gas-burning antiques in our local habitat. Well, partner, Denis lost a perfectly good set of eyebrows that evening, just to prove them wrong.

The hosts had a quaint notion to celebrate Halloween with a supper composed of only curries.

As we had held ourselves to be triple-threat India aficionados, we now had to devise a menu of remarkably hot delights. First seviche; then a velvety-saffroned curry of spiced lamb, thickened with coconut cream and mushrooms; shrimp curry, a thinner version of the former, just as goldeny hot in taste, but tranquilized with slivers of candied ginger and black currants; and finally, a madras of thin, thin strips of beef enveloped in a tomato-curried sauce of hot sour cream. Pure nirvana on Central Park West.

The fifteen or twenty accompanying condiments were reassessed by almost daily telephone communication with the host. Bombay duck was an absolute imperative. The Store in Amagansett would comply even if it meant that my mother must traverse every exotic food department in the city of New York before she could come up with the odiferous stuff.

Besides being successful, the host was a man of parts. He loved the good life, and more than merely loving it—he loved to discuss it. "Would the salad be merely endive or perhaps endive and arrugola mixed?"

We would think that one through, in concert, and call him back later.

"Is a lemon mousse the absolutely rightest . . . absolutely coolest thing for the palate, afterward?" What he really wanted was an out-of-season snowstorm.

And were we sure we would make a *mountain* of rice? He adored rice with his curry. All of his friends adored rice, too. A mountain? O.K., we promised him a mountain.

Phone calls proliferated. Should the flowers on the tables be white or pink or palest yellow to match the curries?

"But, Jerry, you have such good taste yourself." That was obviously not in question. "Besides, if we do the flowers . . . we will have to add a service charge for that. Be a man and decide it on your own."

Arrangements! Arrangements! The logistics of the bar-flow transportation as opposed to the passage to and from the buffet was discussed so often on so many endless long-distance calls that we began to feel like honorary traffic commissioners. It became obvious that the caterer did not merely provide the food in New York—he staged and mounted a Radio City Music Hall production as well.

When All Hallows' Eve arrived, we borrowed my sister's large West Side kitchen for the preparation. My mother and a few well wishing neighbors had been pressed into service, but the curse of the twenty condiments was punishment that not one of them could truly survive.

There was coconut to be peeled and grated, white grapes to be seeded and sprinkled with rum, bacon to be fried and dried and crumbled, eggs to be chopped, peppers to be chopped. Cucumbers and cashews, sweet Brinjal pickles and bananas, Bombay duck, sunflower seeds, pepitas and pickled limes, candied ginger and glacé oranges, green tomatoes, and mangos all had to be chopped.

Some mighty limp wrists were the residual of that evening's enterprise, I can tell you. And they were not only in the kitchen. Being neophytes at the business of hiring waiters and bartenders, we had, with some trepidation, turned to old theatrical friends to bail us out—for one performance only. Several actors we knew to be "at liberty" made their catering debuts (in supporting roles, it is true) that evening.

One of them, an excellent young character actor of some

standing, actually had to be dissuaded from donning a rather flamboyant red wig that he honestly felt would conceal his true identity from any theatrical folk who might recognize him on the wrong side of the footlights and embarrass the caterers. And so it goes. . . .

The evening's curries were prepared to the point where they could be assembled on the host's professional kitchen range. The lemon mousse was chilling in a styrofoam coffin of its very own. All the wretched condiments were sealed in plastic for instant transportation across town, when we realized, with certain dread, that no one had remembered to bring a pot large enough to prepare that promised *mountain of rice.* It was almost five o'clock, and we were due to appear at six sharp. In an absolute frenzy, we called several neighboring Chinese restaurants hoping to buy even a molehill—but none of them would consider selling us that amount of cooked rice at such short notice, particularly sans chow mein.

With a fierceness that all soldiers muster at the last ditch stand, we borrowed saucepans and measured out cups full of rice. No watched pot ever boiled faster.

The rice itself, gummy from being strained before it was properly done, was heaped into a gigantic colander to be steamed later at the host and hostess's apartment.

Rice we brought. A mountain? No, rather a mountain range of it. Wet, sticky, gluey, starchy rice.

This epic congealment was saunaed and sifted and dried, grain by grain, while the drinks and canapes were served, while the curries were arranged and heated, and while the stove's oven blew up in Denis' face. Even after he was sprayed with Solarcaine and laved with softened butter, that dreadful rice steamed on.

In a confidential aside, we were told later that the oven had always been a trifle erratic, but then, they hardly ever ate at home, and the cook eschewed any food preparation other than heating up those frozen things from the supermarket.

The curry survived; it was pronounced delicious. The rice survived. Even Denis survived. His eyebrows grew back blonder and more luxurious than ever—only to be burned off again at another soirée some years in the future.

The actors were charming. All Stanislavsky students, they actually believed they were waiters that night and were generously tipped for their performances.

The Store personnel fared less glamorously. We had never realized that the caterer did not merely mount a Radio City Music Hall production—he cleaned the backstage later, as well.

As the guests departed and the host and hostess kissed us all goodnight and their "Thank you darlings—it was wonderful! Wonderful!" rent the air, we washed and dried and did the scrub-up.

As their bedroom lights were gently extinguished, we straightened and swept and set to right all that had so recently been the scene of such triumphant chaos, packing the remains of the feast in those same little pots and plastic containers to feed friends and family for the weeks ahead. One thing remained, however; the *mountain* of rice. Large as life, still arranged in the great silver salver in which it had made its initial appearance.

"Enough to feed two hundred Chinese for a week," Denis murmured uneasily.

But where do we throw it? Garbage bags would leak. Incinerators were dangerous, and toilets (even the five in the apartment) were out of the question. A mountain of rice could put them out of commission for weeks.

Slowly, in the dawn hours, we dragged ourselves out of the grandest, most prestigious co-operative on Central Park West and dumped our paddy of rice, in one fell swoop, over the park wall—where it may have very well taken root by this time.

The memorable parties are few and far between. Leonard Bernstein once turned fifty and The Store in Amagansett turned inside out to do him midcentennial honor.

The host, a distinguished book publisher, thought it would be kicky in the extreme to take over a posh East-side eaterie lock, stock and barrel, and give all their chefs a day off while we were smuggled into their kitchen—sans union cards.

The staff had been dutifully paid *not* to appear—so, of course, they all showed up, not to work, but merely as spectator sportsmen.

At the fray, in their whited finery and toques blanche, they stared in utter disbelief at the sight of us. Four demented, blue-jeaned interlopers, falling all over each other in a welter of alien restaurant equipment. Snipping parsley with manicuring scissors and whisking quarts of cream by hand while a stunning array of stainless, steely electric beaters sat idly by.

But we were hardly in any position to explain that we did not have the slightest clue how to use those monstrous objects, let alone to reveal our personal paranoia of death by electric shock, a premonition we had cheerlessly nourished for years.

Our onion chopping was a particular point of their derision. Trying to master the skill in public had left the cutting board bereft and the rest of the kitchen ringleted with aromatic golden droppings. So it was with mixed emotion that we allowed ourselves to be dissuaded from the task.

Murmuring soft Spanish imprecations at the state of his domain, the master chef lifted his shiny knife in the air and split all asunder in seconds. Like a true banderillero, he diced and shaved and slivered onions to a fare-thee-well as we wept honest-to-goodness tears of frustration.

As I recall, that party was awash with several hundred of New York's more glittering names. Rumors of Lauren Bacall having a second or third helping of rapée Morvandelle, or of a Comden and a Green gluttonizing over the celeriac rémoulade leavened somewhat that fall from grace in the galley.

In retrospect, all the food *was* pretty fantastic. Most of it had been prepared in advance in the kitchen in Amagansett where we could tap dance on grapes for vinegar without causing an eyebrow to raise. And we had truly cooked up a veritable storm.

By kindly nature, man has been afforded several stout companions to sustain him through the ravages of the cocktail party. They are, of course, wines and spirits. And to fortify his equanimity, add a bit of pâté and a crust of good French bread.

Our own pâté is truly not a paste at all. Technically it is a terrine, a rough country loaf, laved with glacial pork fat and concocted of varying proportions of veal, chicken, pork loin, and chicken liver. It is sweetened with onion and garlic and bathed in odorous Madeira and cognac till it hurts.

At the party of the moment, mounds of this sleek, truffle-studded pâté sat on each bar, rising like twin bosoms from a sea of baguettes. Cool and coarsely pink, barely redolent of spice and garlic, these mountains of fleshly delight were polished off with a consuming passion rarely seen these weight-watching days.

Since both Denis and I hold the canapé in mutual contempt, our base concession to the pre-meal cocktail hour is usually a bit of cheese or some toasted almonds and black olives, or on major occasions, radishes and butter. This occasion was the exception to our rule.

The drinks were man-sized and the cocktail hour went on forever. Invitations were inscribed for noon and lunch was not to be served until three. Needless to say, the dizzying array of hors d'oeuvres taxed the physical and mental constitution of the culinary quartet in the kitchen.

To begin with, there were crudités by the yard and huge salvers of raw vegetables slivered into matchsticks, surrounding ample bowls of tapenade for group dunking. And there were shrimp, all pink and perfumed of court bouillon, nesting around a tub of cold curry sauce so sharp that the recollection still sets the salivary glands afire. There were patachou puffs, flaky bits of golden air baked just long enough to melt their hearts of cheese and béchamel sauce, Swedish meatballs, and lobster-stuffed cherry tomatoes, each rosy jewel holding a treasure of vinaigrette-tossed lobster meat, with a feather of greenish dill capping each orb. And, oh Lord, those were just the hors d'oeuvres.

Later we served poached fish with herbs. Or was it salmon with a tarragon-dill mayonnaise or a striped bass soused in gribiche? Memory kindly draws a curtain. Sliced shards of beef, I do remember, and jambon en croûte, which I will never forget, possibly because on the day of the great event, with the station wagon duly laden with goodly treasure at dawn, emergency necessitated the additional passage of one small child and two Scottie dogs to New York. Even barricaded a respectful distance from the hams, their yelps and cries could shatter glass, no less pâté brisé.

We collectively prayed that the precious coating would stay together long enough to be seen and admired at the maestro's groaning board, before being whisked to the kitchen for reparation and Elmer's glue.

I am a good cook so I can admit that anything *en croûte* fills me with dismay. Yet, with all the awful ambivalence of my Libran nature, I go right on foisting these damn crusts on the world at large, as if I really enjoyed the paralysis that comes from watching each avalanche of shattered pastry as the car hits pothole after pothole on the Long Island Expressway.

The ham en croûte survived that party better than I did.

Dessert had been requested by the hosts and promptly acquiesced to by me. Never mind that I had never made it before. Roulage Leontine is a rich, infinitely chocolate mousse-like cake, whose chief ingredient is the cloud of air inside it. The stuff of which dreams are made, perhaps, but a nightmare for the pastry chef even in ideal circumstances. It is barely baked, then scooped up quite warm in a dampened tea towel, and rolled and unrolled and swabbed with whipped cream more times than I care to recollect. My hands still quake at the promise of one in the oven. That day, we made five. If some split slightly from the heat of the moment and some over-tempestuous manhandling, no one ever knew; an inch-high drift of sifted cocoa destroyed the evidence.

Other parties have earned larger checks and more verbal accolades, but the warmest reward I have ever received was uttered that day: "Bert, Marlene adored your chocolate roll." And so it goes. . . .

For me, all party food breaks down into two mildly loath-some categories: the kind you eat on the fly or the kind you eat on the hoof.

In my lexicon, "fly-food" is anything that can be wolfed down while waiting for another turn at the bar.

On the other hand, "hoof-food" is pure hell. Consisting of a holding pattern for imbibing quantities of commestibles while remaining perfectly vertical, it is only inflicted on unwary guests by a commission of professional ball-throwers and those few sado-hostesses who knowingly pre-ordain a multi-course buffet rather than a sit-down dinner.

The best "fly-food" I can think of is an enormous quantity of iced, fresh vegetables, served with something tart and abra-sive.

I was once only half-jokingly offered a bribe of a thousand dollars for the following recipe. Nobly, I refused the stunning stipend, and now, with open heart, I pass it on to you—absolute-ly gratis!

GREEN TAPENADE

1 can flat anchovy fillets, 2-ounce-size (plus the oil in the can)
2 teaspoons capers

2—3 tablespoons good wine vinegar
2 tablespoons fresh chives, shallot, or onion, finely chopped
¼ cup chopped parsley
1 ½ cups homemade mayonnaise
a good grind of fresh pepper
watercress leaves for garnish

I.   Blend the anchovies, capers, vinegar, chives, and parsley in an electric blender for about three minutes at high speed. It may take several stops and starts of the blender to liquefy all the ingredients.

II.   Stir in the mayonnaise. Season with the pepper. (The mixture will be a light avocado color and quite thick.) Refrigerate until chilled.

III.   Garnish with watercress leaves and serve as a dip for slivered raw vegetables.

The Store's Swedish meatballs are probably not one hundred percent Scandinavian, but they are unusually tender-hearted imitations, redolent of caraway and cream, and fringed with snippets of green dill. Toothpicked, they make a fine hors d'oeuvre, well worth preparing in large quantities and easily frozen for emergency suppers after the ball.

THE STORE SWEDISH MEATBALLS

1 pound round steak, ground
½ pound veal, ground
½ pound pork, ground
1 cup stale bread crumbs
1 large yellow onion
½ green pepper
2 tablespoons fresh dill
2 tablespoons fresh parsley
1 clove of garlic
2 shallots
1 packet G. Washington brown bouillon powder
½ cup milk
1 tablespoon caraway seeds
¼ teaspoon nutmeg

2 eggs
salt and freshly ground pepper
1 stick sweet butter
2 tablespoons oil
1 ½ cup heavy cream
1 cup sour cream
½ cup strong beef broth (if needed)
dill for garnish

I. Have your butcher put the beef, veal, and pork through the meat grinder several times. Place the meat mixture and bread crumbs in a large bowl.

II. Place the onion, green pepper, dill, parsley, garlic, and shallots, along with a packet of bouillon powder and ½ cup of milk, in the blender. Blend at high speed until the mixture is quite soupy. If there is not enough liquid to homogenize the onions, add a bit more milk.

III. Pour the onion-herb mixture over the meat and add the caraway seeds, nutmeg, two eggs, and salt and pepper. Mix well with your hands.

IV. When the meat has absorbed the other ingredients, shape the mixture into forty or fifty small meatballs. If the mixture is too thick, add a few drops of milk. If it appears too thin, sprinkle on some extra bread crumbs for body.

V. In a large skillet, melt the butter and oil. As the foam subsides, brown some of the meat balls. Shake the pan as they cook, so they brown uniformly.

VI. As the meatballs brown, transfer them to a large sauce-pan. Pour cream on the cooked meatballs and simmer them on low heat until all the meat in the skillet has been done. Browning the meat will use up all of the butter.

VII. Turning the meatballs in the saucepan gently, add the remainder of the cream and the sour cream as well. Cook over a low flame, barely simmering, for about an hour. Use beef broth if cream sauce needs thinning. Garnish lavishly with fresh dill. Serves 8 – 10.

Seviche, if the name does not ring an immediate bell, is one party pick-up that can be made without a passing glance at the kitchen range. A spicy, raw fish appetizer, pickled in citrus juice, it is astringent and different and I love it in the extreme for a diet lunch. It is a traditional South American classic and can be made with many different raw fish. An inventive variation takes red snapper. It is also delicious with a cup of slivered bay scallops added.

We make ours with fresh lime juice. In South America, I hear they vary the mix with orange and lemon. Enterprising partygivers will try it either way.

SEVICHE

1½ pounds flounder
1 cup fresh lime juice
¼ cup chopped shallots
1 clove of garlic finely minced
¼ cup chopped parsley
¼ cup peeled and seeded tomatoes, cut into strips
3 tablespoons finely chopped green chili peppers
1½ teaspoons salt
1 teaspoon freshly ground pepper
good dash of Tabasco sauce
¼ cup chopped cilantro (fresh coriander)
½ cup olive oil

I.   Cut the flounder into thin strips about 2 inches long and ¼ inch thick. Cover the fish strips with lime juice. Set aside while you chop the shallots, parsley, tomatoes, peppers, and garlic.

II.   Add the chopped ingredients and the salt, pepper, Tabasco sauce, and chopped cilantro to the fish. Add oil and toss well. Refrigerate about 5–6 hours. Serves 6–8.

Shrimp and curry, like corned beef and cabbage, are rare culinary matings, made in heaven. The secret of this sauce is homemade mayonnaise and generous driblets of Tabasco to hotten it.

COLD SHRIMP WITH CURRY MAYONNAISE

2 pounds raw shrimp
½ cup water
¼ teaspoon salt
1 small onion, peeled
1 thick slice of lemon
3 sprigs parsley
¼ cup dry white wine or vermouth
2 cups cold curry mayonnaise (page 25)

I.   Clean the raw shrimp by peeling off the outer shell and rinsing off the grit. With a sharp-pointed knife, remove the black vein down the back. (When shrimp are served as appetizers, you may leave the tails on for easier handling.)

II.   In a saucepan, combine water, salt, onion, lemon slice, parsley sprigs, and white wine or vermouth. Bring to a boil and add the shrimp. Simmer for 3 to 5 minutes, according to size, until shrimp turn pink and cook through. Drain in cold water and chill.

III.   Arrange the shrimp on a platter around a bowl of cold curry sauce. Serves 8-10.

In my time, I have invented two hors d'oeuvres and lived to regret both. They are delicious, but a bother to make. Precisely because they are so very delicious, I am bothered making them—a lot.

LOBSTER OR CRAB STUFFED CHERRY TOMATOES

1 box cherry tomatoes
salt
½ pound picked lobster meat or frozen king crab meat
    (defrosted)
1 shallot
¼ cup fresh dill
¼ cup vinaigrette dressing
a good grind of fresh pepper

I.   Slice tops off the tomatoes and squeeze lightly to remove the juice and seeds. Sprinkle with salt and turn upside down on a cookie sheet until ready to use.

II.   Mince the shallot and the dill. In a bowl, combine lobster or crabmeat with shallot and dill. Add the vinaigrette dressing and a good grind of fresh pepper. Toss well.

III.   Stuff each tomato with about half a teaspoon of the filling. Decorate with a feather of dill. Serve chilled. Serves 8-10.

OEUFS CRESSONIERE

1 bunch watercress
3 tablespoons heavy cream
2 sprigs dill
1 large shallot
½ cup mayonnaise
salt and pepper
dash cayenne pepper
6 hard-boiled eggs, quartered

I.   Purée half the watercress in an electric blender with the cream, dill and shallot—or chop to a fine paste, gradually stirring in the cream.

II.   Mix the blended watercress mixture with the mayonnaise. Season with salt, pepper, and cayenne. Arrange the eggs on a serving dish and cover each quarter with the green mayonnaise. Garnish with sprigs of remaining watercress.

III.   Serve with black bread or toasted rounds of French bread. Serves 8—10.

Puff pastry is the most blessed single contribution to party fare that I know. Bad-mouthed by bad cooks, it has gained a false reputation somewhere along the line for being tricky to manipulate. Nothing could be farther from the truth. With or without an electric mixer, puff pastry is no hardship. You must mix well, beat quickly after the addition of each egg, and remember to slit the hot puffs as soon as you can manage to handle them, so they do not get a chance to go soggy.

Made in advance, filled and frozen, puffs take the sting away from a surprise guest or two. Made fresh, they are better. But then, what isn't?

PATACHOU PUFFS

PUFFS
1 cup water
6 tablespoons butter cut into pieces
1 teaspoon salt
⅛ teaspoon pepper
pinch of nutmeg
1 cup sifted all-purpose flour
4 large eggs
1 egg beaten with ½ teaspoon water

FILLING
1½ tablespoons butter
3 medium-sized shallots, finely chopped
1 cup ground ham
4 tablespoons Madeira
½ cup béchamel sauce (recipe follows)
¼ cup finely grated Jarlsberg cheese

I.   Preheat oven to 425°. In a 1½-quart heavy saucepan, bring the water to a boil. Add the butter and seasonings and continue to boil slowly until the butter has melted.

II.   Remove from the heat and immediately pour in all the flour. Beat vigorously with a wooden spoon to blend thoroughly. Then beat over a medium heat for 2 minutes or until the mixture leaves the sides of the pan, forms a mass, and begins to film the bottom of the pan.

III. Remove the saucepan from the heat and make a well in the center of the paste with the spoon. Immediately break an egg into the center of the well. Beat it into the paste for several seconds until it has been absorbed. Continue with the rest of the eggs, beating them in one by one. The third and fourth eggs will be absorbed more slowly. Beat for a moment more to be sure all is well blended and smooth.

IV.   A pastry bag makes the neatest puffs and is the easiest way to success. However, if you do not have one, drop the paste on the baking sheet with a spoon. To use a pastry bag, fold the top 3 inches of the bag over your left hand. Using a rubber spatula, fill the bag with the warm paste. Squeeze the paste onto 2 buttered baking sheets, making circular mounds about 1 inch in diameter and ½ inch high. Space the mounds 2 inches apart.

V.   Then dip a pastry brush into the beaten egg and flatten each puff very slightly with the side of the brush. Avoid dripping egg down the puff and onto the sheet, as this will prevent the puff from rising.

VI.   Set the sheets in the upper and lower thirds of the preheated oven, and bake for about 20 minutes. The puffs are done when they have doubled in size, are a golden brown, and are firm and crusty to the touch. Remove them from the oven and pierce the side of each puff with a sharp knife. At this point, check for any uncooked centers in the puffs and scoop out to prevent the puffs from becoming soggy. This procedure must be done quickly. Then return the puffs to the turned-off oven and leave the door ajar for 10 minutes.

VII.   Remove and cool on a rack. Makes 36-40 small puffs.

VIII.   To prepare the filling, melt the butter in a large skillet. Add the shallots and sauté until golden. Add the ham and stir until all pieces are coated with shallots and butter.

IX.   Add the Madeira and raise the heat until all liquid is absorbed. Remove from the heat and stir in the béchamel. Slightly cool before filling puffs.

X.   Preheat the oven to 375°. Remove the tops of the puffs and insert the filling with a teaspoon, filling the bottom portions only. Put a pinch of the Jarlsberg on each and replace the tops. Before serving, place in a preheated oven for 10 − 12 minutes. Serve hot.

Puffs may be made well in advance. Freeze or keep in a cool place until serving. Allow 25 – 30 minutes in the oven for frozen puffs.

BECHAMEL SAUCE

½ stick butter
1 tablespoon flour
1 cup hot chicken broth (bouillon or stock)
¼ cup vermouth
¼ cup heavy cream
pinch of salt
pinch of white pepper
dash of Tabasco

I.   In an enamel or glass saucepan, melt the butter until it is just golden. Do not scorch! Remove from the heat, sprinkle in the flour, and whisk the mixture to a fine paste. Return to the flame and add the hot chicken broth and vermouth, constantly whisking vigorously. This will thicken considerably. Thin with the heavy cream. Add the salt, pepper, and Tabasco and whisk until smooth. It should be like a very thick, clotted cream. (Cool before using in the above recipe.)

I like to keep béchamel on hand at all times. A bit of béchamel will thicken sauce or gravy better than any added flour or cornstarch. It may be stored in the refrigerator in a covered glass jar for up to five weeks.

Every year we get myriad requests for the secret of our pâté. The answer is simple: good ingredients and hard work. Our pâté is difficult to make. It requires the chopping arm of Attila the Hun, and a single ingredient of its complex seasoning cannot be fudged or faked.

THE STORE COUNTRY PÂTÉ

8-cup loaf pan
4-5 sheets of fresh pork fat (back is preferable) about ⅛ inch
  thick
4 tablespoons good cognac

½ *cup white onions*
3 *large shallots*
3 *tablespoons butter with a few drops of oil (for sautéing the*
    onions)
½ *cup Rainwater Madeira*
4-5 *canned black truffles and the juice from the can*
1½ *cups lean pork*
1½ *cups lean veal*
1 *cup fresh pork fat*
1 *cup uncooked chicken*
6 *chicken livers*
3 *lightly beaten eggs*
1½ *teaspoons salt*
pinch of black pepper (freshly ground)
½ *teaspoon épices fines (recipe follows)*
½ *teaspoon crushed fresh thyme*
2 *cloves garlic, mashed*

I.   Preheat oven to 350°. Line the bottom and sides of a
     loaf pan or terrine with the fresh pork fat. Moisten it
     slightly with cognac and set aside.

II. Mince the shallots and onions together. In a saucepan,
     cook the onions and shallots in butter and oil for about
     7 or 8 minutes, until they are translucent and soft. Do
     not brown. Scrape them into a bowl.

III. Pour the Madeira and the remaining cognac into the
     saucepan, and boil it down until the liquid has reduced
     itself by half. Then scrape the mixture into the bowl
     as well. Add the truffle juices and set aside.

IV. At this point, grind the lean pork, lean veal, pork fat,
     chicken, and chicken livers, using the finest blade of
     your grinder. Put through the mill twice, making sure
     the mixture is very smooth.

V.   Add the ground meat mixture to the wine and onions.
     Add the beaten eggs, salt, pepper, spices, and mashed
     garlic. Beat well with a wooden spoon so that the
     mixture has a light and airy texture and is very well
     blended. For a test, sauté a spoonful in a pan and taste
     it to make sure the seasonings are correct. If it is not

flavorful enough, add salt or a drop or two of cognac
to bring up the taste.

VI.   Divide the mixture into two parts. After wetting your
hands in cold water, arrange one half of the mixture
inside the lined loaf pan. Take a strip of the fresh
pork fat that is left over from the lining and lay the
four or five truffles inside it. Cover one side of the strip
with the other—so that you have a sort of tube of
truffles. Carefully place this on the top of the first layer
of pâté mixture so that it makes a row down the center
of the loaf pan; cover this with the remaining portion
of the mixture.

VII.   Fold the pork fat over the top so that it meets. If there
is not enough pork fat from the sides to cover, cut a
slice the length and width of the pan and place it over
the filled pan, making sure the sides are pressed together carefully where the seams of pork fat meet.

VIII. Enclose the loaf pan entirely in aluminum foil and
set in a pan of boiling water. The water should come
up to the halfway point of the pan. (Add boiling water
during the cooking period if necessary.) Place bake-pan
in the lower third of the preheated oven and bake for
about 1½ hours. The pâté is done when it has shrunk
slightly from the sides of the pan and when the surrounding fat and juices are golden and have no traces
of rosy color.

IX.   Take the pan from the water and set it on a large plate.
On the top of the aluminum foil covering, place a
weight of about 2-3 pounds. An iron or the parts of a
meat grinder might do, but the pan must be weighted
so that it packs the pâté, leaving no air spaces inside.
Allow the pâté to cool at room temperature for several
hours and then chill it, still weighted down, in the
refrigerator for about 6 or 7 hours.

X.   When thoroughly chilled, unwrap the aluminum foil
and place on a small board or platter. Decorate with
chopped parsley and a good grind of black pepper.

EPICES FINES

1 tablespoon each:
 cloves, bay leaves, nutmeg, cinnamon, paprika, mace,
 thyme
1½ teaspoons each:
 dried basil, allspice, oregano, marjoram, sage, savory, ginger
1 teaspoon whole black peppercorns
½ cup white peppercorns

I.   Place all of the above ingredients in a blender jar and pulverize at high speed for about 2 minutes. Make sure all of the seeds are broken up. Store in a little jar. It makes about 1 cup.

"Hoof food," you asked for? Try curry of anything. We developed the knack of producing them, early on, without karma. There is a secret, of course. The vegetables are put in raw and barely cooked in the sauce. The crunch is what gives a Store curry its essential bite.

CHICKEN CURRY A LA THE STORE

1 plump-breasted stewing chicken, about 3 pounds
1 large yellow onion stuck with two cloves
1 bouquet garni: bay leaf, sprig of parsley, sprig of dill, tied
 together
1 small clove of garlic
½ lemon, sliced
salt and fresh pepper
stalk of celery
chicken bouillon and about 4 cups water (enough to cover)

CURRY
3 tablespoons sweet butter
12-16 medium-sized mushroom caps
1 cup onion, finely minced
2 cloves garlic, finely minced
1 pared apple, cut up in bite-sized pieces
4 tablespoons curry powder (I prefer the hot kind)
4 tablespoons sifted corn starch
½ cup heavy cream

¼ teaspoon ground ginger
¼ teaspoon ground cardamom
1 tablespoon turmeric
¼ teaspoon cayenne pepper
1 teaspoon salt
½ cup coconut milk*
2 cups strong chicken broth
1½ cups chopped celery (not too finely cut)
½ cup chopped green pepper
2 teaspoons lemon peel, pared and slivered into thin, thin strips
½ cup candied orange slices (cut into thin strips)
¼ cup slivered candied ginger
½ cup dried black currants
¼ cup sliced dried figs
¼ cup chopped parsley

I.   To stew the chicken, place it and the neck and giblets with all of the other ingredients through celery in a large pot. Cover with half chicken bouillon and half cold water. (You may use only water if you wish to economize, but nothing makes the absolutely 40 carat chicken broth for enriching a curry like the combination.)

II.   Over medium-high heat bring the liquid to a boil and then lower the heat so the bird barely simmers: about three-quarters of an hour. Do not overcook or the pieces will shred in the curry later.

III. Let the chicken cool in the broth. When you are able to handle it easily, remove from the broth and place on a large platter. Remove the skin and bones and tear the chicken meat into generous hunks. Reserve.

IV.   Add the skin and bones to the strained chicken stock and boil it down to ½ its original quantity. This will make a marvelously golden, enriched stock. (Refrigerate any that you do not use in the curry for sauces and soups later.)

V.   Sauté the mushroom caps and set aside. In hot butter in a large skillet, sauté the chopped onion and garlic until the mixture turns a golden color and becomes tender, about six minutes.

VI.   Add the apple slices and curry powder and stir well for
        a few minutes longer. Remove from the heat. Mix the
        cornstarch and cream, and add it with the ginger,
        caradamom, turmeric, cayenne pepper, and salt to the
        mixture.

VII.   Over reduced heat, stir the mixture until it becomes
        quite thick and creamy. Thin with coconut milk and
        1 cup chicken broth.

VIII.   Bring to a boil, stirring constantly. Reduce heat and
        simmer the sauce, uncovered, about 15 to 20 minutes,
        stirring it occasionally.

IX.   Gently add the chicken pieces, taking care not to shred
        the meat. Next, add the chopped celery, green pepper,
        and slivered lemon peel. Cook for 7 or 8 minutes, add-
        ing chicken broth as the mixture thickens. Do not
        overcook.

X.   Remove from the heat and arrange the curry in an
        ovenware casserole or serving dish, layering candied
        ginger and candied orange strips, between the chicken
        and vegetables. Sprinkle dried currants and the cut-up
        figs over the top.

XI.   Arrange the sautéed mushroom caps in a pattern over
        the layered curry. You may prepare the curry to this
        point in advance and reheat it in a 300° oven for
        about 15 minutes before serving. Garnish with chopped
        parsley.

XII.   Serve over fluffy rice with appropriate condiments.
        Serves 6-8.**

   *In lieu of fresh coconut, I blend a can of unsweetened,
shredded coconut with an equal amount of milk. Blend on high
speed for a second or two and then strain. Save the softened
coconut for a condiment and use the coconut milk in the
preparation of the dish.
   **Curry condiments are endless. Here are a few we use:
chutney, pickled watermelon rind, diced green pepper, diced
cucumber mixed with yoghurt, diced avocado sprinkled with
lime juice, diced tomatoes, crumbled bacon, chopped cashew
nuts, salted pepitas, chow-chow pickle, imported Brinjal pickle,
India relish, and dried Bombay duck.

SHRIMP CURRY

2-2½ pounds raw shrimp, shelled and deveined (figure 18 to 20
  per pound)
3 tablespoons sweet butter
1 tablespoon oil
1 cup onion, finely minced
4 shallots, finely minced
2 cloves garlic, finely minced
4 tablespoons curry powder
¼ teaspoon ground ginger
¼ teaspoon ground cardamom
½ teaspoon hot peppers (dried)
¼ cup sifted all-purpose flour
2 tablespoons lime juice
1 pared apple, cut up in bite-sized pieces
2 teaspoons lemon peel, pared and slivered into thin, thin strips
½ cup heavy cream
1 cup coconut milk (see preceding chicken curry recipe)
2 cups strong chicken broth
2 teaspoons grated lime peel
1 cup chopped celery
½ cup chopped green pepper
1 teaspoon salt
½ cup dried raisins
½ cup slivered candied ginger
½ cup Bombay chivda (recipe follows)

I.   In a large skillet, melt 3 tablespoons sweet butter with
       1 tablespoon oil. Sauté the chopped onion, shallot and
       garlic until the mixture turns a light golden color
       and becomes tender.

II.   Immediately add the curry powder and the raw shrimp,
       turning them constantly. Add the ginger, cardamom
       and hot peppers as the shrimp begin turning pink.

III.   Remove from the heat. Blend in flour, lime juice,
       chopped apple, and slivered lemon peel.

IV.   Cook over moderate heat, adding the cream and
       coconut milk and stirring constantly.

V.   As the curry thickens, dilute it with chicken broth and
       bring to a boil, stirring constantly. Add the grated lime

peel, chopped celery, and green pepper. Simmer uncovered for about 10 minutes. Add salt to taste.

VI.   Remove from the heat and arrange the curry in an
ovenware casserole or serving dish, layering the raisins
and candied ginger through the curry as you spoon
it out.

VII.   Sprinkle the curry with Bombay chivda and serve.
Shrimp curry may be prepared in advance and reheated
in a 300° oven for 15 minutes. If the curry is to be
reheated, however, do not garnish it with the Bombay
chivda until it is ready to go to the table. Serves 6-8.

BOMBAY CHIVDA

Bombay chivda is my own duplication of the fiery hot
oriental curry adjunctive. I mix it every six months and store it
in a tightly covered jar on my spice shelf.

1 cup Granola dry cereal
½ cup chopped salted pistachio nuts
½ cup sunflower seeds
4 tablespoons hot curry powder
1 tablespoon turmeric
1 tablespoon hot dried pepper seeds
1 teaspoon cumin seed
1 teaspoon Fenugreek
1 teaspoon chili powder
*1 teaspoon crushed candied mimosa**

*Candied mimosa is available by mail from Aphrodisia,
28 Carmine Street, New York, N.Y. 10014.

Cold roast veal is worth a kinetic king's ransom these days.
Save the recipe and make it when the cost-of-living drops
somewhat—or pawn your diamonds and do it now.

COLD ROAST VEAL PARISIEN

4 pounds boneless leg of roast veal
1 large clove of garlic
2 teaspoons fresh thyme, finely chopped, or 1 teaspoon dried
thyme

salt and pepper
½ pound strips of bacon
4 tablespoons dry vermouth
2 tablespoons melted butter

SAUCE
3 cups whipping cream
¼ teaspoon salt and a good grind of fresh pepper
1 tablespoon dry English mustard
2 tablespoons tomato paste
2 tablespoons freshly chopped basil, chervil, or parsley

I.   Preheat oven to 325°. Peel the garlic. With a knife, slash one end and rub the roast well with the cut edge. Place the thyme on the top of the meat. Add salt and pepper.

II.   Cover with strips of bacon and arrange on a rack in a roasting pan. Pour the vermouth and melted butter over it. Insert a meat thermometer in the thickest part of the roast and place in the oven.

III.   Baste often with the pan juices. The roast is done when the thermometer registers 155° to 160° (slightly less than 2 hours). Allow to cool for about 2 to 3 hours.

IV.   Remove bacon strips and slice very thin. Serve with the following sauce.

V.   To make the sauce, simmer the cream, salt, and pepper in a small saucepan for 8 to 10 minutes, or until it has reduced to less than 2 cups.

VI.   Beat the mustard and tomato paste together in a small bowl, then slowly beat in the hot cream. Set aside to cool. It will thicken as it chills.

VII.   Stir in the herbs, correct seasoning, and serve with the veal. Serves 8.

HERBED RICE SALAD

2 cups raw rice
very finely mince and reserve, in separate dishes:

5 shallots
2 stalks of celery
1 small green pepper
1 large raw carrot
1 cucumber
1 medium-sized raw zucchini
4 scallions (tops and bulbs)
slice and reserve:
   ½ cup black olives
   ½ cup radishes
¼ cup toasted slivered almonds
½ cup parsley, finely chopped
2 tablespoons basil, finely chopped
2 tablespoons tarragon, finely chopped
1 cup vinaigrette dressing
salt and black pepper
1 pimiento cut into thin strips
peel of ½ lemon (cut into very, very thin strips)

I.   Cook the rice by throwing 2 cups of raw, unwashed rice into a 5-quart pot of boiling salted water and cooking it uncovered for 15 minutes. Drain the rice in a large colander and place over a pot of simmering water. Cover with a double layer of paper towels. Cook for about 15 – 20 minutes or until the grains of rice are steamed through and separate easily at the touch of a fork. Let rice cool slightly before using it for salad. (Leftover rice works equally well. If it has become hard or sticks together, steam it for 5 – 10 minutes before using.)

II.   Add the minced vegetables to the rice. Add olives, radishes, almonds, herbs, and vinaigrette dressing. Toss well and season to taste. Decorate with strips of pimiento and slivers of lemon peel. Serves 4-6.

Jambon en croûte is a self-serving exercise to which I seem to have devoted far too much space as it is. A well-made crust must be thin enough so there is no floury undertaste, and yet, substantial enough to hold its shape as it is thinly carved, along with its ham tenant. It is no mean trick, I can tell you.

JAMBON EN CROUTE

10-12 pound boneless smoked ham (I prefer the Dubuque
   Fleur De Lis brand)
whole cloves
4 tablespoons Dijon mustard
1 clove garlic, mashed
¼ cup Chinese Duck Sauce
dash of orange juice
½ cup brown sugar

PASTRY
6 cups all-purpose flour
1½ teaspoons salt
¼ teaspoon sugar
½ cup butter
¼ cup vegetable shortening
2 eggs, beaten together
about ⅔ cup cold water
1 egg plus 1 teaspoon cold water

I.   Preheat oven to 400°. With a sharp knife, score the
       top of the ham. Stud with the cloves at every inter-
       section.

II.   Combine the mustard, garlic, and duck sauce with
       enough orange juice to make a syrupy mixture. Spread
       evenly over the tops and sides of the ham.

III.   Sprinkle the surface of the ham with the brown sugar
       and bake in the preheated oven for about 1½ hours.
       Let cool thoroughly (about 4-5 hours) before you
       enclose it in pastry.

IV.   To make pastry, place the flour, salt, sugar, butter, and
       vegetable shortening in a big mixing bowl. Rub the
       flour and fat together rapidly between your fingers
       until it is the texture of coarse oatmeal.

V.   Add 2 beaten eggs and water. Blend quickly with one
       hand. Press the dough firmly into a roughly shaped
       ball. Place the dough on a lightly floured pastry board.
       With the heel of one hand, rapidly press the pastry
       down on the board and away from you in a firm,
       quick smear of about 6 inches.

VI.   Gather the dough again into a mass and knead it briefly into a smooth round ball. Sprinkle it lightly with flour and wrap it in waxed paper. Place in your freezer for about 1 hour or until firm.

VII.   Preheat oven to 400°. Remove the pastry from the refrigerator. Roll ⅔ of the pastry dough into an oval ⅛ inch thick. Lay it on the greased baking sheet. Place the baked ham on the oval, bring the pastry up around the ham, and pat it into place. Roll out the rest of the dough ⅛ inch thick and cut it into an oval to fit over the top of the ham. Paint the edges of the bottom oval with a pastry brush dipped in the beaten egg mixture. Press the top into place. Flute or pinch the edges together to seal.

VIII.   With a cookie cutter or a sharp knife, make decorative pastry cut-outs for the edges and center. (I prefer a pattern of diamond shapes.) Paint the top oval with the beaten egg mixture and press on the pastry cut-outs. Paint with the beaten egg.

IX.   Make a ⅛-inch hole in the center of the pastry and insert a brown paper funnel; this allows the steam to escape. Place the ham in the center of a preheated oven. Cook 15 to 20 minutes or until the crust is brown and firm. Allow to cool well. Serve at room temperature, carefully slicing very thin pieces so the crust does not shatter. Serves 10 – 15.

With the crusted ham and a dab of tart Dijon mustard, I always want celeriac salad. Here is ours, coated lavishly in a lemony rémoulade.

CELERIAC REMOULADE

1 pound celery root
1 ½ teaspoons salt (for preparation of celery root)
1 ½ teaspoons lemon juice
4 tablespoons Dijon mustard
3 tablespoons boiling water
⅓ – ½ cup good oil (I prefer ⅓ olive oil to ⅔ Wesson or poly-
*   unsaturated oil)*

2 tablespoons wine vinegar
salt and pepper to taste
2 to 3 tablespoons chopped parsley or mixed herbs (fresh
*   tarragon or fresh sage is delicious)*

I.   Peel the celery root and cut it into julienne match-
      sticks. (This is a tiresome operation, and the alterna-
      tive is to put the root through the large blade of an
      electric shredder.) Toss in a bowl with 1½ teaspoons
      salt and 1½ teaspoons lemon juice. Let steep for 30
      minutes. Rinse the pieces in cold water, drain, and dry
      them in a towel.

II.   Warm a 2-quart mixing bowl in hot water. Dry. Add
      the mustard and beat in the boiling water with a wire
      whip. Then beat in the oil by droplets to make a
      thick creamy sauce. Beat in the vinegar and season
      to taste.

III. Fold the celery root into the sauce, and allow it to
      marinate for 2 to 3 hours or overnight. Decorate with
      herbs before serving. Serves 6.

A rapée Morvandelle is an extremely immoral mix of
potatoes, cheese, cream and ham—and has absolutely no kinship
with any *au gratin* that I have ever tasted. It makes a fine
marriage with filet of beef or goes its single way as a blessed
early brunch or late supper.

RAPEE MORVANDELLE

½ cup onions, finely minced
2 tablespoons good cooking oil
4½ tablespoons sweet butter
½ cup cooked ham, finely diced
4 eggs
½ clove garlic, mashed
2 tablespoons parsley, finely minced
1 cup grated Swiss cheese
¼ cup heavy cream
¼ teaspoon salt
good grind of fresh pepper
3 medium-sized potatoes

I. Preheat oven to 375°. In a skillet, cook the onions slowly in 2 tablespoons oil and 2 tablespoons butter for 5 minutes or until tender, but not browned. Raise heat slightly, stir in the ham, and cook a minute longer.

II. Beat the eggs in a mixing bowl with the garlic, parsley, ⅔ cup grated cheese, cream, and seasonings. Blend in the ham and onions.

III. Peel the potatoes and grate them, using the large holes of your grater or an electric shredder. Remove them from the bowl a handful at a time, and squeeze out any moisture. Stir the shredded potatoes into the egg mixture. Correct seasoning, if necessary.

IV. Heat 2 tablespoons butter in an 11 to 12-inch flameproof baking dish. When foaming, pour in the potato and egg mixture. Dot with ½ tablespoon butter cut into pea-sized dots. Sprinkle with the ⅓ cup remaining cheese.

V. Set in the upper ⅓ of the preheated oven and bake for 35 minutes or until the top is nicely browned. Serve directly from dish. Serves 6.

Fish poaching is a trick that is easily mastered. Fish cosmetology is a different kettle of ketch. Decorating your skinned beauty requires mayonnaise, magic, and a steady hand. Here are my tips for the party debuts of both salmon and bass:

POACHED SALMON OR BASS

5 — 10 pounds cleaned raw salmon or bass
½ lemon studded with 3 cloves
1 bottle of dry white wine
water
salt
bouquet garni composed of a small stalk of celery, 2 sprigs of parsley, a bay leaf, a raw carrot (cut in 4 pieces), and a sliced onion

MAYONNAISE COLLE TO COVER FISH
2 tablespoons unflavored gelatin (2 packages)
2 cups of clear chicken broth, hot (I use G. Washington)

1 cup mayonnaise
1 cup of sour cream
dash of Tabasco

DECORATION FOR FISH
2 cups of very finely minced parsley
1 large stuffed olive, cut in half
strip of pimiento
carrot curl
*1 large red onion, peeled and cut into ⅛-inch thick slices; then
    cut in half-circles as well*
*1 lemon and 1 lime, peeled and cut into ⅛-inch thick slices
    with each slice cut into half-circles*
*decorative salad greens such as romaine, escarole, bibb, or oak
    leaf lettuce*

I.   Wrap the bouquet garni in cheesecloth and tie with
        string. Have the fish cleaned, but leave the head and
        fins on. To keep the fish intact during poaching, wrap
        it well in a double fold of cheesecloth, tying it from
        top to bottom with white string—and then tying it
        around the middle in three strategic places from head
        to tail.

II.   Place the clothed, trussed fish in a fish poacher with a
        removable rack, so that you can remove the fish from
        the stock and allow it to drain after it has cooked.
        Measuring in cupfuls, pour equal amounts of wine
        and water over the fish. (The liquid should cover the
        fish by about 2 inches. If you are shy—add more water
        and several tablespoons of wine vinegar.) Place the
        salt, bouquet garni and lemon in the poacher as well—
        and set it on top of the stove, covering two burners if
        necessary.

III.   When the liquid has come to a quick boil, lower the
        heat so the water barely simmers. A fish will generally
        take almost 10 minutes a pound to cook. If the water
        begins to simmer, add cold water or an ice cube to
        retard the bubbling. A fish must be cooked slowly so
        the flesh is tender, but does not flake off. When the
        fish is done, lift it out and let it drain well until it is
        cool enough to handle.

IV.   With a sharp knife and a good scissors, carefully remove the string and gently begin to peel off the cheesecloth. (If you are very lucky, some of the skin will peel off with it.) To remove the outer skin, use a sharp knife and make a light vertical incision along the spine from head to tail. Always peel downward—and don't worry if a little flesh becomes disarrayed. When decorating the fish later, one can cosmetically overcome any deficiencies that are incurred. Do not attempt to peel the head. It will be decorated later too. Before decorating, cover the peeled fish with plastic wrap or waxed paper and chill for a couple of hours or preferably overnight.

V.   To prepare the *collé,* dissolve the gelatin in the broth. Beat the mayonnaise and sour cream into the broth. Add a dash of Tabasco and stir over ice until the liquid begins to thicken. Refrigerate while undertaking the next step.

VI.   Place the salmon or bass on a serving platter or fish board. Slip several sheets of waxed paper underneath the fish so that any excess decorating goo will settle on it. By spoonfuls, coat the entire chilled fish with the *collé.* It may require several coats to do the job.

VII.   Once the mayonnaise *collé* is on the fish, you must work quickly, but very carefully. Pat the minced parsley over the entire head section—and then do the same thing to the tail. You may remove the waxed paper at this point.

VIII.   Cut a stuffed olive in half, and place it on the head—where the eye socket was. A carrot curl forms an eyebrow. A curled piece of pimiento makes a fine scarlet mouth.

IX.   I always lay a border of thin sliced lemon pieces, like a collar, just below the head and make a similar border just above the tail section.

X.   Using a wide-bladed knife, lay onion halves in a pattern across the fish's back. Start with two onion slices; then add a row of three below it—then two again, then three, till a whole Pucci-like fabric pattern has been created.

XI.   Tuck decorative lettuce around the entire fish and then make a wall of alternating lemon and lime slices, from head to toe, along both sides of the fish.

XII.   Place the decorated fish in a cool place and let it set well.

XIII.   Serve salmon with homemade mayonnaise or green herbed mayonnaise (pages 24-25). Serve bass with sauce gribiche (recipe follows). Serves 8 — 10.

SAUCE GRIBICHE

6 yolks of hard-cooked eggs
2 teaspoons dry mustard
2 teaspoons salt
1 teaspoon freshly ground pepper
2 cups olive oil
2 tablespoons wine vinegar
6 whites of hard-cooked eggs, finely chopped
2 tablespoons finely chopped dill pickle
2 teaspoons finely chopped capers
4 tablespoons finely chopped mixed herbs: chives, parsley,
*   tarragon, chervil*

I.   Crush egg yolks with a fork and blend well with the mustard, salt, and pepper. Gradually stir in oil. When it is all absorbed, add vinegar, egg whites, and other seasonings. Let sauce stand at least one-half hour to bring out flavor. Serve chilled as accompaniment to poached fish.

POACHED FILETS OF FISH

2 tablespoons shallots, finely minced
2½ pounds sole or flounder filet, skinned and boned, cut into
*   serving pieces*
salt and pepper
1½ tablespoons butter cut into bits
1½ cups fish stock

I.   Preheat oven to 350°. Butter a large bakeproof dish. Sprinkle half the shallots in the bottom of the dish.

Season filets lightly with salt and pepper and arrange them in slightly overlapping layers in the dish. Sprinkle with the remaining shallots and dot with butter. Pour in the stock to cover; add water if necessary.

II. Bring almost to a simmer on top of the stove. Lay buttered, waxed, or brown paper over the fish. Then place dish in bottom third of preheated oven. Maintain liquid at a near-simmer for 8-12 minutes, depending on the thickness of the fish. Fish is done when a fork pierces flesh easily. Do not overcook. Fish should not be dry and flaky.

III. Place a cover over the dish and drain the liquid. Fish may be covered and kept warm over hot, but not simmering water, or covered with the paper and set aside to be warmed later over simmering water. Be sure fish is drained of all liquid before serving.

IV. Serve covered with a blanket of sauce Mornay. Add a grating of fresh Swiss cheese and put it under the broiler briefly (5 minutes). Serves 5-6.

The crowning touch for Leonard Bernstein's birthday was a fabulous chocolate roll. Making it is a test of human resourcefulness, but the result is a thing of such exquisite delicacy that I urge you up and onward.

ROULAGE LEONTINE

8 eggs, at room temperature
1 cup superfine sugar
3 level tablespoons sifted confectioners' sugar
½ pound dark, sweet chocolate
1 tablespoon unsweetened dry cocoa (approximately)
1½ cups heavy cream
fresh vanilla bean
1 tablespoon toasted slivered almonds
oil

I. Preheat oven to 350°. Separate the eggs. Add 1 cup superfine sugar to the yolks and beat with a large wire whip until pale and fluffy. Set aside.

II.   In a small pan or double boiler, place ½ pound dark, sweet chocolate, broken in pieces, with ⅓ cup cold water. Stir over very low heat until the chocolate melts. When cool, mix gently but thoroughly with the beaten egg yolks.

III.   Beat the egg whites into soft peaks. Do not overbeat. Fold the chocolate mixture into the egg whites very gently with a rubber scraper. Do not break the egg whites.

IV.   Oil a jelly roll pan and cover with waxed paper extending 1 inch beyond the ends of the pan. Spread the batter evenly over the paper, smoothing evenly with the scraper. Put in a preheated oven for 17 to 18 minutes. It will puff up and the surface will have a dull finish when done. Do not overcook.

V.   Remove the pan from the oven. Work quickly to soak one layer of paper towels in cold water; wring out excess water. Prepare another layer of dry paper towels. Cover the top of the roll with the wet towels and top that with the dry ones. Let stand for 20 minutes.

VI.   When cool, very carefully peel off the paper towels. Loosen the sides of the roll slightly with a small sharp knife. Carefully lift the extending edges of the waxed paper, first at one end, then the other, to loosen. Then dust the top with dry cocoa (the best way to do this is with a sifter or strainer). Soak a tea towel in cold water and then wring it dry. Place the towel taut over the cocoa-sprinkled surface of the roll. Holding the ends of the pan in either hand, lift the pan and towel together and turn over *very quickly*. Lift the pan away and gently peel off the waxed paper. Very carefully, roll up the towel with the cake inside it, (rolling it the long way). This must be done quickly. Let stand for 5 minutes.

VII.   In a chilled metal bowl, pour 1 cup heavy cream. Beat with a chilled wire whisk until the cream begins to thicken. Add confectioners' sugar and some scraped vanilla bean. Continue whipping until the cream holds its shape.

VIII.   Unroll the cake, put 9 mounds of the whipped cream in rows of 3, across the surface of the roll. Spread evenly with the scraper. Then re-roll it like a jelly roll, flipping it quickly towards you. (Do not worry if the roll cracks a bit as you are going to sprinkle on more cocoa.)

IX.   Serve on a jelly roll board or long platter. Garnish with a heavy dusting of cocoa and a sprinkling of toasted almonds. Chill well before serving. Serves 10.

Swim against
the Current

Chapter Five

DENIS VAUGHAN

To swim against the current is not so bad. I realize that I have been doing this very thing all my life, and it is unlikely I will stop now. Oh, I may tread water now and then, giving some the illusion I am going to go with the tide, but eventually it is back to the same old thing—like those poor salmon. In tribute to them, here is a recipe you are going to find festive. It has nothing to do, however, with salmon.

BLANQUETTE DE POISSON

6 large fillets of sole or flounder
12 large uncooked shrimp that have been shelled and deveined
1 bottle of dry white wine
1 slice of lemon
1 small white onion studded with 3 cloves
1 bay leaf
1 sprig of parsley
1½ cups mayonnaise
½ cup finely chopped parsley
½ cup finely chopped dill
¼ cup finely chopped chives
dash of Tabasco sauce (optional)
salt and fresh pepper

I.   Place the wine, lemon slice, and onion studded with cloves in an enamel saucepan. Tie the bay leaf and parsley sprig together and add to the other ingredients. Let this all come to a boil, then quickly throw in the shrimp. They should cook for no longer than 3 minutes, until they have barely turned pink.

II.   Remove the shrimp and let them drain. With a slotted spoon remove the onion and the bouquet garni as well. Lower the heat so that the fish bouillon is barely at a simmer. If it is too hot, add ¼ cup of cold water to the mixture.

III.   Cut the six fillets of fish in half; roll each half around one cooked shrimp. Place the rolled fillets in the same saucepan and cover with a round of buttered waxed paper.

IV.   Fish will poach over low heat for about 4-5 minutes. With a large slotted spoon remove them to a serving dish and chill.

V.   In a mixing bowl, combine 1½ cups mayonnaise, ½ cup chopped parsley, ½ cup chopped dill, and ¼ cup chopped chives. Mix well and test for seasoning. (This sauce might require a squeeze of lemon, a dash of Tabasco, or salt and pepper to give it a little zip.)

VI.   Make sure the drained blanquettes are free from their poaching liquid bath. Pour off excess water. Then spoon the green mayonnaise over the rolled fish fillets. Serve very, very cold as a first course. This dish is somewhere between light and hearty, bland and spicy, plain and indulgently rich. Serves 6.

There was once a rheumy-eyed lady who was an avid admirer of The Store. She was the widow of famed sportswriter and the current wife of a local sanitation worker, a man who spoke so hesitantly that I wanted to shout, "Get on with it!" She, dear lady, seemed always near tears. With experience and a trained eye, I judged it more the effects of the sauce than emotion. She attended The Store cooking class one year and fell in love with the following dish. She reportedly pressed it on her friends with the regularity of a ticking clock.

FILLET OF SOLE DUGLERE

8 fillets of sole or flounder
2 sticks sweet butter
salt
dash of Tabasco
3 firm, large mushrooms
1 tablespoon lemon juice
freshly ground pepper
1 cup dry white wine

⅓ *cup water*
4 tomatoes
4½ tablespoons flour
cayenne pepper
1 cup heavy cream
½ cup grated Swiss or Parmesan cheese plus 2 tablespoons for
*   garnish*
1 tablespoon chopped parsley
1½ tablespoons buttered bread crumbs

I. Preheat oven to 350°. Blanch the fish, then dry well on paper towels. Melt a little butter and coat a large baking dish with it. Season outer sides of fillets with a little salt and a dash of Tabasco. Fold fillets lengthwise and arrange on the baking dish.

II. In a saucepan, melt 4 tablespoons butter. Slice the mushrooms; add to the pan, shaking so that the mushrooms are well coated. Add 1 tablespoon lemon juice, a dash of salt, and pepper; cook for a minute or two.

III. Add the white wine and water. Bring to a boil and spoon carefully over the fish. Cover the dish with buttered waxed paper and poach in the oven for 15 minutes. Remove from oven and keep warm.

IV. Strain the poaching liquid and set aside. Seed and juice 4 tomatoes. Blend ¾ of them and shred the rest. Set aside.

V. In a saucepan, melt 6 tablespoons butter. Off the flame stir in 4½ tablespoons flour, ½ teaspoon salt, a dash of cayenne pepper; whisk until smooth. Gradually add the strained fish stock and the blended tomatoes. Stir over low flame until mixture thickens and boils. Add the heavy cream and ½ cup cheese. Over a low flame stir in 1 tablespoon butter, by bits, and let the sauce simmer for 5 minutes.

VI. Add 1 tablespoon chopped parsley and shredded tomatoes and spoon over the fillets. Sprinkle with 1½ tablespoons buttered bread crumbs and remaining cheese. Sprinkle with pea-sized bits of butter and brown quickly under the broiler. Serves 6 to 8.

There is a dish we do in The Store—only on demand—that is not so complex as it is tedious. But the Queens of Love and Beauty adore it and so it is done. You will adore it, too, if you have the patience to see it through. It is done with shrimp, limes, and love.

THE STORE SHRIMP SALAD

3 pounds uncooked shrimp
1 quart court bouillon
1 whole clove of garlic
1 large bunch of celery and 3 stalks of fresh fennel, minced
    together, very fine
4 shallots, finely minced
2 limes, sliced into thin, thin rounds, plus the juice of 1 lime
1 large can of pitted black olives
½ cup of chopped fresh basil
1½ cups vinaigrette dressing
salt and freshly ground pepper
chives for garnish

I. Make a court bouillon by combining the following ingredients in a large kettle and bringing to a boil: 1 cup dry white wine, 1 cup clam juice, half a sliced lemon, three parsley stems, the tops of several celery stalks, one large yellow onion studded with 3 cloves, and 1 bay leaf.

II. Place the uncleaned, raw shrimp in the court bouillon and boil for about 3 to 4 minutes, until shrimp turn pink. Do not overcook! Clean and devein shrimp under cold running water. Do not remove the tails.

III. Rub a bowl well with garlic, then discard it. Add the minced celery and fennel, shallots, and the juice of the lime. Toss well.

IV. Add the shrimp, black olives, and basil. Marinate the mixture in vinaigrette dressing for about an hour. Season to taste. Toss. Serve with lime slices and more black olives as garnish. Chop a few chives over all and serve. Serves 6-8.

With lofty detachment, condescending eyes, impeccable continental manners, and a voice laced with quiet steel, Mrs. Oscar Kolin, a lady of brittle grace, makes her needs and wants clear, direct, and to the point. No fooling around here. You have the picture in a flash. She is giving a dinner for twenty. She has her own kitchen help, but would like a presentable bartender and waitress. Provided. Her husband, now the head of Helena Rubinstein, loves lobster. What can we do? Here is what is done.

LOBSTER THERMIDOR

2 boiled lobsters, 1 to 1½ pounds each
4 tablespoons butter
2 teaspoons flour
1 cup stock or bouillon
¼ cup heavy cream
salt
pinch of paprika
pinch of celery salt
pinch of cayenne pepper
1 tablespoon sherry
1½ cups white bread, shredded
bread crumbs for garnish

I. Preheat broiling unit. Split the lobsters in half; remove the hard sack near the head and the intestinal vein. Take the meat out of the body; crack the claws, and remove their meat as well. Dice. Reserve the shells.

II. In a skillet, melt 1 tablespoon butter and stir in the flour until well blended. Add the lobster. Gradually add the stock, and then the cream. Simmer, stirring, for 10 minutes. Season with salt, paprika, celery salt, and cayenne. Remove the lobster from the pan and keep warm.

III. Add the sherry, 3 tablespoons of butter, and the bread to the skillet. Cook and stir until all the butter is absorbed.

IV. Wash the lobster shells thoroughly. Fill them with the lobster mixture, and spread the tops with the crumbs. Place under the broiler until brown. Serves 2.

"Why do your hands shake? You're too young for your hands to shake. And why do you always lie across that chair on your stomach on Fridays?" came the voice of my father, who was a doctor. Would he not be the logical one to have the answers to those questions? Instead he invariably pulled this district attorney number on me, a pre-teen boy raised in a strict Roman Catholic family who detested Fridays because that day meant fish. And always the same fish—cod—done in my mother's style, boiled, swimming in a tasteless white sauce, and served with boiled white potatoes and cauliflower. This virginal white meal not only gave me the stomachache that caused me to lie across the chair, but paralyzed my senses as well. Since parents and all friends from those days have either died or vanished, I have come to liberate my thoughts on the subject of cod—and all fish. Here is a delicious recipe for cod.

COD FLORENTINE

6 large fillets of cod
2 cups of freshly cooked spinach, roughly chopped
nutmeg
¾ cup sauce Mornay
4 tablespoons grated Parmesan cheese

I.   Preheat broiling unit. Poach the fillets according to instructions given on page 88. Arrange the poached fillets on a bed of chopped, cooked spinach that has been lightly sprinkled with nutmeg.

II.   Pour the sauce Mornay over the fish and sprinkle with the cheese. Run under the broiler flame until nicely browned. Serves 6.

If you want to knock 'em dead at your next fiesta or *enkai* (the Japanese word for party) try tempura. It is relatively simple to cook, but infuriatingly complex to prepare. It helps to have a Japanese in residence, as I do, to show you how to chop. Chopping is all in the wrist movement, an action I could not possibly explain unless I had you here to show you. Tempura is, however, sensational party food.

TEMPURA

24 shrimp, shelled and deveined with tails on and with 4 slits
    made halfway through across the back of each shrimp
½ pound fillet of flounder, cut into ½-inch strips
6 medium-sized white onions, cut in half, sliced into ½-inch
    wedges, and skewered with toothpicks
2 carrots, scraped and cut into match sticks about 2-2½ inches
    long
1 sweet potato, halved and cut in ¼-inch slices
½ head cauliflower, flowerets cut into bite-sized pieces
24 string beans, trimmed, halved, and made into pairs by
    skewering with toothpicks
12 medium-sized mushrooms, cut in half
½ bunch watercress, stalks separated
½ bunch parsley, stems removed (allow 3-4 sprigs per person)
6 canned sweet chestnuts, drained and skewered with toothpicks
6 mint leaves
2 pieces of ginger, skinned and sliced ⅛ inch thick
salt and white pepper to taste

SAUCE
4-inch square sheet of **Dashi Konbu** (seaweed)*
5 cups water
1 ounce dried bonito (dried fish known as Hanakatsuo)*
1 cup Mirin (Japanese rice wine)*
1 cup soy sauce
2 tablespoons of bonito*
1 tablespoon Accent
¼ teaspoon hot chopped peppers (or to taste)
1 teaspoon salt

BATTER
1 cup cold water
1 egg, beaten
1½ cups sifted flour
1 ice cube

FINAL PREPARATION
vegetable oil
1 cup flour (approximately)

I.   Prepare the ingredients as called for; season with salt
and white pepper, and set aside until ready to use.

II.   To prepare the sauce, wipe the seaweed with a damp cloth on both sides. Place the seaweed and water in a saucepan on a medium flame. Remove the seaweed just before the boiling point is reached, discard, and replace it with 1 ounce of dried bonito and extinguish the flame. Let the mixture stand until the bonito settles at the bottom of the pan and then strain through several thicknesses of cheesecloth.

III.   Combine 4 cups of the sauce you have just made with 1 cup Mirin, the soy sauce, bonito, Accent, hot peppers, and salt. Place over a medium flame for 8 minutes. Strain through cheesecloth. This is the finished sauce. Cool and use as a dip for the tempura.

IV.   To prepare the batter, pour the cold water into a bowl and slowly add the beaten egg. Blend. Add the sifted flour little by little to the mixture and blend lightly. Add the ice cube to the mixture and continue blending until the cube dissolves.

V.   In a deep skillet, pour vegetable oil to the ¾ depth. Place over high heat until very hot. To test the temperature, place a drop of batter in the oil. If it sinks to the bottom and surfaces quickly, you are in business.

VI.   Roll each of the tempura ingredients lightly in the flour, dip in the batter, and deep fry for 1-2 minutes. The cauliflower and sweet potato will take a little longer—3-4 minutes. When all this is done, drain on paper towels and serve immediately, using the tempura sauce as a dip. (You may want to throw the finished tempura in a very hot oven for a few minutes to insure a hot, crispy final touch). Serves 6.

        *These ingredients may be obtained at any friendly, inscrutable neighborhood Oriental grocery across the land—or from the following by mail: Katagiri and Company Inc., 224 E. 59th Street, New York, NY, or Asia Mart, 41-96 Bowne Street, Flushing, N.Y.

"Princess, princess, Mr. Denis is here to talk about your party," she called up the impressive staircase in the impressive entrance hall of the equally impressive Tudor house in exclusive Sands Point, Long Island. "She" is Margaret, a warm, friendly black woman of a certain age whose main function seems to be the smooth operation of the household of the princess. The princess is Mrs. Maurice Cohn, a petite, dark-haired beauty who looks as if she subsists on a lettuce leaf or two and possibly an occasional dab of cottage cheese. Actually she has a rather robust appetite and doesn't shrink in horror when the fare I suggest becomes heady and frankly fattening. She heartily agrees. We have a very good working relationship. I admire her, and her choice of menus, and her appreciation of our food. The following is a first course for which she always clamors:

SHRIMP WITH GREEN SAUCE

1 ½ pounds shrimp, shelled and deveined
salt
slice of lemon
stalk of celery, chopped
1 onion, halved
¾ cup white wine
1 small onion, finely minced
2 tablespoons olive oil
1 cup minced parsley
1 small garlic, minced
¼ cup water
pinch of saffron
pinch of cayenne pepper
12 pitted green olives, chopped
¼ cup coarsely chopped green olives
1 crushed shallot
¼ cup vinaigrette dressing

I.   Cook shrimp in salted water with lemon slice, celery, halved onion, and ½ cup white wine for 4 minutes, or until pink. Drain and set aside.

II.   Cook the minced onion in olive oil until soft. Add the parsley and simmer for 30 seconds. Add the garlic, ¼ cup white wine, water, saffron, cayenne, and the 12 pitted olives. Simmer for 5 minutes and purée in a blender. Chill well.

III.   Add the shrimp to the green sauce; toss, and add ¼ cup chopped olives, shallot and vinaigrette. Chill and serve cold. Serves 4.

Living in Amagansett are two people who more than once have been the joys of my life. The man is a painter of volatile nature, well known, and respected, who has been known to hoist persons twice his weight high in the air. The other person is a woman of parts. Not only is she a designer, but also an indefatigable hostess and a splendid cook. I would not pilfer one of her recipes, but I will include this one that she has admired. We traveled together through the Soviet Union two years ago, eating the worst food known to mankind. Their name is Gwathmey: he—Robert; she—Rosalie. During our travels through Mother Russia, beautiful as it is, but gastronomically bereft, we never got this:

CRABMEAT VINAIGRETTE

1 head fennel, finely minced
1 bunch scallions, finely minced (keep whites and greens separate)
8 shallots, finely minced
4 pounds king crab, frozen or fresh
½ pound soybean sprouts (bean and stalk)
1 large can pitted black olives
½ cup finely minced parsley
4 limes
1½ cups vinaigrette sauce
salt and pepper to taste

I.   In a large bowl, place finely minced fennel. (Reserve the feathery fronds for garnish.) Add the minced scallion bulbs, shallots and the crabmeat which has been broken into bite-sized pieces.

II.   Break the bean sprouts into about ½-inch sections and place in the bowl. Slice the olives in half and add. Add the parsley and toss in the juice of 2 limes. Then pour in the vinaigrette, toss well, and chill thoroughly.

III. Before serving season to taste with salt and pepper and garnish with paper-thin slices of lime. Serve on a piece of lettuce if desired, and decorate with the minced fennel fronds and minced scallion ends (green part). Serves 10 – 12.

The glamorous, legendary, and late Gertrude Lawrence was appearing in Chicago in *Lady in the Dark* more years ago than I care to remember, and one evening she elected to dine at the Pump Room in the Ambassador East Hotel. My mother, father, and I were seated at the table next to Miss Lawrence, and we were going to see her performance that night. With my father's usual lack of servility, he introduced himself to the lady, told her he had admired her for many years, and that she was a pretty classy-looking babe. She was charming. My mother and I shrank visibly in our chairs. He and "Gertie" (his name for her, not mine) carried on an animated conversation about medicine (I am sure she could not have cared less) and then proceeded to the subject of food.

"What are you having tonight, you cute little vixen?" he asked. Miss Lawrence allowed as how she always ate lightly before a performance. My mother and I by this time were emotionally under the table.

"What do you mean by light?" from the good father.

"Fish," was the reply, and they were off and running.

"The brook trout is divine here," she said. They both had it. I don't remember what I had, chagrin having got the better of me.

"Well, little lady, you'd better be good tonight," he sallied as she rose like a star from her table. "We'll be cheering for you. Let's get together again and swap more fish dishes. I have a couple of my own." She flashed an incandescent smile and departed. The brook trout at the Pump Room is delicious: I have had it since.

BROOK TROUT

4 brook trout, each 8 inches long
flour, seasoned with salt and pepper

¼ cup butter plus 3 tablespoons
lemon wedges
chopped parsley

I.   Clean and wash the trout, removing the fins. Leave the head and the tail on.

II.   Dip the fish in the flour and sauté until nicely browned and tender in ¼ cup of butter. Remove to a hot platter.

III.   Add 3 tablespoons butter to the pan; permit it to brown slightly, and pour over the fish. Place lemon wedges around the fish and sprinkle with parsley. Serves 4.

"Oh, but you're so expensive!" she wailed. This from the lips of Anne Jackson, Mrs. Eli Wallach, a sometime customer of The Store. "And I can do that, and I can do that, and that, and that, and probably better—or just as well." Well, probably. However, if you are having thirty people and you want to impress them and you do not want to do anything yourself because of pressures—one sort or another—sometimes you come to the expensive Store. We settle on a traditional lobster salad with a French bread, a green salad, and whatever wine she elects to choose. It should be white and good . . . real expensive.

A SIMPLE LOBSTER SALAD

greens: lettuce or romaine
2 cups diced lobster meat
mayonnaise
2 hard-cooked eggs
2 teaspoons Pernod
capers

I.   The amounts of the above to be used depend on personal taste and the amount you need. Serve with a little mayonnaise or much; the same with the eggs and capers. Sprinkle Pernod on, and toss lightly.

II.   Line a bowl with greens. Mix the lobster meat with mayonnaise and heap it into the bowl. Cut the eggs into quarters. Garnish with the eggs and capers.

Here is another seafood recipe I love. It has nothing to do with anyone else, but try it.

BROILED SCALLOPS

1 pound scallops
olive oil
4 tablespoons butter
1¼ tablespoons minced chives
1½ tablespoons lemon juice
salt and pepper

I.   Preheat broiling unit. Wash and dry the scallops between paper towels. Then dip them in olive oil and drain. Place them in a shallow ovenproof serving dish.

II.   Melt 4 tablespoons of butter in a skillet, and add the chives and lemon juice. Cook for 2 minutes.

III.   Place the scallops under the broiler for about 5 minutes, basting with the sauce, turning once. Season with salt and pepper. Serves 3.

And here is another I like that has nothing to do with anyone else—except maybe you:

BAKED SWORDFISH STEAK

2 large swordfish steaks
flour
oil
fresh dill
½ onion, thinly sliced
butter
salt and pepper
1 cup white wine
1 cup cream
3 egg yolks
chopped parsley

I.   Preheat oven to 425°. Dust each steak with flour and brush with oil. Place one of the steaks in a well-oiled baking dish. Spread a layer of dill and then onion slices over it. Dot with butter and season with salt and pepper.

II.   Place the second steak over the first and dot well with butter. Season lightly with salt and pepper. Pour ½ cup of white wine into the pan. Bake for about 25 minutes, basting several times during the cooking.

III.   Remove the fish to a hot serving platter. Add ½ cup wine to the pan; bring to a boil, and gradually stir in the cream mixed with the egg yolks. Stir until thick and smooth. Pour over the fish and serve. Garnish with chopped parsley. Serves 6.

"It will be divine, won't it?" she said, as she hurried to the bathroom. Toilet is more the word, since The Store comes equipped with a loo and a sink, and that is it. In the years when she summered out here, Claire Bloom had an energetic need to use the w. c.

"Here she comes," the hired summer help would mutter. "Do you suppose she wants anything—or just the use of?" Always she wanted something and I never minded as long as she didn't—since our w. c. is not the most pristine place on the face of the earth. (Board of Health, blind your eyes.) Miss Bloom, a lovely lady, fine actress, and person of good taste (I hope there are enough w.c.'s around to care for her needs), ordered this several times:

QUENELLES DE POISSON

PANADA
1 cup water
½ stick sweet butter cut into small pieces
1 teaspoon salt
1 cup sifted all-purpose flour
2 eggs
2 egg whites

QUENELLES
2 cups finely ground raw fish fillets (pike, halibut, flounder)
6 to 8 tablespoons heavy cream
pinch of fresh nutmeg
salt and white pepper

I.   Bring the water, butter, and salt to a simmer in a 3-quart, heavy-bottomed saucepan. As soon as the butter has melted, remove the saucepan from the heat. Put in all the flour at once, beating vigorously with a wooden spoon till thoroughly blended. Return to moderate heat and continue to beat until the mixture forms a ball which leaves the sides of the pan, leaves the spoon clean, and finally begins to film over the pan bottom. Remove from heat again; make a hole in the center of the hot panada, and break an egg into it. Working quickly, return to heat and vigorously beat until the egg is entirely absorbed. Repeat the process with the other egg and then with the egg whites.

II.   Spread the paste in a flat, buttered dish and cover with buttered waxed paper. Chill thoroughly for 30 minutes in the freezer.

III. Chill the fish and grind it in a blender at high speed. Place in a mixing bowl and measure out 2 cups of chilled paste. Add to the fish and beat quickly for several minutes until the paste is thick and holds its shape as a solid mass.

IV.   Start beating in the chilled heavy cream 2 tablespoons at a time, beating a good minute between additions. The aim is to beat in as much cream as possible, while allowing the paste to retain enough body so that it can be poached without disintegrating. Test the mixture by poaching for a few minutes in a small pan of not quite simmering water. If the sample is too dry, add more cream. Beat in nutmeg, salt, and white pepper to taste.

V.   For cylindrically shaped quenelles, take a dessert spoon of paste and roll with the palm of your hand on a floured board, making sausage shapes about 3 inches long.

VI.   Bring 2 inches of lightly salted water to a simmer in a large saucepan. Gently slip the quenelles into the water. Poach, uncovered, 12-15 minutes. They will increase their size twice and roll over easily.

VII.   Remove the quenelles with a slotted spoon and drain on a plate lined with paper towels. They are very delicate in texture and must be handled gently. Serve immediately with sauce Nantua (recipe follows), or arrange in a lightly buttered dish, brush with melted butter, cover with waxed paper, and refrigerate. They will keep for one to two days. Serves 4—6.

SAUCE NANTUA

1½ cups fish stock or clam broth
1 small onion studded with a clove
1 bay leaf
slice of lemon
¼ cup white wine
2 cups raw, unpeeled, deveined shrimp
2 tablespoons butter
2 tablespoons flour
2 egg yolks
½ cup heavy cream
salt, pepper, lemon juice, Tabasco to taste
1½ tablespoons Madeira
shrimp butter

I.   Simmer fish stock with the onion, bay leaf, lemon slice, and wine for several minutes. Add the shrimp and cook until pink. Reserve stock. Peel shrimp and clean, saving the debris.

II.   Boil down fish stock until you have 1 cup. Meanwhile melt the butter in a large saucepan. Blend in the flour; stir over heat for 2 minutes without browning. Remove from heat and beat in the stock, using a wire whisk. Return to heat, boil for 1 minute, and remove from heat.

III.   Blend egg yolks and cream with a whisk and beat into the sauce by driblets. Stir over moderate heat until the sauce comes to a boil. Simmer for a moment, adding more cream to thin out the sauce. It should coat the spoon. Taste for seasoning, and add salt, white pepper, lemon juice, and Tabasco as you deem necessary. (This is now a sauce Parisienne.)

IV.   Fold in the cooked shrimp. If you are not using immediately, float a spoonful of cream over the top to prevent from crusting and refrigerate.

V.   Prepare shrimp butter as follows: heat ¼ pound sweet butter to bubbling in a saucepan. Warm the jar of your blender in hot water. Blend 1 cup cooked shrimp debris (peelings, etc.), 2 whole cooked shrimp and the butter at high speed for a minute or so. Rub through a sieve. Beat the strained butter over ice and cold water for a minute until it is cold and creamy. Excess butter can be frozen or stored in the refrigerator for 3 or 4 days.

VI.   Before serving bring to a simmer for a minute to blend flavors. Immediately add 1½ tablespoons Madeira and as much shrimp butter as you wish. Do not reheat after shrimp butter is added as the sauce will thin out.

"I wonder what it will be tonight?" one mused, preparing to repair to the dining board of Mrs. Ralph Rofheart. If one had one's wits about one, musing was only masturbatory—always it was baked bluefish. Martha Rofheart, also known as Martha Jones when she acted with Alfred Lunt and Lynn Fontanne, was very partial to bluefish and prepared it with authority. I fancy she has given up the preparation of bluefish for the more lucrative streams of writing. After retiring from acting, her first novel, *Fortune Made His Sword,* took her away from the stove. We do not know what she is doing now—maybe making peanut butter sandwiches. Here is her recipe.

BAKED BLUEFISH

bluefish (buy fresh and pick out according to the sizes available
    and the amount needed)
butter
salt and pepper
lemon wedges
chopped parsley

I.   Preheat oven to 425°. Clean and split a bluefish. Place it on a well-buttered baking dish. Dot it heavily with butter; sprinkle with salt and pepper, and bake for about 20 minutes. Test with a fork to see if the fish flakes easily. Serve surrounded with lemon wedges, and sprinkle with chopped parsley.

As a variation stuff a bluefish with a few sprigs of parsley, fresh dill, and 3 slices of lemon. Dot the interior with butter. Sprinkle with salt and pepper. Butter a baking dish, and cover the bottom with finely chopped shallots and green onions. Lay the fish on top; dot with butter, and lightly sprinkle with salt and pepper. Add a cup of white wine and bake at 425° for about 20 minutes, basting often. Remove the fish to a serving platter, and take out the herbs. Add them to the pan; boil for 2 minutes, and strain the juices into a small saucepan. Add ½ cup heavy cream and 2 egg yolks. Stir until thickened, but do not boil. Season and pour over the fish. Top with chopped parsley.

Here are some other excellent fish entrées:

FILLET OF SOLE CALENDALE

6 large fillets of sole or flounder
juice of 1 lemon
3 cups water
about 18-20 large cooked shrimp shelled and deveined
½ bottle dry white wine (approximately)
1 onion stuck with 2 cloves
slice of lemon
bouquet garni: 1 sprig parsley, 1 bay leaf, and a sprig of fresh
  thyme or a pinch of dried thyme tied in cheesecloth

1 cup heavy cream
2½ tablespoons butter
⅛ teaspoon fennel seed
pinch of salt
dash of black pepper
2 lightly beaten egg yolks

I.   Preheat broiling unit. Place the fillets in lemon juice and 3 cups of water to whiten the flesh of the fish. Let stand for 5 minutes.

II.   Cook shrimp for 3 minutes in court bouillon (page 5). Then cut the fillets in half and roll each half around a cooked shrimp.

III.   Place rolled fillets in a saucepan. Pour in enough white wine to half cover; add 1 onion studded with cloves, a slice of lemon, and the bouquet garni. Cover the saucepan with heavily buttered waxed paper. Poach over low heat 4-5 minutes or until the fish flake when tested with a fork. Drain well and transfer to a heated flameproof serving dish.

IV.   Reduce fish stock by half; add 1 cup cream, butter, fennel seed, and seasoning to taste. Heat to boiling and gradually stir in egg yolks. When the sauce is thick, pour over the fish; broil to glaze the surface. Garnish with extra cooked shrimp, fresh fennel, or dill. Serve immediately. Serves 6—8.

ROUGET EN PAPILLOTE

6 sea bass or whitings, ½-pound size, cleaned and filleted
1 scant cup of oil
juice of two lemons
2 tablespoons chopped parsley
2 medium-sized onions, chopped
2 shallots, chopped
2 large cloves garlic, finely chopped
½ fennel root, chopped (reserve the feathery inner stalks)
12 anchovy fillets
3 tablespoons butter, room temperature
6 sheets heavy oiled paper (I use heavy vellum tracing paper)

I.   Preheat oven to 400°. If not already done, trim the tails and any head bones off the fish. Marinate for 30 minutes in a mixture of the oil, lemon juice, chopped parsley, chopped onions, shallots, garlic, and fennel.

II.   Mash the anchovy fillets until smooth and blend with the butter. Spread this mixture in the middle of the oiled papers. Place the fish on top of the mixture, and place a small stalk of fennel top inside each fish cavity. Top each fish with a spoonful of the marinade.

III.   Either fold or roll the paper around the fish and twist the edges to seal tightly. (Make sure they are water-tight.) Bake for about 18-20 minutes, watching carefully to make sure the paper does not burn.

IV.   The fish should be served in their paper cases, so the full fragrance of the dish can be appreciated as they are opened. Slice down the center with a sharp knife or kitchen shears to open. Serves 6.

If simplicity is your forte—and God knows it is mine—the recipe I am about to give you is utterly spare, but will please your palate and that of those to whom you serve it:

BAKED FISH FILLETS DENIS

4 large fish fillets
2½ tablespoons butter
½ cup mixed chopped parsley and chives
flour
salt and pepper
¼ cup dry white wine or vermouth
½ cup fresh bread crumbs sautéed in 1½ tablespoons butter
lemon wedges
chopped parsley for garnish

I.   Preheat oven to 450°. Put 1½ tablespoons butter in a shallow baking dish; place in a hot oven. When the dish is hot, remove it; arrange the cut herbs on the bottom. Place fillets on top of the bed of herbs. Sprinkle with flour to cover; add salt and pepper, and dot with the leftover butter.

II.   Sprinkle with the wine and cook for 12 to 14 minutes, or until tender when tested with a fork. Baste occasionally.

III.   Serve sprinkled with the bread crumbs; garnish with lemon wedges and more parsley. Serves 4.

Autumn's Child

Chapter Six

BERT GREENE

For me the saddest day of the year is not the one after Christmas, but rather, the golden tag that invariably follows the last, long spell of heat in August.

On that particular morning the air seems to change as the winey, ripe smell of summer gives way to a slightly burnt-out incense of singed landscape. And although all is still green below, clouds race farther across the sky than they did the day before, and one's field of vision is so intense that the sight of birds in passage stings the retina like a snowstorm. It is a day of false alarm: fall, a full month before it is due. But it is more disturbing than any white-eyed summer scorcher that precedes it because it is precisely a harbinger of time drawing to a close.

I always recognize the signs of this counterfeit equinox because it is at that moment that people start to fade from my orbit. Oh, I know they are there. I see them at The Store or in the swim, talking of their tennis and their traffic, but somehow their presences become less real . . . less important. Their tanned and sunkissed existences grow less consequential by the second, because we have no immediate future together once another season is over.

On that day, I grow inward as a toenail and only perfunctory in any response I must make to the happy band of late party-givers who feel they can exact my attention span along with their hors d'oeuvres. They are still planning their damned luncheons on the boat and bash buffets even as I have mentally stripped the windows bare and put up the "Closed for the Season" signs, half dreading, half dreaming of that precious, free moment when they will all disappear.

This is the time then, to think, to revitalize, I tell myself every fall as we shutter down. The time to paint or write or go see the China coast. The time for me to be me again.

But it is a false declaration of independence because I am saddened anew, year after year, by the inevitability of the break in continuity.

No matter how hard we struggle through those frazzled summer days, the game is always called for weather. Everything vanishes once September comes.

Birds have better sense; they fly south. We tried their route one fall and found it wanting. Perhaps because we had stayed too long in northern climes to be willing to make the kind of mental transplantation that branching out in alien territory requires, perhaps because our blood was too thick or our skin too thin, the Palmed Beach airs seemed too rarified for any real co-existence.

Some are born to riches and others are destined for fame. I am fated to live and die in a four season cycle, and I accept that equity with uncommon good grace.

I was born in October. It has always been a vagrant theory of mine that people flourish best during their natal months. In a superficial sense, I consider that I look better and am more in control of my mind and body for that one month than I am for the nine others that precede it and the two that follow. Certainly I am more awash with energy to store up the yield than I am at any other time of the year.

Just as the autumn garden is my eye's favorite, with its ochre and purple swallowing up what had been ablaze and brilliant such a short while before, so the autumn harvest, sour as the aftermath of a green tomato and sharp as dried pepper, is the rightest season for my tongue. It is a season so pregnant with the possibility of accomplishment that I literally suffer guilt pangs if I ignore my inner call to "put up."

My sanctus is the sound of the boiling jampot, and my canon is the storehouse of gleaming pint jars that bear golden testament to still another year's vintage. Some make hay; I pickle and can.

I suppose I inherit all this preserve of energy from my maternal, Jewish grandmother, who, young and newly freed of the rigors of farm life in Poland, was deposited with some sub-order cousins in France to wait while her husband worked in the new land to earn enough money to pay her passage to America.

What happened to her there, what mysteries of sight and smell assailed her imagination in a French kitchen almost a hundred years ago, I can never know. But the legacy of her stay remained with her to the end of a long, forceful, and food-loving life.

The tiny white onion and the bit of lettuce she always added as pot-herbs to fresh peas; the slivers of garlic carved into pin-strips and inserted into a leg of lamb; indeed, even the roasting technique itself, with the exterior crisp and gold, the flesh subtly pink inside, were examples of pure francophilia in Queens.

My earliest memories are of waking up in the den off the kitchen in my grandmother's house. I watched as she braided her long hair into one enchanted coil like a silvery black snake on the top of her head, stabbing it into place with a hundred hairpins and combs. Aware that I was watching because she had caught my reflection sometime before in the mirror of the huge black coal stove, she would jab harder than ever.

My grandmother's house revolved around that coal stove. Mornings, after she had walked through her large garden snipping a rusty rose leaf here or pinching an errant chafer between her fingernails there, and before she fed her animals, she would always shake out the ashes and lay a new supply of coal and kindling for the day.

How I would wait, impatient for the day to begin, while she threw seeds to the blue jays and the tame pigeons that lived above the garage.

"Grandma, it's time to light the stove."

She would nod, but first she would permit the yard squirrel to approach, poking his nose in her apron pocket for peanuts, and then Snoozy, the fine, fat Scottish terrier bitch who followed her everywhere, must surely be given a snack too.

"It's late. It's really getting late, Grandma."

But it was never too late to put the fresh coals in and light the shiny, black monstrosity. Never too late to sit near the isinglass window, where a small child could watch the flames dance while the coffee percolated for my grandfather's breakfast and Postum boiled for mine.

A practical woman, my grandmother could produce banquets on that stove or just bake bread, as her will took her.

Even after the pressures of modern living disenfranchised my grandmother's coal stove and the centrifugal gas burner was forced upon her by the household, her jams and jellies and her catsup and conserves were still made of the finest produce that she could hand-pick from the vegetable-man's wagon. His patient horse, halfway through Long Island at this point, was always given a bag of oats at my grandmother's—because she took so much time weighing one rosy peach or pear against a less blushing neighbor.

"Don't be fooled by what just looks good. Fruit must be firm to begin with—even if you're going to smash it up later," she would say. "The flavor starts with just what's inside the skin." Then with an investigator's thumb, she would slit a grape or press a tangerine ever so slightly, so that a fine mist of fruitiness would spray the air.

"We'll take five pounds today, please, Mister Joe. It's a marmalade day, I think." It would happen on these marmalade days or grape jelly days that great vats of sweet fruit would stew, and sometimes bags of purply stained cheesecloth would be hung from the pot-latch to catch the winey essence as it dripped below. And the entire house, even the attic and the cellar, would be perfumed with the redolent airs of "putting-up" for weeks and sometimes months afterward.

"But my own grapes were better," my grandmother would say as she pried the wax from a jar of jelly she had just made from Mister Joe's best blue Concords.

"No comparison with that junk he sells. Mine were the best!"

And they were. The biggest, sourest, indigo cat's eyes I had ever seen had grown on an arbor beside the garage. My grandmother, in a spate of energy, which filled her often like a sudden rage until she was a very, very old lady, quixotically pulled up all the roots and planted a rock garden there instead.

"It makes a change. Besides, Prohibition is ended now and your grandfather still makes too much wine in the cellar because he don't like to see the grapes go to waste."

Her look was pure unadulterated matriarch.

"We can't all become *shikkers*—just because of a few *verfallene* grapes!"

It will come as no surprise that my grandmother's rules of thumb for "putting-up" are practically the same as mine today. Here are the rules she made:

1. Use only prime fruit or vegetables for preserves. Examine fruit particularly for dark spots or bruises. If you can

remove blemishes with a paring knife—all well and good. If not, set aside. Always smell or taste any doubtful bit—one bad apple can spoil the batch of apple butter.

2. All produce should be cleaned or washed before you use it. Damp paper towels and elbow grease will not bruise even the ripest peach. Acidy fruits like apples or pears should be kept in cold water after they are peeled to prevent their turning brown. Water-logging destroys the taste somewhat, but a cut lemon half in the water lessens the destruction.

3. When making jam or jelly, always use a large porcelain or enamelware kettle. (My grandmother always called any pot over a quart a kettle.) Make sure yours is very clean before you use it, and only stir what is in it with a long wooden spoon or fork.

4. Always taste what you are making. If the stuff does not taste right on the stove, it is bound to taste worse in the jar. Too much sugar in the jam can be rectified by adding more fruit or small quantities of lemon juice to taste.

5. Never, never use short-cut pectins or commercial thickeners. All fruit has varying degrees of natural pectin in it, and that plus the boiled down sugar syrup will always thicken them sufficiently. If you do not have the patience to wait, do not can!

6. Remember that all jars, tops, and other canning equipment must be sterilized before preserves or pickles can be packed and sealed. A large pot makes a good home sterilizer. All equipment should be put inside it, covered with a good inch of cold water, and then brought to a boil. A good rule is to simmer everything for about 15 minutes. Let the jars and caps stand in the hot water until just before you are ready to use them. Then invert and drain on several thicknesses of paper towels. They can still be warm when you fill them. Baby bottle tongs work wonders removing jars and caps from the hot water.

7. Never pack a jam or pickle jar to the very top. Always leave at least one-half inch between the glass rim and the goodie inside so there is room for atmospheric contraction or expansion.

8. Sealing a jar means making it air-tight. My grandmother sealed hers with a ¼-inch paraffin wax. My mother used screwtop jars with sterilized rubber rings inside. For The

Store, I always use Ball Jars with automatic sealing tops. Even they must be screwed on within an inch of their very lives, to create a proper vacuum; a strong man around the kitchen works wonders at a jam session.

9 When you pack hot pickles or preserves, always fill one jar at a time using a wide-mouth funnel and wipe the jars before sealing so residual drippings do not spoil their appearance later. I usually wipe them three times. A hot towel, a cold towel, and a dry towel works best. Never put hot, sealed jars in the refrigerator or in any excessively cold place to cool as they may crack or explode as the glass contracts.

10. *A safety tip:* When canning vegetables or pickles, it is cautious to give the packed jars an extra bath after they are sealed. Place them in a large pan in about 2 to 3 inches of water (preferably, on a metal cake rack) and simmer for about ten minutes. Remember that bacteria cannot live in a sterilized jar. Extra boiling helps to retard all spoilage, but jams and jellies are usually ready for packing after they have simmered and thickened in an open pan.

11. Always store sealed preserves in a dark, dry place for at least a month before you use them. (I save the boxes the Ball Jars come in and just repack them again.) The breathing spell seems to give the taste time to properly fuse and ripen.

12. Do not worry if jar tops make a popping sound. It is usually just an excess air bubble, formed as the jar expands or contracts in temperature changes. Do worry, a lot, if pickle or jams seem to ferment, or if a jar top buckles. Do not wait to open or taste it, for goodness' sakes. Just throw it out!

My grandmother's grape jam always took a bit of cinnamon and a pinch of clove. I sometimes add a little grated orange rind and some orange liqueur as well, but essentially, this is her recipe:

GRAPE JAM

4 pounds of Muscadine or Concord grapes
1 ½ cups water
2 ½ pounds sugar

1 stick of cinnamon bark
¼ teaspoon powdered cloves
rind of half an orange (grated or slivered into fine shreds)
¼ cup Grand Marnier

I. Skin the grapes. (It is best to use rubber gloves for this.) Save the skins and the pulp in separate bowls.

II. Combine the grape pulps and water in a large kettle and cook over fairly high heat for 15 minutes. Put the cooked pulp through a fine sieve to remove the seeds. Save the pulp and grape juice; discard the seeds.

III. Mix the pulp with the skins. Add the sugar and cook slowly until slightly thickened. Then add the cinnamon stick, cloves, and grated orange.

IV. Return to stove and cook slowly until the jam is quite thick. Add the Grand Marnier and simmer for 5 minutes longer.

V. Let the grape jam stand until slightly cool. Remove the cinnamon stick and pour into sterilized jars and seal. Makes about 7 pints.

PURE RASPBERRY JAM

8 cups of raspberries
8 cups of sugar
juice of half a lemon
juice of half an orange

I. Wash and mash the berries. Put in a kettle over a low heat and cook the berries in their own juice for about 30 minutes, stirring often.

II. Add 2 cups of sugar and slowly bring to a boil. Gradually add the lemon and orange juice alternating with the remaining sugar. Bring the syrup back to a boil after each addition.

III. When the jam is thick, remove it from the heat and ladle it (hot) into half-pint jars and seal. This makes about 8 to 10 half-pints of jam.

My grandmother made tomato catsup and tomato chile sauce. Denis' Aunt Leda left The Store a legacy of her Illinois Tomato Conserve.

LEDA FOLEY'S TOMATO CONSERVE

6 pounds ripe tomatoes, peeled and chopped
1 pound raisins, chopped fine
3 pounds brown sugar
1 pint of vinegar (I use an apple cider type)
4 sticks of cinnamon bark
1 tablespoon ground cloves
1 nutmeg, grated
4 lemons (seeded and skinned, cut in thin slices)
peel of 4 lemons, shredded into thin strips
½ teaspoon freshly ground black pepper
1 tablespoon salt

I.   Put the peeled, chopped tomatoes into a large kettle. Add all the other ingredients and cook slowly for about two hours, until nicely thickened.

II.   Remove the cinnamon sticks and seal in sterilized jars. Makes about 8 to 10 half-pints of conserve.

My grandmother always put up cherries, and sometimes apricots and peaches, in spirituous liquors. She would serve them to us along with cold roast meat and a salad for a Sunday night supper—or more often, a jar would be opened when some specially prized relative from Ohio appeared.

I believe brandied fruit over vanilla ice cream is probably the most useful adjunct an unexpected host or hostess can have—let the Sara Lee be damned.

BRANDIED CHERRIES

1½ quarts cherries, washed and drained
½ cup sugar
¼ teaspoon cinnamon (powdered)
cognac

I. Trim the stems of the cherries so that each cherry will have about an inch of stem. Mix the sugar and cinnamon together.

II. Pack the cherries (unpitted) and sugar mixture in alternate layers in sterilized jars. Do not fill the jars within one inch of the tops. Add enough cognac to cover the fruit and seal.

III. Let the brandied fruit stand at least a month. Turn the jars upside down each day for a week or so to make sure the sugar and cognac will blend well. Store in a cool dark place until you use them. Makes about 3 half-pints.

BRANDIED PEACHES

6–8 pounds firm ripe peaches
3½ pounds sugar
juice of one lemon
peel of a large orange (slivered into shreds)
½ teaspoon grated nutmeg
2 pints of good brandy or bourbon

I. Peel the peaches and leave them whole. Cover with sugar and lemon juice and let them stand for about 2 to 3 hours. Turn the fruit mixture into a kettle; add the slivered orange peel and nutmeg. Bring slowly to a boil. Simmer the peaches until they are tender when pierced with a toothpick or a gentle fork. Remove the fruit and cool in a bowl. Save the syrup.

II. Boil the syrup down until it becomes quite thick.

III. Pack the peaches in sterilized pint jars and fill half way up with syrup. Add enough brandy or good bourbon to cover the fruit. Seal well and store in a dark place for about a month. Makes about 6 pints.

BRANDIED PLUMS

4 quarts ripe plums
1 stick of cinnamon bark (broken into small pieces)
2 cups of sugar

1 cup of orange juice
¼ teaspoon salt
4 whole cloves
½ lemon, sliced paper thin
Grand Marnier liqueur

I.   Select plums that are ripe and juicy. Wash well and pack in sterilized pint jars. Add a piece of cinnamon bark to each.

II.   Bring 2 cups of sugar, a cup of orange juice, ¼ teaspoon salt, and four cloves to a boil. Add the lemon slices and simmer until the fruit becomes transparent.

III.   Cover the plums halfway with syrup, making sure each jar has a slice of lemon as well. Fill with Grand Marnier and seal. Store in a cool dark place for about a month. Turn the jars upside down once each week. The longer the plums stand, the better they taste when served. Makes about 5 pints.

Judith Leiber, the noted handbag designer, and her husband have a wonderful house and an even more wonderful garden in Amagansett. One summer she brought us a golden treasure of gooseberries; The Store's shelves gleamed with the provender all summer.

GOOSEBERRY CONSERVE

8 to 10 pounds gooseberries
6 pounds of sugar
¼ teaspoon salt
1 teaspoon cinnamon
¼ teaspoon grated nutmeg
¼ teaspoon cloves
4 cups of orange juice (freshly squeezed)
peel of 4 oranges, cut into fine slivers
½ cup Grand Marnier liqueur

I.   Put the orange peel slivers to soak in the Grand Marnier, at least 30 minutes. Remove the stems from the gooseberries. Wash the berries, and put them in a large kettle with the sugar, salt, spices, and orange juice.

II.   Bring to a boil; simmer over a low flame until quite thick. Add the orange peel slivers and the Grand Marnier in which they have been soaking. Cook 15 minutes longer. Pour into sterilized jars and seal. Makes about 12 half-pints.

BLUE-BLUE PLUM CONSERVE

5 pounds of blue plums
1 teaspoon almond extract
2 quarts of blueberries
2½ pounds of granulated sugar
1½ pounds of brown sugar
1 teaspoon cinnamon
½ teaspoon ginger
1 cup of water
1 cup of orange juice
½ cup good cognac

I.   Wash and split the plums. Sprinkle with almond extract and let stand for 30 minutes while you wash and hull the blueberries.

II.   Combine plums, blueberries, both sugars, spices, water, and orange juice in a kettle and bring to a fast boil. Reduce the heat and simmer for about 1 hour or until fairly thick, stirring often.

III.   Thin with cognac and simmer an additional 10-15 minutes. Cool slightly and seal in sterilized jars. Makes about 12 half-pints.

STRAWBERRY PRESERVES

6 cups fresh strawberries, cleaned and washed
5 cups sugar
pulp of an orange, well blended (seeds removed)
¼ cup lemon juice
slivered peel of one bright-skinned orange
½ cup of Grand Marnier liqueur

I.   Layer berries and sugar in a large kettle, making sure to start with a layer of sugar. Pour orange pulp over and bring slowly to a boil. When the whole mass is simmering, add the lemon juice and bring back to a boil.

II.   Remove from the heat and let stand until cool (preferably overnight). On the second day, add the orange rind and Grand Marnier and boil for about 15 minutes only. Cool and pour into sterilized jars. Makes from 6 to 8 half-pints.

The consistency of any good home-made preserve is always a bit more syrupy than ordinary commercial jams, but it is always sweeter and truer to real fruit in flavor.

Store chutney is a tactical experience. Each spring and fall, the very air of Amagansett's main street is beclouded with the heady gift of its incense. We have cooked up storms of pineapple, pear, and even nectarine chutneys on occasion. The recipe that follows is a classic version concocted of apples, melon, tomatoes, nutmeat, onions, and pepper. Hot, brown, and velvety—no self-respecting curry should have to make its way without a dab of it.

STORE CHUTNEY

1 pound of tart apples, peeled and chopped
6 firm pears, peeled and sliced into vertical strips
2 large cantaloupe, peeled and sliced into 1 inch cubes
2 mangoes, peeled and sliced thin
1 can crushed pineapple
12 hard tomatoes, peeled and chopped
5 large onions, peeled and chopped
3 cloves garlic, peeled and minced
6 fresh hot red pepper pods
2 green peppers, seeded and chopped
6 cups brown sugar
1 quart of cider vinegar
1 cup of yellow raisins
½ cup dried black currants
1 cup of roughly chopped walnuts

1 tablespoon white mustard seed
1 tablespoon yellow mustard seed
½ teaspoon powdered ginger
½ teaspoon powdered cloves
1 pound preserved ginger, chopped

I.   Mix all chopped fruit (including tomatoes), onions, garlic, red and green peppers, sugar, and vinegar in a large kettle. Cook until the mixture is thick and smooth, stirring frequently. Add the remaining ingredients and let the mixture simmer for about 45 minutes.

II.   Remove the mixture from the heat and let it cool overnight. Return to medium heat and bring it to a boil again on the second day. Pack in sterilized jars while quite hot. Makes about 18 pints of chutney.

This chutney, incidentally, makes a wonderful and welcome house-gift any time of the year.

Another Store favorite is this hot, mustardy anomaly called "Hot, Hot Kansas City Chow Chow." It's good and unusually spicy.

HOT, HOT KANSAS CITY CHOW CHOW

1 gallon of cabbage, chopped
½ gallon green tomatoes, chopped
½ gallon red tomatoes, chopped
1 whole cauliflower, cut into flowerets
4 large green peppers, chopped
4 tablespoons dried hot red peppers
2 pounds of dark brown sugar
1 quart of onions, chopped
4 cloves of garlic, minced
kernels of 4 ears of corn, sliced off the cob raw, or 1 package of
*   frozen corn kernels*
2 tablespoons ground ginger
1 tablespoon ground cinnamon
1 tablespoon ground cloves
3 tablespoons turmeric

1 tablespoon curry powder
1 tablespoon celery seed
2 tablespoons kosher salt
4 tablespoons cornstarch
4 tablespoons ground Colman's mustard
1 quart cider vinegar

I.   Mix all but the last three ingredients in a large kettle. Mix cornstarch and mustard into vinegar and pour over vegetables. Place over medium heat, bring to a boil and boil for about an hour, stirring frequently. Pour hot into sterilized jars and seal. Makes about 16—18 pints.

Here are two versions of bread and butter pickles that I like. One has shallots, garlic, and red pepper added to a basic recipe, but it gives a spicy fillip to the old-fashioned summer staple.

STORE BREAD AND BUTTER PICKLES

3 quarts medium-sized cucumbers, sliced
3 medium-sized onions, sliced
½ cup kosher salt
water, to cover the cucumbers
2 cups cider vinegar
½ cup water
2½ cups sugar
2 tablespoons mustard seed
1 teaspoon celery seed
1 teaspoon turmeric

I.   Combine the sliced cucumbers and onions, and mix them well with kosher salt. Let them stand an hour and then pour cold water over them and let them stand 2 hours longer. Drain well.

II.   In a large kettle, combine the remaining ingredients and bring to a rolling boil. Add the cucumbers and onions and heat to simmering for about 10 minutes. Avoid over boiling the pickles to keep them crunchy. Pack while hot in sterilized jars and seal. Makes about 6 pints of pickles.

GRANDMOTHER'S BREAD AND BUTTER PICKLES

4 quarts cucumbers, sliced
2 quarts of onions, sliced in rings
1 dozen shallots, sliced
½ cup kosher salt
1 large clove garlic, minced
2 tablespoons hot red pepper
2 cups vinegar (1 cup cider mixed with 1 cup wine)
2 cups brown sugar
2 tablespoons each:
mustard seed
celery seed
turmeric
allspice

I.   Combine sliced cucumbers with the onions and shallots and sprinkle with salt. Let stand about 2 hours.

II. In a kettle, combine the vinegar, brown sugar, spices to taste, and minced garlic; bring to a boil. Drain the vegetables and immediately add them to the boiling mixture. Simmer for 7 minutes. Pour into sterilized jars and seal. Makes about 8 pints.

At the Store we make a delicious series of herbal jellies: mint, tarragon, basil, dill, and mixed herb bouquets. The base is always made of pure apple jelly. This is how it is made:

APPLE JELLY

5 pounds of tart apples
5 cups of cold water
¾ cup lemon juice
sugar

I.   Wash apples and cut into quarters leaving peels, seeds, and cores intact. Put into a large kettle with a cover. Add the water and lemon juice. Place over medium heat and steam through until the apples are soft (about 30 minutes).

II.   Pour into a jelly bag (or a baby's pillowcase) and let
          the jelly (it will be liquid) drip over a large bowl until
          the pulp is well drained. Do not press the bag; it turns
          the jelly cloudy.

III.   Measure the liquid; measure out ½ cup sugar for
          each cup of juice. Heat the juice and slowly add the
          sugar. Bring to a quick boil and keep it boiling
          until the syrup becomes sticky and forms a ball when
          put on a cold surface.

IV.   Skim any foam or sediment. Pour into sterilized jars
          and seal or use in the recipes that follow.

MINT JELLY

Add 4 cups of freshly chopped mint leaves, ½ cup crème
de menthe, 2 tablespoons of good wine vinegar to 6 cups of
cooled apple jelly. Whisk well. Immediately pour into sterilized
jars and seal. Makes 6 to 7 half-pints.

TARRAGON JELLY

Add 2 cups of freshly chopped tarragon, ½ cup Pernod,
and 2 tablespoons good tarragon wine vinegar to 4 cups of
cooled apple jelly. Whisk well. Pour into sterilized jars and
seal. Makes 4 to 5 half-pints.

PARSLEY JELLY

Add 4 cups of finely minced parsley, ¼ cup Galliano,
and 2 tablespoons of white wine vinegar to 4 cups of apple jelly.
Whisk well. Pour into sterilized jars and seal. Makes 4 to 5
half-pints.

For apartment dwellers and instant gourmets, there is
also an unorthodox mint jelly that can be made quickly and
stored in the refrigerator. It is delicious, if a trifle larcenous of
the cook: take 1 jar of commercial mint jelly, 4 tablespoons of
crème de menthe, 1 cup of chopped mint leaves, 1 tablespoon of wine vinegar, and a good dash of black pepper. Combine, whisk well, and serve, answering no questions afterward.

The Meat Rack

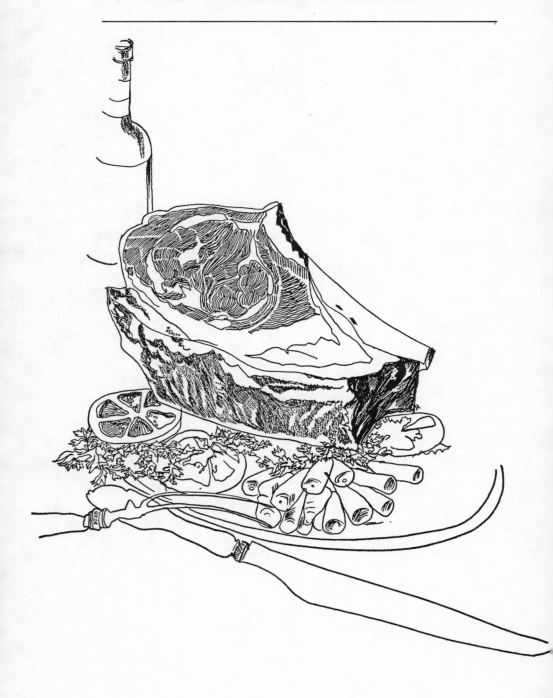

Chapter Seven

DENIS VAUGHAN

"You go too far!" she shouted at me, eyes ablaze. I suppose I did, I always have, but I didn't know in which direction. I never do—or can't remember. I have always admired a quote attributed to Ingrid Bergman: "I have good health and a bad memory." I have, too. At any rate, the lady with whom I went too far, verbally, was Zelda Dorfmann, sometime manager of the New York City Center Ballet and duenna to the company of "Porgy and Bess" that marked the initial invasion of the United States into the Soviet Union—in the arts, of course. One never heard the end of that. It was like Waterloo. Zelda, however, a tense, nervous, jittery, chain smoker with unfocused eyes, but not Long Island lockjaw, loved to eat.

When I was in the theater, Zelda was the business manager of the show I was directing. She never listened to a damned thing one said, but kept nodding her head affirmatively and breathing yes, yes . . . no matter that what was being said was negative or positive. It made me slightly tense. Suddenly she would summon from her birdlike body, "You go too far!"

Since my own temperament is one of ups, downs, acrosses, and circles, I find it difficult to harbor rages. Even though I indulge in them, they are gone in a flash. Zelda clutched her rages to her heart, and often would not speak to me for days, leaving me mystified by the enormity of my felony. Since Zelda loved to eat, here is a dish I made for her one day when I was feeling paternal, maternal, and warm and tender towards her. It warmed her, too. It may amaze you, but it is not difficult, and if you like oysters, you will be delighted. Zelda loved it.

MEDALLIONS OF BEEF WITH OYSTERS

This is such a simple recipe that I am going into a lot of elaborate detail about it. Cut as many slices as you need, two inches thick, from the top of a filet of beef. Shape them into circles by beating them lightly with a wooden mallet or with the edge of a plate. Brown on both sides over high heat in enough butter to cover the bottom of your skillet. Turn constantly with meat tongs for no longer than six to eight minutes. Place the medallions on a hot earthenware platter, sprinkle with salt and pepper, coat with melted butter and chopped chives, cover with small pyramids of raw, well-drained oysters, and bake in a hot oven (425°) for a few watchful moments until the oysters curl around their edges.

With this dish I prefer the simplest accompaniment: fresh string beans or broccoli and a hot, crusty French bread.

Have a pot of boiling, salted water on your stove. Cut the broccoli into strips. If you are using string beans, take a pair of scissors, which you should have handy at all times in your kitchen, and snip off both tips and cut the bean in two. Rinse either vegetable in cold water, plunge into the violently boiling water, hum a few bars of your favorite song, and count to forty. Instantly upon arriving at the magic number, remove the vegetables from the flame, pour into a colander, and douse with cold water to retard further cooking. The vegetable will be *al dente,* but this is the way it should be, so I'm not going to tell you any other way to do it. If you wish to punish vegetables, that's up to you. Doing it my way retains all the vitamins and also an absolutely superb color. An unassuming Beaujolais with this meal is chic and understated.

If perhaps you'd like to be more festive—and British— here are recipes for roast beef and Yorkshire pudding that are marvelous and not difficult, but you must be watchful.

ROAST BEEF

At The Store we always use a 10 to 12 pound sirloin of beef, rolled and tied for roasting, because it is easier to carve by hand. At home a rib roast of three or more ribs makes a fine English beef roast.

Wipe the roast with a damp cloth and dry it well. Rub it with salt and pepper and place in a roasting pan, preferably on a rack to keep the meat from sizzling in the drippings. Slice a large white onion very thin and cover the top of the roast with it. Place the roast in an oven that you have preheated to 450°. Cook the meat for 25 minutes until it is well seared and then lower the temperature to 325° until it is done to your taste. It is not necessary to baste.

For rare beef, figure on 16 to 18 minutes per pound, or, if you are using a meat thermometer, it is ready when it registers 120°. For medium-rare, 20 to 22 minutes a pound or 130°. And for well done (although that is not a pleasant thought) 30 minutes or 150°.

Let the meat stand for 15 minutes before carving as it will continue to cook in its own juices. Serve accompanied with a boat of pan juices, or make the following gravy: take 3 tablespoons of drippings and 3 tablespoons of flour. In a skillet, blend the two together. Cook and stir until lightly brown. Add ½ cup of milk and almost a cup of degreased drippings. Stir constantly while adding the liquids. Add a dash of soy sauce and season to taste.

YORKSHIRE PUDDING

2 eggs, beaten
scant cup of flour
1 cup of milk
salt
2 tablespoons plus ¼ cup beef drippings

I.   Preheat oven to 450°. Beat the eggs until light and fluffy. Very slowly blend in the flour, beating vigorously to avoid lumps. Slowly blend in the milk. Add a dash of salt and about 2 tablespoons of drippings from the roast. Stir well.

II. Heat an earthenware soufflé dish or a tin mold in the oven for a few minutes and pour ¼ cup of beef drippings over the bottom. Swirl the pan around so that the entire bottom and sides are coated. Pour in the batter.

III. Bake in a 450° oven for 10 minutes, reduce the heat to 350°, and continue baking for another 10 to 15 minutes or until puffy and browned. (This should be done after the roast has come out and the juices are settling.) To serve, slice in pie-shaped wedges. Serves 6−8.

"Ability to do more, but will to refrain." These cogent words came from the cigarette-drooped lips and hooded eyes of Judith Kandel, a world-weary lady from Bucks County, Pennsylvania, and a great and good friend to the aforementioned Zelda Dorfmann. "Lap, pan, dissolve," her husband Aben Kandel would say repeatedly through his myriad "dream-factory" stories. I was listening so hard, my senses reeling with the magic names of Ann Sheridan, Humphrey Bogart, and John Garfield, that it took me several moments to realize what he was talking about. "Lap, pan, dissolve" is movie jargon for setting the camera up for a "take," bringing it in on the scene, expanding the horizon, and then dissolving. Fade out. Aben Kandel wrote so many screenplays that it would take another whole book to list them. His wife Judith made periodic trips to New York and it was on one of those occasions that she dropped the quote above in regard to me and a show I had directed. It was a quote I have never forgotten.

An unimportant footnote is that Judith lives in a sensational farmhouse on five or six hundred acres of land, with a view that boggles the mind. She invited me, my partner, Bert Greene, and his sister Myra for Thanksgiving dinner some years ago. The implication on the phone was "weekend." We weren't sure, but packed accordingly and with innate good taste left our bags in the car when we arrived. We were given the inevitable tour of the house, which was a breathtaking step into the past; endless drinks, to which I've never objected; and no words such as, "Where are your bags?" "When would you like to eat Thanksgiving dinner?" "This will be your room —and this—and this—or perhaps you'd like to share?" Acolytes sometimes have their place in the world, but on a truly empty stomach, it can become a bit to bear.

"The roast is in the oven," Judith gasped between coughs, as she lit another cigarette.

I thought, "Does she mean turkey or roast?" She meant roast and monstrously overdone at that.

She cried not too over-perilously into the air, "Oh, what shall I do?"

With as much aplomb as I could muster, I muttered things about onions, green peppers, tomatoes, potatoes, and tomato juice, and maybe we could salvage this debacle. She had them all—perhaps heaven-sent. Once again to the burners to set to. This is an old and tried recipe belonging to my mother—not exactly recommended for Thanksgiving dinner, but if you're bizarre enough to have a rather mediocre cut of beef that out of negligence or lassitude you overdo, the following recipe may evoke cries of approval from your friends.

ROAST BEEF HASH

4 — 5 pound chuck roast or rolled roast of beef
butter
6 medium-sized potatoes, peeled and boiled for ten minutes
6 medium-sized yellow onions, roughly chopped
3 green peppers, roughly chopped
3 large tomatoes, roughly chopped
salt and pepper to taste
1 tablespoon Worcestershire sauce
can of tomato juice

Roast the beef for an hour at 375°. Remove from the oven and cut into 2-inch chunks. Place in a large iron skillet with enough butter to film the bottom. Chop the potatoes and add them, along with all the other ingredients. Moisten the mixture with tomato juice. This can cook on a low light for hours. When all has come together, place under the broiler for about 10 minutes. Serve with a green salad, French bread, and beer. Serves about 6.

Incidentally, Bert, Myra, and I departed the Kandel's for New York again at midnight, our bags fortunately still packed for instant flight.

Viveca Lindfors once breathed throatily to me, "But, darling, food is so boring. What can you possibly give me that I haven't seen, eaten, and am tired of?"

It gave me pause. Viveca, whom I love, is a woman of erratic nature. Her moods are as swiftly changing as the wind and to try to "plan" for her is a sometime thing. (By contrast, her daughter Lena, seems to be as constant as the setting sun and rising moon—or the other way around.) Viveca and I established a significant hate relationship when we worked together many years ago. I was monumentally star-struck and the name "Lindfors" loomed imposingly, as did the lady. When

I heard her murmur "amateur" to a friend in her dressing room after a performance, my instant reaction was to flee to the nearest medicine cabinet and devour all the sleeping pills in sight. Clearly I did not. Rather than that, I thought, some years later when we got back in touch, "I'll make you a meal, baby, that you won't forget."

I invited; she accepted, and this is what she got—with a deep bow to Alfred Lunt. It is simple, and so good, but you must get a fillet of veal with all the fat trimmed; otherwise you're off the meat rack into the soup.

FILLET OF VEAL WITH COFFEE, CREAM, AND COGNAC

1 fillet of veal, 3—4 pound size trimmed of fat and lightly rubbed with a bruised clove of garlic
salt and freshly ground black pepper
½ stick sweet butter
1 cup good strong black coffee
2 teaspoons sugar
¼ cup heavy cream
1 small glass of cognac
1 teaspoon cornstarch (approximately)

I.   Preheat oven to 375°. Coat the garlic-rubbed fillet of veal with a light shower of salt and ground black pepper.

II.   Place the veal on a rack in a roasting pan and dot it with ½ stick butter. Place in the preheated oven for about 30 minutes or until the juices start to run.

III.   Combine the strong coffee, sugar, cream, and cognac. Pour over the veal and reduce heat to 350°. Now you are on the rack! You are going to have to baste this little bugger every 10 minutes for an hour.

IV.   Remove from the oven and place on a tray. Pour all the drippings into a saucepan. Put the roast back in the turned-off oven while you make the sauce.

V.   Bring the drippings to a boil, and add a little cornstarch to thicken.

VI.   Now you are ready to serve. Do not pour the sauce

over the veal—use it for what it is—a fillip to the meat. Also serve: rice done the simplest way possible; fresh green peas or string beans (be sure you follow the instructions I have given you—furiously boiling, salted water. Plunge in. Count to 40—out and under the cold water). To warm, swirl in a pan with melted butter and to the table. Serves 6–8.

An excellent white Côtes du Rhone or an equally excellent red wine can make this meal a delight. A salad should go along as an added treat. I prefer watercress and endive with a sliver of Brie. Dessert? Thank you no, but if you want—choose a mousse. Thank you, Alfred Lunt.

While we are on the subject of veal, let me tell you of a hearty little peasant dish, French, of course, and completely disarming. Unfortunately, I have no name to drop on your foot with this one, but I think its verdant elixir will more than compensate.

VEAL WITH A SAUCE AS GREEN AS A FIELD

5 pounds stewing veal
7 tablespoons sweet butter
3 tablespoons flour
1½ cups chicken bouillon
1 cup dry white wine
bouquet garni made of: 1 bay leaf, a sprig of thyme, 6 stalks
    of parsley, 2 green onions, and 2 cloves garlic
2 pounds fresh spinach
6 egg yolks
¼ cup heavy cream
salt and pepper

1. Cut the veal into 2-inch cubes. Melt butter in a Dutch oven over low heat and add the veal. Stir with a wooden spoon until the pieces are covered with butter, without browning. Add the flour and continue to stir. Add bouillon and wine, along with the bouquet garni. Cook over medium heat for ¾ hour, turning meat frequently. Add 2 teaspoons salt and 1 teaspoon pepper.

II.   Chop the raw spinach fine. Remove bouquet garni from the Dutch oven and place the spinach in with the meat and juices and cook for 15 to 20 minutes longer.

III.   Stir 6 egg yolks in a bowl with ¼ cup heavy cream; slowly add some of the juice from the meat. Add to the sauce in the Dutch oven, stirring until the spoon is coated. Do not allow to boil or eggs will scramble.

IV.   Serve hot, accompanied by noodles with croutons (recipe follows). Serves 10.

NOODLES WITH CROUTONS

2 packages very wide egg noodles
1 stick sweet butter
8 slices white bread
¾ stick butter

I.   Drop noodles into 8 quarts of rapidly boiling salted water and boil for 10 minutes. Drain in a colander. Blanch. Reheat quickly in pan, tossing in butter.

II.   Meanwhile, cut bread (crusts removed) into cubes and sauté in ¾ stick of butter in a skillet until golden brown. Place on top of the noodles and serve. Serves 10.

If you are the wife of a painter, a patroness of the arts, and also one of the wealthiest and seemingly one of the most unassuming women in the world, what would your name be? Well, if you were in residence on the South Fork of Long Island and your stately mansion burned to the ground one winter's night leaving you in your nightdress shivering on the road, and you had a gleaming new mansion and swimming pool erected in record time—it would be Castro-Cid (last name, not first). You would also smile beguilingly at workmen, shopkeepers (me), pay your bills with alacrity—and get things done. You might also want whole suckling pigs on occasion, on which your dour German cook would turn thumbs down, offering Wiener schnitzel, red cabbage, and mashed potatoes instead. Still smiling, you would allow her to retreat to her room to look at the telly while you called me.

"For tonight—suckling pig? Christophe! Amagansett is the end of nowhere! I'd have to be running a pig farm to provide that for you. I haven't seen a suckling pig close up in twenty years."

We chatter on as merrily as possible—if not too briskly. She smiles so much, even on the telephone, that the words have a certain tentative quality. Thankfully, she is not one of those "And-what-else?" ladies. If you are quick enough to remember her tastes, you know that she likes veal. Here are two recipes, one rather elaborate, the other, simpler, that you might enjoy.

VEAL PRINCE ORLOFF

5-pound boned and tied roast of veal
1 small glass of brandy
3 tablespoons butter, more if needed
3 tablespoons oil
2 sliced carrots
2 sliced onions
bouquet garni made of: 5 parsley sprigs, 1 bay leaf, and
    ¼ teaspoon thyme
½ teaspoon salt
¼ teaspoon pepper
2 strips of fat bacon, simmered for 10 minutes in a quart of
    water, then rinsed, drained, and dried

RICE AND ONION STUFFING
¼ cup raw white rice
2 quarts salted boiling water
3 tablespoons butter
4 sliced yellow onions
1 tablespoon salt

MUSHROOM ENRICHMENT
½ pound fresh mushrooms, squeezed dry, then minced
3 tablespoons minced shallots
2 tablespoons butter
1 tablespoon oil
salt and pepper

VELOUTE SAUCE
6 tablespoons butter
8 tablespoons flour
1 cup boiled down veal juice
2 cups hot milk
¼ teaspoon salt
pinch of nutmeg
⅛ teaspoon pepper
½ cup heavy cream

FINAL ASSEMBLY
cooked rice and onion stuffing
mushroom enrichment
¼ cup whipping cream (more if needed)
salt and pepper
remaining velouté sauce
⅓ cup and 3 tablespoons grated Jarlsberg cheese
3 tablespoons melted butter

I.   Preheat oven to 325°. Rub the veal with brandy and let it dry. Place a large ovenware casserole over moderately high heat and add 3 tablespoons of butter and 3 tablespoons oil. When the mixture foams, add the roast and brown lightly. Remove. If the fat burns, pour it off, and add some more butter. Stir in 2 sliced carrots and 2 sliced onions. Add the bouquet garni. Cook over low heat for 5 minutes without browning.

II.   Sprinkle salt and pepper over the veal, return it to the casserole and baste with the butter in the casserole. Lay the bacon over the meat and then cover with aluminum foil. Cover the casserole and set in a preheated oven. Cook the meat slowly for about 1½ hours, or until the juices run clear. Baste every 15 minutes. Then remove the meat and allow it to cool at room temperature for about half an hour.

III. Strain the roasting juices into a small pan and skim off the fat. Boil juices down rapidly to reduce to 1 cup. Reserve for the velouté sauce.

IV.   While the veal is roasting, prepare the rice and onion stuffing. Drop ¼ cup raw white rice into 2 quarts of boiling salted water for 5 minutes. Drain. Meanwhile, melt 3 tablespoons butter in a large casserole and stir in 4 sliced yellow onions. Add 1 tablespoon salt and blend, making sure the onions are well coated. Stir in the rice. Cover and cook over very low heat for 45 minutes or until tender. Mixture should not brown.

V.   To prepare the mushroom enrichment, squeeze ½ pound mushrooms in a cloth napkin to extract the juice. Then mince and sauté them with 3 tablespoons minced shallots in 2 tablespoons hot butter and 1 tablespoon oil for 5 minutes. Salt, pepper, and set aside.

VI.   When the roast is done, prepare the velouté sauce: Melt 6 tablespoons butter in a saucepan. Stir in 8 tablespoons flour and cook slowly, stirring together until they foam. Remove from the heat, pour in 1 cup boiled-down veal juice and 2 cups hot milk, and beat vigorously with a wire whisk. Beat in ¼ teaspoon salt, pinch of nutmeg, ⅛ teaspoon pepper; bring to a boil and boil for 1 minute. Pour 1 cup of this sauce into the cooked rice and onion mixture. Beat ½ cup heavy cream into the rest of the sauce and set it in a pan of slowly simmering water while you begin the final assembly.

VII.   Purée the rice and onions in a blender and add to the mushrooms. Pour in ¼ cup of cream and simmer for 5 minutes, stirring constantly. The filling should be thick enough to hold its shape. Boil down if too thin. If too thick, thin with 2-3 tablespoons cream.

VIII.   Preheat oven to 375°. Carve the veal into very thin slices, piling them in the order in which you slice them. Then transfer to a lightly buttered ovenware serving platter. Place the last piece carved on the platter, sprinkle lightly with salt and pepper, and spread with a spoonful of filling. Overlap the next slice, and repeat the process until all the meat is on the platter. Spread any extra filling over and around the meat (as if you were making an icebox cake).

IX.   Bring the remaining velouté sauce to a simmer and add more salt and pepper if necessary. It should be thick enough to coat a spoon. Off heat, beat in ⅓ cup of grated Jarlsberg cheese. Spoon the sauce over the meat, sprinkle with 3 tablespoons grated cheese, and dribble on 3 tablespoons melted butter.

X.   About 30 to 40 minutes before serving, set the veal in the upper third of a preheated oven, and heat until the top has browned lightly. Take care not to overcook. Serve at once. Serves 10 – 12.

VEAL MARENGO

3 pounds veal stew meat, cut into 2-inch pieces
2 tablespoons sweet butter
2 to 3 tablespoons olive oil
1 cup yellow onions, minced
salt and pepper
2 tablespoons flour
2 tablespoons granulated sugar
2 cups dry white wine or vermouth
1 pound ripe tomatoes, juiced and roughly chopped
½ teaspoon basil
½ teaspoon thyme
3-inch strip of orange peel ½-inch wide
2 cloves garlic, mashed
3 tablespoons cognac
½ pound fresh mushroom caps, lightly sautéed in butter
½ tablespoon cornstarch mixed with 1 tablespoon water
¼ cup fresh parsley, chopped fine

I.   Preheat oven to 325°. Dry the veal on paper towels. Heat the butter and oil in a skillet until smoking. Then quickly brown the meat, a few at a time, and arrange in a 4-quart fireproof casserole.

II.   Lower the heat, pour almost all the oil from the skillet, and lightly brown the onions. While the onions are browning, toss the meat with 1 teaspoon salt, ¼ teaspoon pepper, and the flour. Stir over moderate heat for 3 to 4 minutes to brown the flour lightly. Add 2 tablespoons sugar to carmelize the meat and remove from the heat.

III.   Add the wine to the skillet with the onions. Boil for 1 minute, scraping up the juices. Pour the wine and onions into the casserole and bring to a simmer. Stir. Juice the tomatoes by cutting them in two and squeezing out the pips. Then roughly chop and stir them into the casserole. Add the herbs, orange peel, and garlic. Bring back to a simmer and season lightly to taste. Cover and set in the oven to simmer slowly for 1¼ to 1½ hours or until the meat is almost tender when pierced with a fork.

IV.   Taste the sauce for seasoning. Add 3 tablespoons cognac and the mushrooms to the casserole and baste them with the sauce. Bring to a simmer on top of the stove again, then cover and return to the oven for 15 more minutes.

V.   Remove from the oven and pour the contents into a sieve placed over a saucepan. Remove the orange peel and return the meat and vegetables to the casserole. If sauce is greasy, skim the fat off in the saucepan and boil the sauce down rapidly until reduced to 2½ cups. If too thin, blend in the cornstarch mixture. Correct seasoning and return to the casserole. Serve or set aside to be warmed up slowly later. Serve garnished with chopped parsley. Serves 4—6.

Veal Marengo is excellent over rice or noodles, but my favorite way to serve it is with small potatoes that have been parboiled for 20 minutes, drained, laved with butter, and tossed in G. Washington golden bouillon powder, and then put in a casserole in the lower portion of the oven (along with the veal) for 45 minutes or until the potato develops a golden crust on all sides. Drench with parsley and serve with a hearty wine. A Spanish Valdepenas is just peasanty enough to enhance the whole wonderfully.

Let us retreat to beef for a moment. If I had the patience, or the taste for it, I would tell you about Beef Wellington, but since I loathe it, I shall tell you instead how to make the same cut of beef in a Madeira sauce. You can find the Wellington in other cookbooks—and you are welcome to it.

STEAK AU FOUR

5 pounds prime or choice boneless fillet; 2½ inches thick,
    excess fat removed
olive or cooking oil
2½ tablespoons butter
1 tablespoon coarse salt
1 teaspoon dried thyme
8 cloves garlic, unpeeled
1 cup beef bouillon
1 cup red wine
1 tablespoon cornstarch
¼ cup Madeira
½ cup cream
1 tablespoon butter
freshly chopped parsley for garnish

I. Preheat oven to 375°. Dry the steak thoroughly on paper towels and rub lightly with oil. Film the bottom of an iron skillet with a layer of oil and heat until smoking. Brown the steak for a minute or two on each side. Pour off the oil.

II. Spread 2½ tablespoons butter over the steak and sprinkle on the salt and thyme. Place the unpeeled garlic cloves around the meat and bake in the preheated oven for 20 to 25 minutes. (Meat is medium-rare when red juices begin to pearl up at the surface.)

III. Remove and set the steak on a hot platter. Spoon out any excess fat. Add the bouillon and wine; set over high heat. Mash the garlic into the juices; discard the peels, and boil down until liquid is slightly syrupy. Mix 1 tablespoon cornstarch with ¼ cup Madeira and slowly add to the sauce. Slowly add the cream and heat until thickened. Remove from heat and swirl in 1 tablespoon butter until absorbed. Pour over steak, garnish with chopped parsley and serve. (Steak should be sliced thinly on the diagonal.) Serves 6.

Or if you're feeling provincial:

SANS BIKINI

1½ cups fresh Swiss chard or spinach or 1 package frozen
    mustard greens, finely chopped
¼ cup finely minced onions
2½ tablespoons sweet butter
1 tablespoon oil
½ cup ground round
3 tablespoons Madeira
2 cups ground cooked beef (left over roast-beef or pot roast)
¼ cup raw sausage meat
1 teaspoon salt
¼ teaspoon pepper
¼ teaspoon allspice
¼ teaspoon mace
¼ teaspoon oregano
2 cloves of garlic (minced in a press)
¼ teaspoon Tabasco sauce
½ cup grated Parmesan cheese
2 beaten eggs
flour
1 cup homemade tomato sauce (recipe follows)

I.   Preheat oven to 375°. Throw a cup and a half of finely chopped Swiss chard, spinach, or mustard greens into boiling water to blanch. Press the cooked vegetable in a fine strainer until all liquid is gone. Then cook in a sauté pan along with the onions, 1 tablespoon butter, and the oil, until the mixture is quite dry and any possible liquid has evaporated.

II.   In a sauté pan, over moderately high heat, melt 1½ tablespoons butter. Add the ground round breaking up the meat with a fork and turning it continuously. Sprinkle on the Madeira and lower the heat, cooking until all liquid is absorbed. The cooked meat should be lightly browned but not crusty. Cool slightly.

III.   In a large bowl combine the dry cooked chard with the cooked meat, sausage, ground round, spices, herbs, garlic, Tabasco, and cheese. Beat in the beaten eggs, a bit at a time, making sure the mixture holds its shape.

IV.   Take a part of the mixture in your hand and roll it
        into a fat sausage shape about 1½ by 3 inches. Roll
        it in flour and set aside. After the quenelles are made,
        drop them into a shallow pan of lightly salted sim-
        mering water. Let them simmer for half a minute only.
        With a slotted spoon, remove them to a cake rack
        and let them rest until all are poached.

V.   Arrange the poached sausage shapes together in an
        ovenware dish and dribble the homemade tomato
        sauce over them. Give them a good grating of Parme-
        san cheese and set in a 375° oven for about 20 to 25
        minutes. These naked little devils are delicious served
        hot or eaten cool, later on. Serves 4—6.

TOMATO SAUCE

1 stick of sweet butter
4 large ripe tomatoes
1 medium-sized yellow onion, well minced
1 clove of garlic, mashed
1 packet G. Washington brown bouillon powder
1 stalk of celery, well minced
½ teaspoon basil
½ teaspoon oregano
1 pinch of thyme
1 tablespoon sugar
1 grating of fresh orange peel (¼ teaspoon)

I.   In a saucepan over low heat, melt a stick of butter.
        Cut the tomatoes (like oranges) and squeeze out the
        pulp and seeds. Chop roughly. Add the onion and
        garlic to the butter and sauté until golden—add the
        chopped tomatoes and the bouillon powder. Cook for
        a half hour and then add the minced celery, basil,
        oregano, and thyme; stir the mixture well. Sprinkle
        1 tablespoon sugar and a dash of grated orange peel
        over all and cover. Reduce heat and cook for about
        an hour or until the sauce turns a velvety orange and
        is fragrant. Taste for seasoning. Add salt and pepper
        as desired. Stored covered, this sauce lasts a month
        in the refrigerator.

I would like to digress and tell you about Carol Channing. She popped into my mind because of rock candy. She used to press it on me in what seemed to be tons. She was clearly a devotée and carried mounds of it in her outsized handbag. Carol Channing and rock candy will always be synonymous in my mind. I was working in New York for a rather unscrupulous gentleman who was handling public relations for *Hello Dolly*—it and Miss Channing—the hit of the sixties. He assigned me to her as "go-for," errand boy, or whatever appellation you care to attribute to one who goes and runs, follows, sits, rides in freezing air-conditioned cars (which I love—and she does too). She had the cast and chorus of *Hello Dolly* in torment all summer because the stage and backstage were kept at sub-zero level.

"Are you going to that thing tonight?" she asked as we rolled down Seventh Avenue in beautifully Arctic splendor to a mink-coat fitting. She was getting the wrap in lieu of money for lending her face and name to the merchandise.

"I'm not going anywhere. Hopefully, home," was the reply.

Fishing deeply into her troubled handbag, her over-sized alarm clock that she always wore on a chain about her neck getting perilously in the way, she managed to unearth two pieces of rock candy. I got one; she, the other. "But I won't have anyone to talk to," she wide-eyed and plaintively said.

At the risk of seeming an idiot, I felt I should find out what the good lady was talking about. I had discovered by this time that she operates a great deal in the realm of the non sequitur.

"Where would we talk and what would we talk about?" Sensible questions, I thought to myself. Instead, I offered this: "What thing, Carol?" Mild, at best.

"Oh, that thing they're doing on the top of some building." The top of some building happened to be the Rainbow Grill.

"What is it, a benefit?"

"No, it's a party for those two people. He's in the movie —she's not." It was Richard Burton and Elizabeth Taylor and the occasion was the opening in New York of *Night of the Iguana*. Presumably Carol Channing went, along with her ever-present handbag, alarm clock, organic food, bottled water, and rock candy. I would love to be able to dedicate a hearty recipe to her, but I know she would never be able to eat it. Here is one, however, that is perfect for Miss Channing.

RATAFIA CAROL CHANNING

1 pint of sloes*
½ pound of rock candy (as white and clear as possible)
2 empty bottles of the same size with corks
1 bottle of good dry gin (quart size)

I.   Prick the sloes with a silver fork and crush the rock candy slightly. Put ½ pint sloes and ¼ pound rock candy into each empty bottle. Cover with half bottle of gin in each. Seal with a cork.

II.   Allow to stand for about three months, shaking the bottles every day. Then strain through a fine muslin or several layers of cheesecloth and rebottle the contents. Leave the ratafia at least a year before drinking. The longer it sits—the better. If you have the patience to let it alone for seven years, you are in for a real treat.

*Sloes are the berries of the blackthorn bush. They may be purchased (dried) at fine herb or apothecary shops. Fresh hawthorn berries, picked after the blossoms fade in summer, or beach plums, picked in the fall, make an uncommonly good substitute for this tart liqueur.

If you use fresh berries, rinse them well, and add 1 cinnamon stick and two cloves to each bottle before you cork it.

Well, enough of that. I have been told by partners, friends, and enemies that I indulge in too much frivolity. So back to the serious art of cooking. I indulged myself when I introduced Miss Channing, and now let us go on to the delights of veal. There are several recipes I think you will enjoy.

VEAL MARSALA

3 tablespoons butter
4 veal chops
3 tablespoons Madeira

1 small clove garlic, crushed
½ teaspoon tomato paste
½ teaspoon beef bouillon powder
3 tablespoons flour
1 cup water
¼ cup dry white wine
¼ cup Marsala
salt and pepper
4 tomatoes, skinned and sliced
chopped fresh parsley

I. Heat 2 tablespoons butter in a large skillet. When the butter is intensely hot, put the chops in and brown quickly on both sides. Heat the Madeira in a small pan, ignite, and pour over the meat, shaking the pan until the flames subside. Remove the meat from the pan and set aside.

II. Put the garlic and remaining butter in the pan and cook for 1 minute. Off the fire, blend in the tomato paste, bouillon powder, and flour. Add 1 cup of water, wine, and Marsala. Stir over the fire until it boils. Season with salt and pepper. Return the chops; cover and cook for 40 to 50 minutes until tender. Add the tomatoes and cook for 5 minutes more. Arrange the chops on a hot serving platter. Pour the sauce over; sprinkle with chopped parsley, and serve. Serves 4.

STUFFED BREAST OF VEAL

3½—4 pounds breast of veal
1 pound ground pork
1 cup homemade breadcrumbs
2 finely minced onions
1 teaspoon fresh basil or ½ teaspoon dried basil
1 teaspoon salt
1 teaspoon freshly ground pepper
2 eggs
½ cup finely minced parsley
2 tablespoons good cognac
5 tablespoons sweet butter
1 tablespoon oil

2 cloves garlic, mashed
salt and fresh pepper
1½ cups white wine
1 tablespoon softened butter mixed with 1 teaspoon flour

I.   Preheat oven to 350°. Have the butcher make a pocket for stuffing in the roast. Prepare the stuffing as follows: blend thoroughly 1 pound of ground pork, 1 cup homemade breadcrumbs (toasted in the oven), 2 finely minced onions, 1 teaspoon basil, 1 teaspoon salt, 1 teaspoon ground pepper and 2 well-beaten eggs. Add ½ cup finely chopped parsley and 2 tablespoons cognac.

II.   Stuff the breast, and sew it up using a darning needle and coarse thread.

III. Melt 5 tablespoons of sweet butter in a large ovenproof pot. Add 1 tablespoon oil to keep the butter from burning.

IV.   Brown the veal breast quickly on all sides. Add 2 mashed cloves of garlic, salt and fresh pepper, and 1½ cups of white wine. Cover and cook in a 350° oven for about 3 hours. Cook covered for the first hour and uncovered for the last two. Bast the meat every 15 minutes.

V.   Remove the veal to a hot platter. Skim any excess fat from the pan juices and let them cook down quickly. If sauce is too thin, add a little *beurre manié* (a tablespoon of softened butter combined with 1 teaspoon of flour to thicken and rolled into tiny balls for easy mixing).

VI.   This veal is excellent hot or cold decorated with mounds of jellied chicken bouillon and strips of lemon peel. Cut it into thin diagonal slices. I like to serve it with a sauce composed of 1 cup homemade mayonnaise combined with 2 tablespoons Dijon mustard, 1 tablespoon capers, and 1 teaspoon fresh white horseradish. Serves 6—8.

VEAL A LA BONNE FEMME

4 lean veal chops
1 clove garlic, crushed
4 tablespoons butter
⅓ cup finely chopped shallots
12 very small new potatoes
¼ pound salt pork, diced
2 tablespoons dry white wine or vermouth
1 package beef bouillon powder
½ cup strong chicken broth
salt and freshly ground black pepper
1 teaspoon lemon juice
¼ cup chopped parsley

I. Preheat oven to 350°. Rub the chops with crushed garlic. Heat 1 tablespoon butter in a heavy skillet until very hot, and brown the chops quickly on both sides. Remove the chops from the pan and add the remaining butter. Add the shallots, potatoes, and salt pork. Brown slowly for 15 minutes. Add the wine and stir the vegetables thoroughly to make sure all are glazed.

II. Off the fire, blend in the bouillon powder, broth, salt, pepper, and lemon juice. Return to the flame and bring slowly to a boil. Remove from the heat.

III. Place the chops in an ovenproof casserole and pour the vegetables over. Stir once, carefully. Cover and place in the oven for 30 to 40 minutes or until tender. Skim off the fat if there is any floating on the sauce. If the sauce appears too thin, pour off ¼ cup of it and beat 1 teaspoon cornstarch into it. Then add the thickened *roux* to the sauce, by spoonfuls. Sprinkle with parsley and serve directly from the casserole. Serves 4.

For hardier appetites and fuller wallets, increase the chops to 2 per person. The recipe works equally well, stretched thusly.

VEAL IN BLACK OLIVES

5 tablespoons butter
4 veal chops, about 1½ inches thick
¼ cup minced shallots
1 packet G. Washington golden bouillon powder
1 cup dry white wine
salt and pepper
6 to 8 large ripe olives
1 tablespoon good cognac
4 tablespoons chopped parsley

I.   Melt 3 tablespoons butter in a large skillet. When the butter foams, put in the chops and brown them on both sides. When they are browned, add the remaining butter. Add the minced shallots and the bouillon powder; cook together until the shallots turn a golden color. Add ½ cup wine and season with salt and pepper.

II.   Cover and cook over a low heat for 25 to 30 minutes or until tender. Add the remaining wine a little at a time during the cooking period. Chop the olives finely, and put them in the pan with the chops. Add the cognac and cook for 5 or 6 minutes longer.

III. Arrange the chops on a hot serving dish and spoon the sauce over them. Sprinkle with chopped parsley and serve. Serves 4.

I have in residence a young Japanese man, Tsuyoshi Horita, whom God or whoever is the equivalent in Japan, sent to me. The young man is bright, eager, quick, and burning to learn. Eat your heart out, as they say; they are not easy to come by. For some reason or other he has extreme difficulty with my name—or maybe it is a slant reference to my sex—because Denis invariably comes out "Denise." Well, no matter, I gave up worrying about that sort of thing years ago.

"Denise," he calls gently up the stairwell to my messy suite where I am committing this to paper. "What would you like for dinner?"

I think instantly, "Oh God, do I have to worry about that now?" Words at this red-hot second are more important to me than food.

"Japanese style, French or American?" the voice goes on.

"Japanese." With a shudder of delight, he bustles into the kitchen, and I hear the sound of refrigerator doors opening and closing and merry Japanese tunes tinkling from his whistled lips. Center-cut pork chops had been bought the day before. "Denise," the voice carols, "in ten minutes."

I think, oh, hell, I won't even have time for a proper drink and will have to do what my parents did and take my drink to the table.

I once had an artist friend who was inordinately fond of pigs—and at this moment—or point in time, as the saying now goes, I would love to roast him, but barring that, I turn to the Horita recipe. It not only allows you to take out your hostilities, but fills your belly as well.

PORK CUTLET HORITA

4 thick loin pork chops
salt and black pepper
1 cup flour
2 eggs beaten with ½ cup milk
2 cups bread crumbs
cooking oil
1 tablespoon Tabasco sauce
½ cup Worcestershire sauce
½ cup catsup or chili sauce
1 cup rice
green cabbage for garnish
whole radishes for garnish
watercress sprigs for garnish
2 medium-sized ripe tomatoes, sliced, for garnish

I.   Preheat oven to 400°. Remove the meat from the bone of the chops and shape into 1-inch-by-5-inch sticks. Sprinkle with salt and black pepper and roll in flour. Each chop yields 2 sticks. Dip into the beaten egg and milk mixture and roll in bread crumbs.

II.   Fill ¾ of a skillet with oil. Heat the oil and sauté the pork sticks on each side until brown. Remove from the skillet and place on a rack in a roasting pan. Bake for 10 minutes in the oven.

III.   In a saucepan, bring the Tabasco, Worcestershire, and chili sauces to a boil. Serve with the chops.

IV.   Serve rice as an accompaniment. Use 1 cup of rice to 1½ cups of cold water. Wash and drain it three times. Bring to a boil; simmer 3-4 minutes. Turn off the flame and allow the rice to rest for 5 minutes. Drain. Serves 4.

Accompany this dish with green cabbage finely shredded and immersed in cold water for 20 minutes—then drained. Add whole radishes, watercress, and sliced tomatoes as garnish.

STUFFED PORK CHOPS

4 double pork chops, with pockets
salt and fresh pepper to taste
¼ cup butter
¾ cup chopped onion
¼ cup chopped celery
1½ cups bread cubes
1 teaspoon crushed fennel seeds
½ cup chopped parsley
¼ cup heavy cream, approximately
dry white wine
1 teaspoon cornstarch for each cup of juices to be thickened

I.   Preheat oven to 350°. Sprinkle the chops inside and out with salt and pepper. Let sit for a few minutes.

II.   In a heavy skillet, heat 3 tablespoons butter; add the onions and celery, and cook until the onion is transparent. Add the bread cubes, fennel seeds, and parsley. Remove from the heat. Add enough heavy cream to moisten the mixture.

III.   Stuff the pork chop cavities with the mixture and close the openings with toothpicks. In a Dutch oven melt the remaining butter, add the pork chops and brown on both sides. Add wine to a depth of ¼ inch; cover and bake 1 hour, turning after 30 minutes.

IV.   Transfer the chops to a warm platter and keep hot. Bring the remaining sauce to a boil. Mix the cornstarch with a little water and stir into the sauce. Correct the seasonings and serve with the pork chops. Serves 4.

PORK LOIN ROAST

4-pound loin roast
2 cloves garlic, crushed
salt and pepper
4 tablespoons Dijon mustard (approximately)
1 onion, roughly chopped
1 large carrot, roughly chopped
½ stick butter
4 tablespoons caraway seeds
branch of fresh thyme or a pinch of dried thyme

I. Preheat oven to 350°. Be sure to have your butcher cut through the shin bone to make the roast easy to carve. Wipe the meat with a damp cloth and rub entirely with crushed garlic on all sides. Then rub the fat side well with salt and pepper. Smear the entire surface with Dijon mustard and arrange it with the prepared fat side up, in a roasting pan.

II. Cook 1 onion and 1 large carrot, roughly chopped, in the butter until the onions just turn color. Spread over the mustard-coated meat. Sprinkle caraway seeds on the meat and lay a branch of fresh thyme or a pinch of dried on top of the roast.

III. Roast, uncovered, in a 350° oven for about 30 minutes per pound, or until a meat thermometer reaches 175°. Baste every 15 minutes. Take the roast from the oven and let it stand a few minutes before carving. It will continue to cook with its own heat and the juices will settle. Serves 4.

Lamb of God and all that notwithstanding, this ethereal, delightful delicacy can be one of the most succulent and satisfying meats on this planet. Young lamb which has just begun to graze is a great delicacy with a marked and delicious flavor. In many European countries, lamb is the staple meat because the little fellows take up far less grazing room than beef steers;

and when they are slaughtered so young, they are relatively inexpensive to raise. On that thought, which films my eyes with tears, here is a recipe for roast leg of lamb that I think you will admire.

DIJONNAISE ROASTED LAMB

8 pound leg of lamb
1 clove garlic, cut in slivers
½ cup Dijon mustard
2 tablespoons soy sauce
1 clove garlic, mashed
1 teaspoon ground rosemary or thyme
½ teaspoon powdered ginger
2 tablespoons olive oil

I.   Preheat oven to 350°. Using an ice pick, score the surface of the lamb with a pattern of small incisions. Insert slivers of garlic into the skin of the lamb, and let stand while you prepare the marinade.

II.   Blend the mustard, soy sauce, garlic, herbs, and ginger together in a bowl. Beat in the oil, by droplets, to make a mayonnaise-like cream. Paint the lamb with the mixture using a rubber spatula, and set it on the rack of a roasting pan. The meat will pick up more flavor if it is coated 3 to 4 hours before roasting.

III.   Roast in the oven for 1 to 1¼ hours for medium rare or 1¼ to 1½ hours for well done. Serves 8-10.

If you are feeling grand, nervous, excited, and want to impress someone—lover, friend, husband's boss (or wife of same)—here is a recipe that will do it. It might make you feel your home is on the range, but never mind, I think you will find it worth the stay—and ultimately, you will glow.

RACK OF LAMB

1 small rack of lamb, with 8 chops
6 tablespoons butter
3 teaspoons flour

1 teaspoon tomato paste
1 packet good bouillon powder
1 ½ cups beef broth
salt and pepper
12 small white onions
¼ pound mushrooms, quartered
1 cup each cooked fresh peas, French string beans, and
    sautéed potato balls

I.   Preheat broiling unit. Trim the ends of the rib bones, leaving about 2 inches of the bone free from meat and fat. Place the lamb in a baking pan and dot the top with 2 tablespoons butter. Broil until the lamb is very well browned and the bones charred, turning once to brown both sides. This will take about 30 minutes in all, leaving the outside well cooked and the inside pink and juicy.

II.   Meanwhile, prepare the following sauce: melt 2 tablespoons of butter in a small saucepan and off the fire, blend in the flour, tomato paste, and bouillon powder. Return to the fire; stir in the stock, and slowly bring to a boil. Season with salt and pepper and simmer for a few minutes.

III.   Brown the onions slowly in the remaining butter, more if needed. Add the mushrooms and cook another 3 minutes. Pour in the sauce and simmer slowly until ready to use.

IV.   Place the lamb on a hot serving dish. Spoon some of the sauce over the meat and pour the rest around it. Put cutlet frills on the ends of the bones. Surround the lamb with small mounds of cooked vegetables, and serve, allowing 2 ribs per person. Serves 4.

If you are not niggardly—and you must never, never be—you will have bought more lamb than you needed for that roast. And there is a divine way to dispatch the remains of the little beast. There is a marvelous little East Indian restaurant in Greenwich Village, the name of which constantly eludes me, but I manage to find my way there like a homing pigeon.

It is on Sullivan Street and has the facade of a red barn. After repeated return engagements, I think I have discovered the secrets to the lamb curry they serve. It will enrich your life, get rid of the leftovers, and perhaps induce the person you serve it to—to an added response. Be sure to prepare all the condiments listed—they are a must.

LAMB CURRY

2 pounds lamb
6 tablespoons butter
2 cloves garlic, crushed
salt and freshly ground black pepper
½ cup strong beef bouillon
2 tablespoons good vegetable oil
1 cup finely sliced mixed onion, carrot, celery
1 apple, sliced without skin
4 to 5 tablespoons curry powder, or to taste
4 tablespoons flour
1 tablespoon tomato paste
2 cups beef stock
1 can coconut
1 cup milk
juice of one orange
juice of ½ lemon
2 cardamom seeds, crushed
⅓ cup black currants
2 cups rice, boiled

I.   Remove most of the fat from the lamb and cut it into ¾-inch squares. Heat 2 tablespoons of butter in a heavy skillet; add the garlic, and cook for 1 minute. Then sauté the meat until it is well browned on all sides. Season lightly with salt and pepper, add ½ cup strong bouillon, and simmer until the lamb is tender. (Omit step I if using leftover lamb.)

II.   Meanwhile prepare the sauce. I do mine in an old kettle, because I prefer to serve the curry directly from it, accompanied by a bowl of hot, boiled rice. You may make this dish in any deep heavy saucepan. Heat the remaining butter and the oil until bubbly. Add the onion mixture and the apple. Cook slowly for 5 minutes. Add the curry powder and cook another 10 minutes.

III. Blend in, off the fire, the flour, tomato paste, and lamb juices, or ½ cup bouillon, if using leftovers. Pour in 2 cups of stock and stir over a low flame until the mixture comes to a boil. Barely simmer for 5 minutes.

IV. In a blender, combine the coconut and milk. Blend at high speed until smooth. Strain, reserving ¼ cup of the milk. Also reserve the coconut.

V. To the sauce, add the orange juice, lemon juice, coconut milk, and cardamom seeds. Season with salt and pepper, and simmer for 30 to 35 minutes.

VI. When the lamb is cooked, add it to the sauce with any pan juices. Add the dried currants and the reserved coconut. Serve. (If not to be served immediately, transfer to an ovenproof casserole to be warmed in the oven later.)

VII. Serve directly from the pot or transfer to a serving bowl, accompanied by hot boiled rice and any or all of the following condiments: 1 finely diced green pepper, 3 finely chopped hard-cooked egg whites, 3 finely chopped hard-cooked egg yolks, 1 cup chutney, 1 ripe avocado diced and mixed with 4 tablespoons lime juice, 6 slices crumbled crisp bacon, ½ cup ground cashews, 1 banana cut in spears and sprinkled with lemon juice, 1 cup sliced white grapes, 1 cup chopped sweet-mixed pickles, and 1 cup chopped cucumber mixed with ½ cup plain yoghurt. Serves 4—6.

A decidedly lilting voice tinged with all the emerald green of Ireland emerged from my telephone one day. "I have a serious problem! We're stopping at the Ocean Dune before going to our boat and they won't book unless we give them the money, and we won't be out until tomorrow, and they won't hold. I turn to you because I feel you'll be kind enough to give them their fee. It's $175."

Bad cess to them, I thought. The Ocean Dune, I mean, a chic and expensive motel on the ocean in Amagansett. Up to this point, however, no note of identity had been provided by my caller. My vision may be failing, since I have to use a spy-glass to read telephone numbers and certain parts of recipes, but my hearing is as acute as ever, and I had already divined the identity of the lady in distress.

"We'll need something to tide us over till we get to our boat and I thought if I rang you up you could prepare it and do me this enormous favor. We hate to eat out, and besides, one always has to dress. Oh, I'm terribly sorry, this is Mrs. Stuart Scheftel."

Well, at last! I knew from the second sentence you were Geraldine Fitzgerald, but discretion, the better part of wisdom and valor, silenced my tongue. A check was duly delivered to their lodgings and a suggestion for lamb stew was offered to tide them over. There was a delighted response that would have made my mother—in whatever Valhalla or nirvana she now inhabits—proud of me.

LAMB STEW BAKED IN A CASSEROLE

4 pounds lamb shoulder or breast, boned and cut into 1½-inch
*   cubes*
salt and freshly ground pepper
4 tablespoons oil
¼ cup flour
2 cups finely minced yellow onions
1 tablespoon finely minced garlic
pinch of saffron
½ cup dry white wine
3½ cups peeled, chopped tomatoes
1 cup of good strong chicken broth
1 tablespoon sugar
1 tablespoon sweet butter
1 tablespoon slivered orange peel
¼ cup good cognac
chopped parsley

I.   Preheat oven to 375°. Sprinkle the cubes of meat with salt and pepper.

II.   Heat the oil in a large heavy casserole and add the meat.
        Cook over medium-high heat, stirring frequently,
        for about 20 minutes or so. At first the meat will emit
        a liquid but this will burn off as the meat continues
        to brown. If your pot is not ample enough, it may be
        wise to sauté the meat in smaller amounts, reserving
        the browned portions until all the cubes are sautéed.

III.   When all the meat is browned all over, sprinkle with
        flour. Stir well so that all the pieces are evenly coated.

IV.   Add the onions, garlic, and pinch of saffron. Cook,
        stirring occasionally for about 5 or 6 minutes. Then
        add the wine, tomatoes, and chicken broth. Sprinkle
        the mixture with 1 tablespoon sugar. Cover and bake
        for about an hour.

V.   In a small sauté pan, melt 1 tablespoon sweet butter.
        Add the slivered orange peel (it must be cut in fine
        strips) and toss them for a minute or two until they
        are well coated with butter. Add ¼ cup of cognac
        until it is warmed and then flame it.

VI.   Pour the cognac and orange peel over the lamb in the
        casserole and return it to the oven for an additional
        20 minutes or so, until the cubes are tender and redo-
        lent of a rich Mediterranean sauce.

VII.   Garnish with chopped parsley and serve over buttered
        noodles, rice, or tiny boiled potatoes. This dish takes
        a full-bodied red wine to assert its authority. Try a
        Medoc. Serves 6 – 8.

Speaking of my mother, here are two recipes I learned at
her knee. She was a lamb fancier and had to foist the fare
deceptively on the whole family. She would explain with all
the innocence of the guileful that what they were about to eat
was roast beef done a new way. I do not think it fooled anyone,
least of all me, since I watched her in action. In addition to
which, I had been sent to the butcher shop to buy the meat.

BRAISED LAMB SHANKS

4 lamb shanks, about 1 pound each
3 tablespoons flour
salt and pepper
paprika
2 tablespoons butter
2 tablespoons oil
1 large onion, thinly sliced
¾ cup red wine
1¼ cups water
¼ teaspoon chopped fresh rosemary (or a pinch of dried)
chopped parsley

I.   Preheat oven to 375°. Season 1 tablespoon of flour with salt and a little paprika and lightly dust the shanks. Heat the butter and oil in a deep heavy saucepan and brown the shanks on all sides. Remove from the pan and lightly brown the onion. Put back the meat; add the red wine, ¾ cup of water, and the rosemary. Season with salt and pepper. Cover and cook in the oven for about 2 hours, or until the meat is easily pierced with a fork.

II.   Take the lamb shanks out of the juices, blend the remaining flour with ½ cup of cold water, and add it to the pan juices, stirring over a fire until the gravy thickens and comes to a boil. Simmer for 2 to 3 minutes, then strain.

III. Serve the shanks garnished with parsley. Pass the gravy separately. Serves 4.

SHOULDER OF LAMB, BRAISED PROVENÇALE-STYLE

1 boned, rolled shoulder of lamb (about 4-5 pounds)
3 cloves of garlic (cut into thin slivers)
¼ cup oil
1 teaspoon coarse salt
1 teaspoon fresh ground pepper
1 clove of garlic, finely minced
2 cups diced eggplant (unpeeled)

4 shallots, finely minced
2 medium-sized yellow onions, thinly sliced
2 cups chopped tomatoes (seeded)
½ teaspoon fresh or dried basil
1 packet brown bouillon powder
1 cup good red wine
1 cup ripe olives (pitted)
½ cup chopped fresh parsley

I. Make small incisions in a boned and rolled shoulder of lamb with an ice pick and insert slivers of garlic into every opening. Rub the outside surface of the meat with oil, and then press on coarse salt and fresh ground pepper until it is well coated. Let the meat stand 15 minutes.

II. Heat your oven to a blazing 500°. Place the roast in a large pan and let it sear in the hot oven for about 20-25 minutes.

III. Remove from the oven and turn the heat down to 325°. Add minced garlic, eggplant, shallots, sliced onions, and two cups of the chopped, seeded tomatoes. (I seed mine by cutting them in half and squeezing the pips out, as you would an orange.) Also add a ½ teaspoon basil, a packet of bouillon powder for body, and a cup of red wine.

IV. Put the meat back in the oven and cook for about 25 to 30 minutes a pound (for medium-rare meat). Baste thoroughly every 20 minutes. If you require your meat more well done, leave the lamb in an additional 20 minutes.

V. A few minutes before the roast is done, add 1 cup of pitted black olives and blend them well with the sauce. Remove the roast to a warm platter and cover it with sauce. Garnish the roast lavishly with chopped parsley. Serve with rice and a watercress-and-endive salad. A crusty bread is a necessity here, for the mopping-up operation. And a Châteauneuf-du-Pape makes a sturdy accompanying wine. Serves 8-10.

There is a man, young, wealthy, and supercilious, who owns an art gallery in Soho, that relatively new art colony in lower Manhattan. He shall remain nameless because he would be the first to sue me. His first name is at the end of the alphabet; his wife's name at the beginning, and she shall be nameless, too. These two plagued me for several years about parties they were giving.

"And will it be good? And will the help be right?" That old saw I told you about before. After droning my litany of menus, we always wound up with the same thing. Maybe they just liked the sound of my voice. I say they because they were always on extension phones—a little disconcerting when you are constantly interrupted by two voices chorusing, "Will that be good?"

All I could ever do for them was to arrange the ingredients. The dish cannot be cooked in advance, and the charmless young man fancied himself a master chef. The dish they served, however, is good. I love it, and if you are on your mettle and do it right, you will, too.

SHISH KEBAB

1 small leg of lamb
¼ cup lemon juice
1 cup red wine
¼ cup olive oil
2 cloves garlic, crushed
1 tablespoon salt
freshly ground black pepper to taste
1 teaspoon oregano
½ teaspoon soy sauce
½ teaspoon curry powder
1 teaspoon crushed cumin seed
12 mushroom caps
12 tomato wedges
2 green peppers cut into squares
18 small white onions (can be parboiled 5 minutes for a tender
*   touch)*
2 eggplants, cut into cubes

I.   Have a butcher remove the bone, gristle, and all remnants of fat from the leg of lamb and cut into 2-

inch squares. Place in a deep saucepan, and add the lemon juice, red wine, oil, garlic, salt, pepper, oregano, soy sauce, curry powder, and cumin seed. Marinate for a minimum of 12 hours.

II.   Preheat your broiling unit. Spear the meat on skewers, alternating with mushrooms, tomatoes, green pepper, onions, and eggplant.

III.   Brush with the marinade sauce and then place under the broiler (or over coals on a hibachi or barbecue). Cook until nicely browned on all sides. Serves 6.

I once, when slightly—or maybe not so slightly—in my cups, doused the whole kebab in kerosene, thinking that I was applying lighter fluid to the coals. Try not to do that. Now, on to ham.

During a season in The Store, we prepare a ham daily for take-out consumption. It elicits squalls of ecstasy and cries of delight and approval. "Divine!" "Super!" "Superb!" are the gasps as fingers grasp for the bits that fall to the carving board as the ham is sliced. There are two stipulations you must adhere to if you have it in your head to open your own version of The Store. One is the ham itself; the other, the glaze. The ham should be a Dubuque ham, and it should be boneless except for about an inch of bone at the rear end. Save this for future reference.

THE STORE HAM

10 – 12 pound boneless smoked ham (I prefer the Dubuque Fleur De Lis brand)
whole cloves
4 tablespoons Dijon mustard
1 clove garlic, mashed
¼ cup Chinese duck sauce
dash of orange juice
½ cup brown sugar

I.   Preheat oven to 400°. Line a large roasting pan with aluminum foil.

II.   With a sharp knife, score the top of the ham. Stud with the cloves at every intersection.

III.   Combine the mustard, garlic, and duck sauce with enough orange juice to make a syrupy mixture. Spread evenly over the tops and sides of the ham.

IV.   Sprinkle the surface of the ham with the brown sugar and bake in the preheated oven for about 1½ hours. Serve hot, or at room temperature.

If you are like some of my frantic ladies and giving a party at which you may serve ham, the cry, "How can I slice it for all those people? Will you do it at the Store?" clarions loudly.

The Store, preferring to do things the pioneer way, does not own a slicing machine. We deal with a small butcher shop, Walter's Meat Market, on the corner of Greenwich Avenue and Jane Street in the Village. And they will slice it paper thin for me and tie it together. If you flash an enchanting smile and murmur wistfully, I am sure you can manage the same. Once it has been sliced, bake it exactly as before.

And here is another delicacy:

HAM WITH FIGS

precooked smoked ham
whole cloves
¼ cup brown sugar
¼ cup canned fig juice
dried figs, steamed for 20 minutes or soaked in hot water for
     the same length of time
green grapes

I.   Preheat oven to 325°. With a sharp knife score the top of the ham. Stud with cloves at every intersection. Spread the brown sugar evenly over the top of the ham. Bake in a shallow pan, allowing 18 to 20 minutes per pound.

II.   When the sugar on the ham begins to melt, pour the canned fig juice over it. Baste the ham at 20-minute intervals.

III.   Forty-five minutes before the ham is to be removed from the oven, decorate it with figs, as follows: Nip off the little hard end; cut each fig partially through into quarters. Open it and flatten out on the ham in the shape of a four-leaf clover. Make a small hole in the uncut center of the fig and force a green grape halfway through it. Serve hot or at room temperature. Number served varies with size of ham.

Now that you have all those ham leftovers lying around, what to do, what to do? Well, I can tell you what to do. One of these recipes, a pâté, will make you feel you are suffering the tortures of the damned and that you have been chained to the kitchen in penal servitude. The other is relatively simple. Both are delicious.

JAMBON PERSILLE A LA BOURGUIGNON

large bowl of ham ends
3½ cups chicken broth
2½ cups white wine or vermouth
1 sprig thyme
2 sprigs tarragon
½ cup chopped shallots
1½ cups onion, finely sliced
1 stalk of celery
1½ packages gelatin
3½ tablespoons wine vinegar
2 cloves garlic
½ cup heavy cream
2½ cups fresh parsley, finely chopped

I.   Chop all the meat you can cut off the ham and put it aside.

II.   Put the bones, fatty pieces, and skin in a large saucepan along with the chicken stock, wine, herbs, shallots, onions, and celery. Add water to fill the pot halfway, if necessary. Boil this mixture until it reduces to half the original amount. Remove the bones and discard. Stir in the package of clear gelatin and allow to cool.

III.   Remove any soft pieces of ham from the cooked broth. Roughly chop and add to the chopped ham mixture.

IV.   Scoop out the gristle, ham skin, and end material from the pot and put into the jar of a blender. Add vinegar, garlic, and cream. Blend for a few minutes until it is a thick, creamy mixture. (If more liquid is needed, use the stock from the pot.)

V.   Divide the chopped ham into 2 equal portions. Add half the liquid to 1 portion and set aside. To the other portion, add the remaining liquid and half the parsley.

VI.   Pack into a buttered pan or crock, alternating with parslied ham, plain chopped parsley, and plain chopped ham. Pack tight, pressing down the sides to make a loaf. Cover with saran wrap and chill.

VII.   Serve well chilled, garnished with finely chopped parsley.

JAMBALAYA

3 tablespoons butter
1 cup finely chopped onion
1 cup finely chopped green pepper
2 cloves garlic, crushed
1 cup cooked chicken, diced
1 cup cooked ham, diced
6 sweet Italian sausages, cut in thirds
2½ cups canned tomatoes, undrained
1 cup raw white rice
1½ cups chicken broth
½ teaspoon thyme
1 tablespoon chopped parsley
¼ teaspoon chili powder
1½ teaspoons salt
¼ teaspoon freshly ground black pepper

I.   Preheat oven to 350°. Melt the butter in a large skillet and add the onion, green pepper, and garlic. Cook slowly until tender, stirring often. Add the chicken, ham, and sausages. Cook for 5 more minutes.

II. Add the tomatoes with their liquid, the rice, broth, thyme, parsley, chili, salt, and pepper. Transfer the mixture to a large ovenproof casserole. Cover and bake until the rice is tender, about 1¼ hours. Serves 8.

And here is a recipe that Myra Greene, Bert's sister, sprung on me in Palm Beach two years ago. The two of us journeyed to this manicured Siberia of the western world in a truck accompanied by three Scotch terriers, one cat, twenty-five hams, and other assorted gear that would put a gypsy caravan to shame. Our high-spirited trek from New York to that mausoleum of the rich and mighty was ostensibly for the establishment of The Store in Palm Beach.

"They need you desperately down there," cooed several lovely ladies. "You'll be a smash!"

Well, we smashed all right, with a thud that resounded from Maine to Key West. We rented a picturesque house done in the Spanish style of the late 1920s in Lake Worth, where the mean age of the residents ranges from 85 to 90. We had a particularly sprightly neighbor of 93 who pretended he was blind, but had the sight of a bird dog. He lived with a woman—was she his wife, his housekeeper, his mistress, or his keeper? He referred to her only as "she." Actually, her name was Vera, as we soon learned.

On the second day we were there, I became aware of the repeated wail of sirens and thought Lake Worth must be burning to the ground. Suddenly feeling like Scarlett O'Hara in *Gone with the Wind* about to flee Atlanta, I rushed to our neighbor who was sunning himself in an ice cream chair with an impossibly small, nasty-tempered dog at his feet. Rather nervously, I burbled things about fire engines.

"Them ain't fire engines, sonny. That's the pulmotor squad."

We were to be one in a complex of shops, the entire project masterminded by a highly professional con man. I will spare you the legal, technical, and architectural complications attendant on this enterprise. The Store in Palm Beach never even opened.

Well, now, what do you do with twenty-five hams? You move them from refrigerator to freezer daily. Fortunately, we had two freezers, but this action can lead to hysteria, not to mention nervous breakdowns. A good samaritan approached Miss Greene and myself with the knowledge that Trude Heller, famed lady of the discotheque of the 1960s, was operating a dimly lit palace of dubious festivities in Palm Beach and was thinking of opening a restaurant. God, those hams! A way to get rid of them. I was interviewed, perhaps scrutinized is a better word, by the lady who is possessed of a flinty eye and voice of ground granite. A deal was made—abortive, because Hostess Heller never had any customers, and we wound up feeding the help and giving dinner parties for her guests. At any rate, after this long preamble, here is the recipe:

MYRA'S HAM

Slice some ham ¼ to ½ inch thick, place on a baking sheet, run under the broiler for 10 minutes. Turn and layer the other side with slices of Swiss cheese; put it back under the broiler till the cheese melts and bubbles. Delicious with a green salad.

Here is the last ham recipe you are going to get from me. It was invariably served to me at the home of one of the most unpleasant and awkward girls I have ever encountered. I was in college at the University of Virginia and her doting mother pressed her on me because the poor thing couldn't manage any other "dates." We muddled through, eyeing each other with hostility. This meal, however, even though it had a certain repetitive quality at the time, is delicious. It was prepared and served by a very large and jovial black woman, then the fashion, who seemed to divide her life between the kitchen and the dining room table. The fare was beautiful—albeit the sullen eyes staring at me across the table were not.

ROAST FRESH HAM

1 uncooked tenderized ham
whole cloves
1 cup brown sugar, packed
2 teaspoons dry mustard

I.   Preheat oven to 300°. Place the ham under cold running water and scrub the rind well with a stiff brush. Dry and place it in a roasting pan with the skin and fat side up. Insert a meat thermometer into the thickest part of the ham.

II.   Bake the ham, uncovered, 25 minutes to the pound, or until it registers 160° on the thermometer.

III. When the ham is done, remove it from the oven, and use kitchen shears or a sharp knife to cut off the rind. Score the fat diagonally to make a diamond pattern. Stud each intersection with cloves. Combine the brown sugar and mustard with a little of the ham drippings. Spread evenly over the top of the ham.

IV.   Increase the oven heat to 400° and return the ham to the oven until the sugar forms a glaze.

Honey may be substituted in place of the brown sugar. Some people prefer to leave the skin on during the entire cooking, because it does get very crispy and is good to eat, but is not as elegant as the glazed, diamond look.

My Sister's Store

Chapter Eight

BERT GREENE

A permanent weekender, my sister Myra runs The Store from Friday night to Sunday afternoon—and has for over seven years.

No matter where her city life takes her, no matter what bramble of legal machination she is involved with at the moment (be it maritime law or metropolitan garage arbitration), her heart belongs solidly and four-square to the blue-and-white checked-gingham walls and the marble-topped butcher's table where she is ensconced like a *femme de ménage* from early May to late September.

It is she who, in the late evening, scrubs down the rough pine counter and chivies up after the hired scrubber-upper, who never quite washes well enough to do credit to her station: "The Front."

There is no question that the golden area encompassing the cookie jars, the unused adding machine ("it's too complicated to bother with"), and the solid brass cash register that totes up only dream "coat and dress sales" in memory of some other doomed business venture is absolutely Myra's domain.

And there she rules, by turns a tartar or a Talleyrand, as the spirit or the spiritlessness of the customer of the moment moves her.

Her "Hiya kiddo!" to beloved friends (and surely all the old customers *are* her friends) warms any chill Decoration Day weekend.

And her measured, "Hell-o. How'r you?" to the non-cognoscenti who invariably ask her, "What kind of a *store* is this anyway?" can put an icecap on a day in August.

Myra's domain extends from the ornamental French baker's rack at The Store's entrance, past the geographical boundary of a dessert case and the shelves of antiquary kitchenware that separate a single dining table (always set for four) from the traffic snarl of the cheese board, where she doles out slivers of Havarti and Brie to those in her favor at the moment. Her kingdom ends at the kitchen doors.

"Can we do a Reine de Saba, today?" she will call, ignoring the groans. "Can we take a lemon mousse for fifteen people for tomorrow?"

Blithely disregarding the negative reply she expects full well (one day's notice is simply not enough, Myra), she will put on her half-glasses and peer hard at the other orders pinned to the kitchen wall, seeking logic as a life preserver.

"Aha! Tom and Rustine Guinzburg have ordered a lemon mousse for ten people for tomorrow! And I see that Peter and Mary Stone are having one for eight. Now . . . couldn't we just stretch it a little—and do fifteen portions more?"

Most times she will not wait for a formal answer, aware that the low mutterings are just part of the human condition in a cook's world and, instead, she will sail back to her own safe harbor in the front (now jammed with commerce) and whisper confidentially:

"I think we can arrange that lemon mousse, madam . . . . But you must bring your own bowl. And by 10 A.M."

The counter is unquestionably where she is in full command. Her arrangements of its serving spoons and assorted salvers is legendary. Every utensil, every pencil has its place. And her anger at the weekly displacement of this cache of *tabletterie* by the crew of youthful and undedicated summer workers is worthy of a Cossack quartermaster.

"No system!" she clarions as she retrieves the missing forks and carvers from a welter of kitchen clutter. "Absolutely no system whatsoever! You can leave something in the same place every single Sunday for seven years—and you can bet your bottom dollar that you won't find it there when you come back again on Friday."

She ought to know. She has been there from The Store's first day with only half a Sunday off for illness or vanity a while back, when an errant tooth broke.

My sister, Miss Greene, is The Store's staunchest ally, growing gray in its service, always lending it zeal, willing hands, or money (when the receipts dip perilously). As a matter of record, she was its original co-backer. Since none of the original partners had the cash or a decent enough credit rating at the time to persuade any bank to sponsor it, Myra signed up for

The Store's first loan. And co-signed for a few afterward as well.

Though it is her store on weekends, she is never the first to appear in the morning. But you can always depend on her arrival before the resplendent salads depart from the kitchen. She comes in through the screen door like Ceres, bearing wreaths of summer greenery to fill the back of the blue toile salad case, more to divert the eye from an excess of condensation in our antique equipment than from any passion for greenery.

She will more often than not bring a goody with her in the morning—a crumb cake or some brioche that she will have heretically purchased at a city bakery the day before. Something to be shared at our pre-opening coffee break.

"Myra! This stuff is really awful," we will say, wolfing it down.

"Well, there's no rule that you have to eat it, y'know," my sister will reply, popping a myriad of colored pills into her mouth along with a bit of croissant. "But I simply cannot take vitamins on an empty stomach."

Aside from the smidgen of Brie from the cheese knife (if the Bries are truly running well) this is probably the only sustenance she will get all day. The rest of us usually stop for lunch, or in my case, nosh all day, but Myra just keeps on pacing.

"You want an omelette, Myra?"

"Thanks, but no time, luv. What I'd really like is a cup of instant, though."

It is made, but usually grows cold before it is ever drunk. Most of her day is spent dashing back to her station as each new bell jangle announces another arrival.

"Is that a guest?" she will inquire of her youngest co-worker, Kevis Goodman, who is ten years old.

Shy Kevis, permitted to work in The Store weekend mornings by an indulgent mother and father, will poke her small head around the wall to survey the scene.

"Yes, it's another guest, Myra!"

The late Michael Field once wrote lovingly of The Store in McCall's Magazine: "Run by imaginative and dedicated young cooks . . . The Store prepares a charming conceit called an *Haute Picque-Nique*. Made from scratch . . . are pâtés, quiches, billi bi, gazpacho, cold tarragon chicken, baked country ham, cold herbed omelettes on individual loaves of French bread, fragrant salads of all descriptions, and elegant cakes and tarts. . . .

Each dish is so lovingly prepared that the shock of paying the bill is painlessly absorbed by the sheer euphoria induced by eating this elegant food."

If dear Michael put us into the "Haute Picque-Nique" business in the first place, my sister Myra has surely to take the responsibility for keeping us up to our ankles in it now.

"There was nothing much on the board for Sunday," she will announce at a discreet distance from the kitchen doors, "so I took a Luncheon on the Boat."

A Luncheon on the Boat is comprised of individual containers of icy gazpacho, each swallow a fiery salute down the hatch; fried chicken with Tamar croustade, the chicken sautéed in butter only, and the croustades made of trimmed French breads filled with a garlic-tinged, black olive butter. They are sliced as thin as beach grass. To that, add string beans vinaigrette, pecan tartlets, and, hopefully, a good white wine, supplied by the ship's captain.

Since The Store specializes in a cargo of such comestibles, it is not a surprising sight on a weekend to find Myra along with Kevis, her acolyte in this enterprise, packing fifty or seventy-five of these redoubtable boat hampers before lunch.

Haut picniques (as we spell them) are usually put together in the middle room of The Store. A limbo between kitchen and customer, it is the place where pies cool and lemon sponge cakes sometimes fall, a place where hot-pink and acid-green tissue paper, the elegant lining for every picnic lunch box, swirls about the feet like a Mediterranean sirocco on Luncheon on the Boat days.

The *haut picnique* may be humble. Even the most humiliated, however, is priced at $3.50 per person. But it is generously crammed with pâté or baked ham on crusty bread, a container of one of the salads of the day, a finger of cheese, and a gleaming orb of fruit.

The most elaborate one we ever prepared was for a beach supper some years back to celebrate Andy Warhol's birthday. It consisted of cold lobster with a lemony light mayonnaise, a salad composed of raw tomato and basil, cold, boned chicken tarragon, and a whole Brie cheese. There were fresh strawberries for dessert, and Denis made a mountain of angel food cake crested with whipped cream. It made a hamper of absolutely stunning munificence.

The Hearty Night Picnic is my favorite. It is a huge stew-pot of bouillabaisse, with loaves of crusty bread and cauliflower salad as its only accompaniment, assorted cheeses, and a whole rummed raspberry nut torte for sheer stomach distress later . . . much later.

The Bash Buffet is one picnic listed on our menu that has gone abegging for years—probably more for the formidable quantity of food described than the price. Bash buffets for fifty persons or more run upwards of about twenty dollars a person, and can be ordered, it is stated, with a week's notice.

Partner Denis, with all his dour, Irish pessimism, has always proclaimed that we could not turn one out in a month. A wild mix of comestibles, it runs the gamut of every conceivable alfresco party staple: lobster-stuffed eggs and cold shrimp bathed in a cold curried mayonnaise, whole baked ham, whole roast beef, and a flurry of fresh vegetable salads. Cold lemon chicken nestles beside filled herbed tomatoes; potato and cheese mayon-naise a la Romana anointed with prosciutto vies for prominence inence with a dish of cold white beans crowned with inky black caviar.

This feast ends with a flourish. Cheese and fruit and pie . . . pie . . . pie. Apple, peach, blueberry, and pecan. And probably more than a touch of indigestion for the picnicker.

Such a bash was prepared at The Store one summer's day not too long ago when William Doyle, the prestigious antique dealer and estate auctioneer, decided it would provide the per-fect finale to a long day's dismantling (after he had sold off the contents of a great East End mansion). A *grand bouffe* was requested, a "wall-to-wall," dusk-to-dawn picnic that he could over-host to repay a crew of loyal co-workers, customers, and cohorts.

I never saw much of *the* bash after it left our establishment. Myra reported that it took two large cars and a small pick-up truck to transport the larder to its destination. And that was that—except for reports of a gastronomic Hiroshima that ringed the South fork of Long Island for the rest of the summer. But then, one can hardly be expected to take the responsibility for the overindulgences of one's clients, even if the quantity pro-vided does take on rather epic proportions. (Having Jewish forbears can be contagious, obviously in matters of plenitude.)

My sister's triumph of will over the haut picnique occurs

once every Labor Day weekend when the Roses give their
annual *champs de fête*.

A handsome and vigorous couple who summer in a ginger-
bread, grey Victorian on Ocean Avenue, Dan and Joanna Rose
twice yearly turn their manicured lawns and slopes into a picnic
ground for the artists, writers, and mobile devotées of the good
life in East Hampton and its environs. The Labor Day event is
truly special.

Under some misguided star, six frozen deep-dish chicken
pies were once dispatched for a small Sunday supper, where they
mysteriously turned out to be blueberry pies when the first fork
shattered the pastry. Mrs. Rose acknowledges our talent *and*
our fallibility.

Mrs. Rose, some years ago dubbed the "Sergeant-Major" by
an itinerant Store wag, is a lady permanently pressed with a no-
nonsense demeanor. Her efficiency and total drive can only be
matched by Myra's resoluteness.

Mrs. Rose will want lobster-stuffed eggs for at least seventy-
five or a hundred guests. And she will want them to look
pretty—not your usual routine deviled egg bit.

Myra, who usually wins the opening sortie with Mrs. Rose,
will remind the formidable opponent that our eggs always look
pretty because we pack them in old-fashioned cardboard egg
cartons, with just a snippet of pink tissue paper underneath.
(And we never devil our eggs, Mrs. Rose.) And so it goes.

Mrs. Rose's party fare is always a trial by fire for us because
it must not only be large and various, but it must also bridge the
generation gap as well. Ham and pâté, quiche or cold herbed
omelettes we can take in our stride; peanut butter and jelly is
the rock on which we sometimes perish. If Mrs. Rose comes to
discuss her provender like an army tactician that is her preroga-
tive. In her long experience with us she has learned to forgive
trespasses.

The Roses' picnic is always a prompt affair. And Mrs.
Rose's picnic hampers must always be out of The Store's front
door exactly on time. It is probably the one order of the season
that manages that signal feat.

And that is solely due to my sister's diligence. Early, early
on the day of the great event, Myra, Kevis at her elbow, fords
the streams of multi-colored tissue, counts the containers of
salad, the boxes of cookies, the occasional mousse, Brie, fried

chicken, sandwiches, and other goodies that comprise that lady's order.

"If we have a hundred of everything, I think we're safe," Myra will murmur hopefully.

"What if we have a hundred and one of something, Myra?"

"We're still safe, kiddo!"

The night before Labor Day, when The Store is traditionally closed, the personnel cast a wary glance heavenward.

"Let us all pray for good weather for Mrs. Rose."

"Don't bother," my sister was heard to say. "The Sergeant-Major wouldn't permit it to rain."

One Labor Day it did. The skies poured silvery grey torrents all morning long as Myra counted and recounted the baskets. But the resourceful Mrs. Rose was undeterred. She simply moved her lawn party lock stock, and barrel to her living room floor. And the haut picnique was alive and well in Amagansett.

A respectable *haut picnique* can be composed of any food in the world, I suppose. Shahs probably dine alfresco on nothing but Iranian caviar and vintage champagne.

A bottle of Châteauneuf-du-Pape and a runny Brie will do in a pinch too.

What makes a picnic *haut* I will never know. But tuna fish on rye never makes it to the best-dressed list.

Some sample menus for your own picnic are listed below, exactly as we do them at The Store. The recipes for starred dishes can be found in this book (see index). Some other outdoor originals follow the menus. With your taste buds as your guide, mix and match them at will.

SIMPLE PICNIC BOX LUNCH

Pâté or Baked Ham Sandwich on French Bread
Cucumber Salad*
Wedge of Imported Cheese
Fruit of the Season

PICNIC BRUNCH

Cold Herbed Omelettes on Individual Loaves of French Bread*
Bacon-Filled Brioche*
Strawberries Dipped in Sugar

Sour Cream Coffee Cake*
Coffee

LUNCH ON THE BOAT

Picnique-Stuffed Eggs/Stuffed Mushrooms*
Gazpacho*
Fried Chicken*
Croustades*
Cold String Bean Salad Vinaigrette*
Store Cole Slaw*
Pecan Tarts
Coffee

HEARTY NIGHT PICNIC

Bouillabaisse*
French Bread
Cauliflower Salad*
Fruit of the Season
Assorted Cheeses
Store Raspberry Nut Torte*
Coffee

BEACH SUPPER

Billi Bi*
Cold Lobster with Lemon Mayonnaise*
"Tiens!"*
Cold Breast of Chicken with Saffron Sauce*
French Bread
Whole Brie
Fruit of the Season
Angel Food Cake with Whipped Cream*
Coffee

PICNIC BY THE POOL

Pissaladière Niçoise*
Cold Shrimp and Artichokes
    in Tomato Mayonnaise*
Cold Sliced Roast Beef*

Asparagus Vinaigrette*
Lemon Sponge Cake*
Strawberry/Red Currant Mousse*

PICNIC ALLA CEZANNO

Seviche*
Artichokes and Sour Cream*
Baked Ham with Figs*
Salad Niçoise*
Thin Sliced French Bread with Butter
Brie Cheese
Chocolate Angel Food Cake*
Coffee

"HAUT PICNIQUE"

Slices of Pâté*
Torta Di Spinaci Rusticana*
Cold Sliced Veal*
Herbed Rice Salad*
Bibb Lettuce Salad
Fruit in Champagne
Reine de Saba*
Coffee

BASH BUFFET

Lobster-Stuffed Eggs*
Cold Shrimp in Curried Mayonnaise*
Whole Virginia Ham*
Whole Roast Beef*
Potato and Cheese Mayonnaise alla Romana*
Herbed Tomatoes*
Cold White Bean Salad with Caviar*
Tossed Green Salad
Assorted Breads
Assorted Cheeses
Apple Pies*
Fruit Pies in Season*
Pecan Pies*
Coffee

COLD HERBED OMELETTES ON
INDIVIDUAL LOAVES OF FRENCH BREAD

The ingredients listed below are based on a single serving, so double, triple, and so on, accordingly.

2 — 3 eggs
pinch of salt
pinch of pepper
1 tablespoon cold water
1 tablespoon butter

FILLING
½ cup mixed herbs: chopped parsley, tarragon, chives, watercress, and dill in any combination you wish

small loaf French bread, cut in half and well buttered on both sides

I.   Using a wire whisk beat the eggs, seasonings, and cold water in a mixing bowl for a minute, or until the yolks and whites are blended.

II.   Place an omelette pan over high heat for several seconds. The pan is hot enough to receive the butter when a drop of water sprinkled in the center sizzles intensely.

III.   Place 1 tablespoon of butter in dead center of the preheated pan. As the butter melts, tilt the pan in all directions to film the sides.

IV.   When the butter foam subsides slightly, but before it changes color (melted butter should be deep golden), pour in the eggs.

V.   Hold pan handle with the left hand—thumb at top— and start sliding pan back and forth rapidly over heat. At the same time, using a wooden spatula or fork, quickly stir eggs and spread them over the bottom of the pan. Vigorously scramble the eggs until they thicken into a light but fluffy custard-like consistency.

VI.   The filling should go in at this point. Place it on one side of the omelette.

VII.   Tilt the pan handle to a 45 degree angle over the heat.

Rapidly gather egg at far lip of pan. Still holding the pan tilted, run a fork around and under the edge of the omelette to keep from sticking.

VIII.   Loosen the omelette and curl it over onto itself. Hold tilted pan over the heat for 1—2 seconds, to brown the bottom lightly, but not too long or the eggs will over-cook. The center should be soft and creamy.

IX.   Turn the omelette onto a small half-loaf of French bread (like a Hero) that has been well buttered on both sides. Garnish with a grind of fresh pepper. Serve hot or at room temperature. Do not refrigerate.

Though it may sound less than delicious, a cool omelette is a marvelous creamy concoction. It makes an interesting first course without the bread.

BACON-FILLED BRIOCHE

1 stick of softened butter
½ teaspoon of bouillon powder
2 teaspoons finely minced chives
2 teaspoons finely minced watercress leaves
2 teaspoons finely minced parsley
dash of Tabasco
dash of Worcestershire sauce
salt and pepper
6 large brioche (recipe follows)
¼ pound of crisply sautéed bacon, well drained on paper
    towels

I.   Whip the softened butter to a fine froth with a hand mixer. It should be the consistency of a shiny whipped cream. Add the bouillon powder, chopped chives, watercress, and parsley and mix well. Season with Tabasco and Worcestershire sauce, and salt and pepper.

II.   Pull the cap off a baked brioche. Make a well inside the bun with your finger. Place about ½ teaspoon of herbed butter and a generous crumbling of bacon inside. Replace the cap and let the brioche stand at room temperature so all the tastes mellow together.

III.   Pack each brioche in a separate cone of waxed paper

and then roll up in a colored napkin. This is a most savored picnic party favor.

BRIOCHE

Brioche-making is not easy. I would hazard a guess that it is one of the most complicated numbers in a French pastry chef's repertoire. But the finished result is well worth the time and effort. It is best to allow 8 or 9 hours from the beginning of brioche-making until the fluted cups are oven ready. Plan at least 4 hours for the first rising of the dough, about 2 hours for the second rise—1 hour to chill the dough again, and 2 hours for the final puff-up.

3 large eggs, at room temperature
1 package of dry active yeast
3 tablespoons warm tap water
1¼ cups all-purpose flour
3 teaspoons sugar
1¼ teaspoon salt
1½ sticks of unsalted butter, chilled
1 egg, lightly beaten

I.   Break the eggs into a small bowl. Whisk them slightly so they are blended well.

II.   In another small bowl, mix the yeast with warm tap water. Add a teaspoon of sugar and let the yeast dissolve.

III. In a large mixing bowl, measure out the flour. Make a hole in the center of the flour mound and pour in the beaten eggs. Sprinkle 2 teaspoons sugar on the eggs; add the salt. Using a bowl scraper, blend in the yeast liquid. Mix all the ingredients together until they form a mound of wet, rather sticky dough. Pat it with a rubber bowl scraper for a moment or two to make sure the ingredients coalesce and then set it aside.

IV.   The stick and a half of sweet butter should be chilled before you start to work. Soften it by pressing it (still in its wrapper) with the palm and heel of your hand. Work the butter (out of its wrapper) on a large board or piece of marble until it is malleable. Set aside.

V.   Knead the dough. The dough will be soft and sticky and may need the addition of a bit of flour if it does not become elastic enough. Using the scraper, flip the dough over from right to left and from left to right about 15 times until it begins to develop a firmer texture.

VI.   When the dough becomes firm, lift it up with your hand and throw it down again on the kneading surface. Do this 6-7 times. Sprinkle a bit more flour if it needs it. The dough, when well kneaded, will retain its original shape after it has been picked up and thrown down as directed. When it seems to retain its sense of mass, the dough is ready for the introduction of the butter.

VII.   The butter is kneaded into the brioche by small bits, the size of silver quarters. Start kneading and smearing these bits of butter across the surface of the dough with the palm of your hand. Then, using the scraper, flip the dough over on itself. Press out and start pressing and smearing more butter on the fresh surface. The dough will turn sticky and stringy as you start to work in the butter, but work quickly and make sure to press the buttered dough back into shape.

VIII.   The dough is through being kneaded when all the butter has been used up. This is a difficult trick and you may be forced to scrape the dough together with the flat blade of a knife if it gets too soft or oily. If this happens, refrigerate the dough for a moment or two and then begin the kneading action again.

IX.   For the first rise, place the dough (it will be somewhat less than 3 cups) in the center of a very large mixing bowl. Remember the dough will inflate to about three times its volume—so make sure you leave room for the blow-up. Cover the bowl with plastic wrap and a Turkish towel. Leave it in a warm place, free from drafts. The dough will rise in about 4 or 5 hours. Do not look at it until that time elapses.

X.   When it has risen, using a bowl scraper or your fingers, quickly dislodge the dough from its bowl and turn it onto a lightly floured board. With floured hands, pat it into a rough rectangle shape, about 10 inches or so in length.

XI.   With the flat end of a large knife or a bowl scraper, fold the dough over (like folding a letter). Fold right to center first. Then, fold the left side over it. You will end up with a long narrow case of dough that looks like an unbaked strudel. Pat the dough shape back into a rectangle shape and make all those folds once more to distribute the butter well throughout.

XII.   Put the envelope of dough back in the bowl, cover again, and let stand another 2 hours or so. When dough has doubled in size, remove it from the bowl and re-frigerate it on a large platter covered with waxed paper—and weighed down so there will be no refrigerator rising. Let it cool for about 45 minutes to 1 hour.

XIII.   Brioche are usually made in fluted cups or muffin tins. But any small form will work.

Remove the dough from the refrigerator and set it back in the bowl, uncovered, to rise for about 2 hours. The temperature should be about 75 degrees to assure a nice high rising. Make sure the dough is free of drafts (it might be wise to set the mixing bowl on top of a warming oven as it rises). Dough will double in volume on its third rise.

XIV.   Preheat oven to 475°. To form the brioche: Butter the molds with 1 teaspoon soft butter. Working quickly with lightly floured hands, break off a bit of dough, form it into a small ball, and press it into the bottom half of the mold. With your thumb, press a wide hole inside the ball (so it is doughnut shaped). Roll a bit of remaining dough into another small ball, and shape one end into a cone that can be inserted into the well of the doughnut. Brioches should be one-half their desired size because they double in volume as they bake. Just before baking, paint the surface of the brioche with beaten egg. But be sure not to glaze the area where the cone joins the doughnut for this could prevent the top from rising. To help the top rise during baking, make a few slashes with a sharp thin knife in the upper portion of the doughnut shape, just under the top. Give a second coat of egg to the rest of the brioche.

XV. Bake at 475° in the middle of an oven for about 15 to 20 minutes. Cool on a rack for about 15 minutes before serving. Makes 10-12 brioche.

PICNIQUE-STUFFED EGGS

8 hard-cooked eggs
½ cup mayonnaise
1 tablespoon Dijon mustard
¼ cup finely chopped ham, or ¼ cup cooked shredded lobster meat*
1 teaspoon capers, washed of their brine
1 teaspoon finely chopped parsley
grating of fresh lemon rind
1 small shallot, well minced
salt and fresh pepper to taste
watercress leaves or fresh dill

I. Cut eggs in half lengthwise. Remove yolks, crumble in a bowl, and mash them with the mayonnaise. Add mustard, chopped ham (or lobster), capers, parsley, lemon rind, shallot, and salt. Mix well together. The mixture should be spreadable but not runny. If the mixture is too dry, add a teaspoon of mayonnaise. If it is too wet, add another hard-cooked egg yolk or if you are doing the ham version, a tablespoon or two of finely grated Swiss cheese. (It is a delicious substitute.)

II. Fill each egg half with a nice mound of stuffing. Dust with a grating of fresh pepper and garnish with a leaf of watercress for ham, a sprig of fresh dill for lobster. Serves 8.

*If you are using lobster, add a teaspoon of Madeira to the mayonnaise and cut the mustard by one-half.

STUFFED MUSHROOMS

24 medium-sized mushrooms (allow 4 per person)
1 large package of softened cream cheese (at room temperature)
1 tablespoon sour cream
2 packets of G. Washington brown bouillon powder
3 cloves garlic, minced
¼ teaspoon cayenne pepper
dash of Tabasco
1 teaspoon Worcestershire sauce
freshly ground pepper to taste
fresh chives for garnish

I.   Remove the stems from the fresh mushrooms and with a sharp knife, gently peel the skin from the caps. (If you are not using the mushrooms immediately, sprinkle them with lemon juice to keep the flesh white.)

II.   Whip the softened cream cheese well. Add sour cream, bouillon powder, minced garlic, cayenne, Tabasco, Worcestershire, and fresh pepper. Stir well. The mixture should be creamy and easy to spread.

III. Fill the insides of the mushroom caps with the stuffing and immediately press, stuffed side down, into a plate of finely cut chives. (I cut chives with a scissors, because it bruises them least.)

IV.   Serve as an adjunct to cocktails—at a picnic, or anywhere people lift an elbow. Serves 6.

Left-over mushroom stuffing keeps indefinitely in a tightly covered jar in your refrigerator. One way to vary the stuffing is to add a tablespoon or so of soft-crumbled Roquefort cheese to the cream cheese as you whip it.

PATE OF CORNED BEEF IN CROUSTADE

¼ pound butter, creamed
2 cups cooked corned beef, ground twice
1 tablespoon onion, grated
1 teaspoon minced garlic
3 tablespoons heavy cream
2 teaspoons Dijon mustard

1 teaspoon English dry mustard
1 teaspoon lemon juice
2 tablespoons parsley, finely chopped
2 tablespoons chives, finely chopped
¼ teaspoon salt
¼ teaspoon freshly ground black pepper
2 teaspoons Worcestershire sauce
a fresh loaf of French bread (preferably a baguette), about 8½
    inches long and 3½ inches in diameter

I.   Cream the butter in a mixing bowl by beating it with a large spoon for a few minutes until it is smooth and and pale in color. Then, a few tablespoons at a time, beat in the corned beef and, one after the other, the onions, garlic, cream, mustards, lemon juice, parsley, chives, salt, pepper, and Worcestershire sauce. An electric mixer is a big help, but if you do not own one, continue to beat the pâté by hand until it is as smooth as you can possibly get it. Taste for seasoning, remembering that when the pâté is chilled, its flavor will be considerably muted.

II.   Slice 2 inches or so off the ends of a small French bread. With your fingers and the aid of a long thin spoon or knife, remove as much of the soft insides of the bread as possible without damaging or breaking through the crust. When the bread is a hollow tube, stand it on one end on a sheet of waxed paper and carefully fill it with soft pâté, packing it down as you proceed. If there isn't enough pâté to fill the bread, simply cut off the hollow portion. Wrap each end of the croustade in waxed paper and refrigerate for a few hours until the pâté is firm. Slice into ⅛ or ¼-inch rounds with a serrated knife and serve.

GAZPACHO

2 cloves shallots, roughly cut
2 medium-sized onions, roughly cut
2 cucumbers, pared and roughly cut
6 tomatoes, unpeeled
2 green peppers, seeded

8 raw eggs
½ teaspoon salt
½ teaspoon pepper
½ teaspoon cayenne pepper
dash of Tabasco
½ cup Dessaux vinegar
½ cup olive oil
1¼ cups tomato juice

GARNISH
1½ cups bread cubes
4 tablespoons olive oil
2 cloves garlic, finely minced
1 cucumber, finely diced
1 green pepper, chopped

I.   Roughly blend the ingredients (except for the garnish), a few at a time in a blender. Add the required liquids, and then the eggs, one at a time. Transfer ingredients to a pitcher, add the seasonings, mix well, and taste. Chill well before serving with the garnish.

II.   To make the garnish, brown the bread cubes in hot oil in a saucepan. Add the garlic and stir for one minute. Allow to cool, placing on paper towels to absorb the grease. Add the croutons, cucumber, and green pepper just before serving. Serves 10–12.

PATE OF POT ROAST IN CROUSTADE

2 cups cold pot roast, trimmed of all fat and gristle and coarsely chopped
8 anchovy fillets, drained, washed, and dried
¾ cup good strong beef stock
½ pound sweet butter, softened
1 tablespoon onion, finely grated
1 shallot, finely minced
1 clove garlic, peeled and pressed
dash of Tabasco sauce
1 teaspoon lemon juice
½ teaspoon salt
freshly ground black pepper
a fresh French bread, 8½ by 3½ inches

I.   In the jar of an electric blender, combine the pot roast, anchovies, and ¾ cup beef stock. Purée at high speed, stopping from time to time to scrape down the sides with a rubber spatula, adding more stock when necessary to produce a smooth, fairly fluid purée. Use a little more than the suggested amount of liquid if the blender should clog. (To make the pâté by hand, chop the meat and anchovies as finely as you can, then with a mortar and pestle pound them vigorously until they are reduced to a paste.) Rub the purée through a sieve with the back of a large spoon to achieve as smooth a paste as possible.

II.   Cream the butter in a mixing bowl by beating it with a spoon for a few minutes until it is smooth and light in color. A spoonful at a time, mix the butter into the meat purée, and continue to beat the mixture until the butter and meat are completely combined. Add the grated onion, shallot, garlic, Tabasco, lemon juice, salt, and pepper. Mix well and check seasonings.

III. Prepare the bread and fill as in the recipe for Pâté of Corned Beef. Chill for at least 4 hours before serving. Serves 6–8.

CROUSTADE OF TAMAR

1 large can of pitted black olives, thoroughly drained
1 large clove of garlic
2 shallots
¾ pound sweet butter, at room temperature
dash of Tabasco sauce
½ teaspoon lemon juice
½ teaspoon salt
grind of fresh pepper
fresh loaf French bread, 8½ by 3½-inches

I.   Crush the olives, garlic, and shallots in a blender until they are a fine mash. Scrape into a wire sieve and let all the liquid drain off.

II.   Put the softened butter into a large bowl and whip until it is light and creamy. Gradually add the olive mixture and beat together until it is a light grey caviar-like color. Season with Tabasco, lemon juice, salt, and pepper.

III. Prepare the bread and fill as in the recipe for Pâté of Corned Beef. Chill well before serving. Serves 6-8.

THE STORE COLE SLAW

1½ medium-sized heads cabbage
3 carrots
2 green peppers, seeded
1 large yellow onion
2 small shallots
½ pound bacon well cooked—reserve drippings
1¼ pints mayonnaise
1 packet G. Washington brown bouillon powder
½ pint sour cream
1 teaspoon chili powder
½ teaspoon salt
1 teaspoon Dijon mustard
1 tablespoon wine vinegar
¼ cup milk
chopped parsley

I. Grate all vegetables in a large bowl. Set aside.

II. Mix the bacon drippings with half the mayonnaise. Add the bouillon powder and sour cream; beat until it is the consistency of very thick cream. Slowly add chili powder, salt, mustard, wine vinegar and remaining mayonnaise, beating well after each addition.

III. Mix the cream mixture in with the vegetables; add the milk to thin. Toss very well till all the vegetables are well coated with dressing.

IV. Crumble the cooked bacon into small bits and sprinkle over cole slaw. Toss entire mixture again so bacon is well distributed. Garnish with chopped parsley.

BOUILLABAISSE

6 tablespoons olive oil
1½ cups chopped leeks
6 cloves garlic, finely minced

1 cup chopped onion
3 cups chopped tomatoes
2 sprigs fresh thyme or ½ teaspoon dried
4 sprigs fresh parsley
1 bay leaf
2 cups dry white wine
2 cups fish stock (fish heads, bones, and trimmings, boiled with
    a small amount of salt)
1 heaping teaspoon leaf saffron, crumbled
salt
freshly ground black pepper
1 teaspoon Tabasco
2 lobsters, 1½ pounds each
6 tablespoons butter
1½ teaspoons all-purpose flour
2½ pounds fresh red snapper, striped bass, porgy or cod cut
    into serving pieces
1½ quarts fresh mussels, scrubbed well
4 dozen cherrystone clams
36 raw shrimp, peeled, shelled, and deveined
3 tablespoons Pernod
garlic croutons (recipe follows)

I.   Heat the olive oil in a large saucepan and add the leeks, garlic, and onions. Cook until the vegetables are wilted. Add the tomatoes, thyme, parsley, bay leaf, wine, stock, saffron, salt, pepper to taste, and the Tabasco. Simmer ten minutes.

II. Plunge a knife into the place where tail and carcass meet on the lobster. This will kill the lobster immediately. Split the tail and carcass and cut the carcass in half lengthwise. Scoop out the liver and coral from the carcass and place in a small mixing bowl. Cut the tail section into four crosswise pieces and set aside.

III. Add the carcass and any scraps of lobster to the tomato mixture, cover and simmer for 30 minutes.

IV. Meanwhile, blend the butter and flour with the fingers and mix with the reserved coral and liver.

V.   Strain the tomato mixture through a sieve, pushing through as many solids as possible. Bring to a boil.

Add the red snapper, mussels, clams, shrimp, and reserved lobster tail. Simmer 15 minutes. Stir in the coral mixture, and when the mixture comes back to a boil, add the Pernod. Scoop into hot soup plates and serve with garlic croutons on top. Serves 8.

For a picnic supper outdoors, one would prepare the bouillabaisse in an agateware clam and lobster cooker. Do not, however, add the coral and Pernod until just before you are ready to serve. Prepare the rest in advance and keep warm until ready to serve.

GARLIC CROUTONS

Bake eight thin slices of bread in a 400° oven until crisp and brown. Rub with garlic and brush with melted butter. Cut into squares.

THE STORE RASPBERRY NUT TORTE

½ pound sweet butter, softened
1½ cups granulated sugar
1½ pounds ground walnuts and pecans
¾ cup raspberry preserves
1 tablespoon vanilla extract
6 eggs, separated (at room temperature)
¼ cup good dark rum
1 cup cake flour sifted with 1 teaspoon baking powder
confectioners' sugar

I.   Preheat oven to 350°. Mix the softened butter with the granulated sugar and beat until the mixture is light yellow in color. Add the ground walnuts and pecans, stir well, and add the raspberry preserves and vanilla.

II.   Add the yolks to the batter, one at a time; beat well after each addition. Stir in the rum, and quickly add the sifted flour and baking powder, mixing well.

III. Beat the egg whites until they are stiff, but not dry, and carefully fold them into the cake batter.

IV.   Put in a buttered cake tin that has also been floured, and shaken free of any excess flour. Depending upon the cake tin (you may use a loaf or a small round—or a deep spring-form pan), bake in the oven for 35 to 40 minutes. A deep pan may take a little longer. Test for doneness by inserting a straw or toothpick into the center; if it comes out clean, the cake is finished.

V.   Cool well on a cake rack and dust with powdered confectioners' sugar before serving. This makes a delicious dessert with coffee-flavored whipped cream as a garnish.

BILLI BI

2 pounds mussels
2 shallots, coarsely chopped
2 small onions, quartered
2 sprigs of parsley
salt and freshly ground black pepper
pinch of cayenne pepper
1 cup dry white wine
2 tablespoons butter
½ bay leaf
½ teaspoon thyme
2 cups heavy cream
1 egg yolk, lightly beaten

I.   Scrub the mussels well to remove all exterior sand and dirt. Place them in a large kettle with the shallots, onions, parsley, salt, black pepper, cayenne, wine, butter, bay leaf, and thyme. Cover and bring to a boil. Simmer 5 to 10 minutes, or until the mussels have opened. Discard any mussels that do not open.

II.   Strain the liquid through a double thickness of cheesecloth. Remove the mussels from the shells and reserve them for garnish.

III.   Bring the liquid in the saucepan to a boil. Add the cream. Return to a boil. Remove from the heat. Add the beaten egg yolk and return to the heat long enough for the soup to thicken slightly. Do not boil. Serve hot or cold, garnished with the mussels. (This dish may be enriched, if desired, by stirring 2 tablespoons of hollandaise sauce, page 5, into the soup before it is served. Either way, it is excellent.) Serves 4.

COLD LOBSTER WITH LEMON MAYONNAISE

Allow a 1½-pound lobster for each person. In a large kettle put enough water to cover the lobsters and add 1 tablespoon of salt for each quart of water. Bring to a rolling boil. Grab the live lobsters, one at a time, at the back of their heads just behind the pincers. Be careful not to let the claws or pincers reach you. Plunge them into the boiling water head first. Cover and simmer for 5 minutes for the first pound and 3 minutes for each additional pound. A 1½-pound lobster will cook in approximately 8 to 10 minutes.

Remove from the water and put on a board or work table on their backs. Using a heavy, sharp knife and a mallet, split each lobster in half the long way, from head to tail. Remove the stomach and intestinal tract, but do not discard the green liver or any reddish deposit. Crack the claws with a nutcracker so that the meat will come out easily. Let it cool and serve with the lemon mayonnaise.

LEMON MAYONNAISE

To a cup of mayonnaise (homemade is preferred), add the grated rind of a lemon and 3 tablespoons of lemon juice. Mix well. Then add 1 packet of G. Washington golden bouillon powder and a dash of Tabasco sauce. Stir and serve.

"TIENS!"

2 tablespoons sweet butter
3 tablespoons olive oil
2 pounds fresh spinach, roughly chopped
2 pounds Swiss chard, roughly chopped
3 medium-sized onions, chopped
3 cloves garlic, finely chopped
6 small zucchini, finely diced

1 small green pepper, finely diced
1 cup chopped, fresh basil leaves
½ cup finely chopped parsley
1½ teaspoons salt
¼ teaspoon freshly ground black pepper
8 eggs, beaten
¾ cup freshly grated Romano cheese
¾ cup finely grated Jarlsberg or Swiss cheese
½ cup soft bread crumbs

I.   Preheat oven to 375°. Place the butter and oil in a large, heavy kettle. Add the spinach and chard and cook covered until leaves wilt.

II.   Remove the greens to a fine strainer and press out all the liquid. Return greens to the kettle. Add the onion, garlic, zucchini, and green pepper. Cook covered until vegetables are barely tender, stirring occasionally.

III.   Transfer vegetables to strainer and press out every vestige of liquid. Combine the dry mixture with the basil, parsley, salt, and pepper, and divide between two well-buttered 9-by-10-inch, scalloped earthenware quiche pans or pie plates.

IV.   Pour half the eggs over each pie. Sprinkle half of the cheese and bread crumbs over each. Bake 25 to 30 minutes. Serve hot or chilled. Serves 12.

Save the pressed liquids to be used in soups, stews, gravies.

COLD BREAST OF CHICKEN WITH SAFFRON SAUCE

6 supremes (the skinned and boned breast-halves from 3 frying chickens)
1 teaspoon lemon juice
salt and white pepper
6 tablespoons butter
SAUCE
6 large ripe tomatoes
4 scallions
6 tablespoons oil

1 medium-sized onion finely chopped
3 large shallots finely chopped
2 cloves of garlic, crushed
½ cup dry white wine and ½ cup cold water
good grind of fresh black pepper
½ teaspoon saffron, crumbled
1 lemon sliced thin
½ can pitted black olives for garnish

I.   Preheat the oven to 400°. Rub the supremes with drops of lemon juice and sprinkle lightly with salt and pepper. Heat the butter in a heavy ovenware casserole with a cover, until it is foaming. Quickly roll the supremes in the butter.

II.   Cut a piece of waxed paper large enough to cover the casserole. Butter it and place it over the chicken. Put the cover back on the casserole and place it in a hot oven. After 6 minutes, press the top of the chicken with a finger. If it is still soft, return it to the oven for a few more minutes. When the meat is springy to the touch, it is done. Drain the supremes; allow them to cool to room temperature; cover with waxed paper, and chill while you prepare the sauce.

III.   To make the sauce, first dip the tomatoes in a pan of boiling water and remove their skins. Cut them in half and gently squeeze out their seeds. Place the seeded tomato halves in a chopping bowl and mince them fine.

IV.   Split the green part of the scallions from the white bulbs. Chop both sections to a very fine mince, separately and reserve the greens for garnish. In a sauté pan, heat 6 tablespoons of oil and add the chopped scallion ends and the finely chopped onion and shallots. Cook until they just begin to brown, stirring well with a wooden spoon. Add the minced tomatoes and garlic and cook for about 5 minutes. Add ½ cup white wine and ½ cup water. Season to taste with salt and pepper and add ½ teaspoon saffron.

V.   Simmer the sauce for about 10-15 minutes, stirring it

as it cooks. Remove from the heat and allow to cool before placing it in the refrigerator to chill really well.

VI.   Before you are ready to serve it, arrange chicken on chopped scallion greens in a cold serving dish and spoon the saffron sauce over it. Garnish with lemon slices and black olives. Dust well with chopped parsley. A crisp French bread, a curl of sweet butter and an iced blanc de blanc makes the picnicker wax eloquent. Serves 6.

PISSALADIERE NIÇOISE

2 pounds minced onions
5 tablespoons olive oil
1 bouquet garni: 4 parsley sprigs, ¼ teaspoon thyme, and
    ½ bay leaf tied in washed cheesecloth
2 cloves unpeeled garlic
½ teaspoon salt
1 pinch of powdered cloves
⅛ teaspoon pepper
8 canned anchovy fillets
16 pitted black olives
8-inch pastry shell, partially cooked and placed on baking sheet

I.   Preheat oven to 400°. Cook the onions very slowly in 4 tablespoons olive oil with the bouquet garni, garlic, and salt for about 1 hour, or until very tender. Discard bouquet garni and garlic. Stir in the cloves and the pepper. Taste carefully for seasoning.

II.   Spread the onions in the pastry shell. Arrange the anchovy fillets over it in a fan-shaped design. Place the olives at decorative intervals. Drizzle on 1 tablespoon of olive oil. Bake in upper third of the preheated oven for 10 to 15 minutes, or until bubbling hot. Delicious hot or cold. Serves 4 – 6.

COLD SHRIMP AND ARTICHOKES IN TOMATO MAYONNAISE

1 stalk of celery
1 sprig of parsley
½ lemon

1 small onion stuck with a clove
1 clove of garlic
1 bay leaf
3 whole black peppercorns
2-2½ pounds raw shrimp, peeled and deveined
2 packages frozen artichoke hearts
2 tablespoons lemon juice
3 shallots, finely minced
2 tablespoons capers (washed and drained)
¼ cup freshly chopped basil leaves
½ cup chopped fennel
2 tablespoons good cognac
1½ cups tomato mayonnaise
pinch of salt
dash of freshly ground pepper

I.   In a kettle or an enamel saucepan place a stalk of celery, a sprig of parsley, a half lemon, 1 small onion stuck with a clove, and a peeled clove of garlic. Add a bay leaf and 3 black peppercorns and water to cover. Bring to a boil and simmer uncovered.

II.   Place the peeled, deveined shrimp in this bouillon and cook them for 5 minutes exactly. Drain the shrimp, saving the liquid; allow them to cool.

III.   Strain the fish bouillon and return to the heat. When the liquid is boiling, add the 2 packages of frozen artichoke hearts and simmer for about five minutes. Drain in a colander and let cool.

IV.   Place the cool shrimp in a large mixing bowl and add lemon juice, chopped shallots, capers, basil, chopped fennel, and cognac. Toss well.

V.   Add 1½ cups of tomato mayonnaise, salt, and a good grind of pepper to taste, and toss until all the ingredients are well coated. Add the cooked artichokes and gently toss again. If the dish seems bland, add a spot of Tabasco. Serves 10-12.

This cold shrimp is wonderful stuffed inside an avocado or gracing a bark of endive as a first course.

ASPARAGUS VINAIGRETTE

1 pound fresh asparagus
a pan of salted boiling water
½ cup vinaigrette sauce
3 teaspoons capers
2 hard-cooked egg whites
½ pimiento, cut into strips

I.   Wash and peel the lower half of asparagus with a potato parer. My rule for peeling asparagus is to bend the stalk at the point where it breaks, then peel the stem upward for an inch or so. Do it carefully; asparagus is a fragile vegetable.

II.   Have a large skillet half-filled with boiling, salted water. Place the asparagus in the boiling water and cook for 6 minutes. Immediately place the pan under cold running water and keep the asparagus stalks there until they are cold to the touch. Then drain them well and chill till 30 minutes before you are ready to serve.

III.   Place the asparagus stalks on a serving dish and pour the vinaigrette sauce over them. Add the capers and let stand.

IV.   Chop the hard-cooked egg whites until they are fairly fine and sprinkle them over the asparagus just before you serve them. Decorate the stalks with pimiento strips arranged over the crisp, blanched vegetable like the inevitable red string that rings every bunch in the market place. Serves 4–6.

ESCABECHE OF FLOUNDER

2 pounds flounder fillets
½ cup lemon juice
¼ cup all-purpose flour
1 stick of sweet butter
2 tablespoons oil

SAUCE
½ cup oil
3 tablespoons wine vinegar

¼ cup chopped shallots
¼ cup chopped green pepper
2 teaspoons fresh tarragon (or 1 teaspoon dried)
2 teaspoons chopped chives
¼ cup chopped fresh parsley
½ cup pitted green olives, sliced
salt and fresh pepper
black olives and lemon wedges for garnish

I.   In a shallow dish, place 2 pounds of flounder fillets and cover with lemon juice. Let the fish marinate for at least 1 hour. Then dust the individual pieces with flour, transfer to a pan and sauté them in butter and oil until golden in color. When the fish is entirely sautéed, arrange neatly in a deep dish.

II.   To make the sauce, mix the oil, vinegar, remaining lemon juice, shallots, green pepper, tarragon, and chives together. Blend with a scraper and add the parsley and green olives. Season to taste and pour over the fish. Marinate in refrigerator for at least 24 hours. The longer the fish absorbs the sauce, the tastier the escabeche.

III. Serve garnished with black olives and lemon wedges. Pass the crusty French bread and butter. Serves 8.

ARTICHOKES AND SOUR CREAM

This is different picnic fare. But there *are* imperatives. For one thing the artichokes must be tender and tiny enough so they can be eaten in two bites without the drama of leaf-by-leaf peeling. That scene is meant for another occasion. I find that small artichokes are available at the vegetable counter year-round, if one asks for them, but there is a preponderance at my market in spring and fall. Use only artichokes that are young enough not to have the choke removed.

Clean the stems with a sharp knife and trim the outer leaves with a scissors. Set the small artichokes in an enamel pan half full of cold water to which you will add ½-cup wine vinegar, a bay leaf, a clove of garlic, half a cut lemon, and 2 tablespoons of salt. Bring to a boil and then let them simmer for about 15 minutes.

Then plunge them under cold running water till they are no longer hot to the touch. Drain them well and store covered with saran wrap in your refrigerator until they are well chilled. (Artichokes absorb the taste of other foods if they are not covered tightly.) Serve with a sour cream sauce made of:

1 pint of sour cream
½ cup very strong beef bouillon, cooled
   (I make this by boiling down 1 can of beef broth until it
      reduces to half the quantity)
3 tablespoons mayonnaise
2 shallots, minced in a garlic press
¼ cup fresh dill
salt and pepper to taste

Beat the sour cream and bouillon together. Add the mayonnaise, shallots, and dill. Stir well, season to taste, and let the mixture stand (covered) in the refrigerator for several hours so the flavors coalesce.

Sometimes I throw all the artichokes into the sauce and toss them in a large bowl and let the picnickers spear them out. Other times, I just serve a bowl of the sauce separately and let everybody dunk his own. Either way, it's an uncommon alfresco treat.

SALAD NIÇOISE

3 cups cold, blanched string beans
3 or 4 quartered tomatoes.
1 cup vinaigrette dressing
1 head Boston lettuce, separated, washed, drained, and dried
3 cups cold potato salad Provençale
1 cup canned tuna chunks, drained
½ cup pitted black olives
2 or 3 hard-boiled eggs, cold, peeled, and quartered
6 to 12 anchovy fillets, drained
2 to 3 tablespoons minced, fresh green herbs

I.   Just before serving, season the beans and tomatoes with several spoonfuls of vinaigrette. Toss the lettuce leaves in the salad bowl with ¼ cup of vinaigrette, and place the leaves around the edge of the bowl. Add the potato salad, making a mound in the center of the bowl.

II.   Decorate with the beans and tomatoes, interspersing them with a design of tuna chunks, olives, eggs, and anchovies. Pour the remaining dressing over the salad, sprinkle with herbs, and serve. Serves 6—8.

SCALLOPS AND SHRIMP IN A BLANKET OF MAYONNAISE

1 ½ pounds fresh bay or sea scallops, quartered
1 ½ pounds raw shrimp, peeled and deveined (about 36)
¾ cup vermouth
10 peppercorns
3 sprigs fresh parsley
2 sprigs fresh thyme or ½ teaspoon dried thyme
½ bay leaf
1 tablespoon shallots or onions, chopped
1 clove garlic, sliced
salt
1 cup homemade mayonnaise
2 tablespoons finely minced shallots
4 tablespoons finely minced parsley

I.   Combine the wine, peppercorns, parsley, thyme, bay leaf, chopped shallots or onion, garlic, and salt to taste in a saucepan. Simmer 5 minutes and add the scallops. Cover and simmer 3 more minutes. Set aside to cool.

II.   Pick out the scallops and let them chill in the refrigerator. Bring the liquid in which the scallops cooked to a boil. Add the shrimp. Simmer 3 minutes and let cool. Remove the shrimp and chill in the refrigerator.

III.   Blend the scallops and shrimp with the mayonnaise and minced shallots. Spoon the mixture into a serving dish, dredge with parsley, and serve cold as a first course or serve in scooped out halves of crusty French bread for an "Haut Picnique." Serves 6-8.

TORTA DI SPINACI RUSTICANA

PASTRY
3 cups flour
½ teaspoon salt

1 cup butter, cut into pieces
1 egg yolk
3 tablespoons cold water (approximately)

FILLING
3 tablespoons olive oil
2 large onions, finely chopped
1½-2 pounds fresh spinach leaves
3 smoked pork chops, 1 inch thick, trimmed and diced
1½ cups freshly grated Parmesan cheese
1 cup ricotta cheese
salt and freshly ground black pepper
4 eggs, lightly beaten
1 egg white

I.   To make the pastry, place the flour, salt, and butter in a bowl. With a pastry blender or fingertips, work the butter into the flour until the mixture resembles coarse oatmeal. Mix the egg yolk with 3 tablespoons water and sprinkle over the mixture. Stir with a fork, adding only enough extra water to make a dough that just holds together. Wrap in waxed paper and chill briefly.

II.   To prepare the filling, heat the oil and sauté the onion until tender but not browned. Place the washed spinach leaves, with stems removed, and just the water that clings, into a large saucepan. Cover tightly and cook until the leaves wilt. Drain well and chop. Combine the spinach with the onions and let cool.

III. Add the diced smoked pork, Parmesan cheese, ricotta cheese, salt and pepper to taste, and eggs to the cooked spinach mixture.

IV.   Preheat oven to 425°. Roll out half the pastry; use it to line a 10-inch pie plate. Brush the bottom and sides of the shell with the lightly beaten egg white. Pour in the filling. Roll out the remaining pastry and cover the filling. Seal and decorate the edges, make a steam hole and place leaves, cut from extra pastry, around the hole but not over it. Bake 40 minutes, or until the pastry is golden and done. Let stand 10 to 15 minutes before cutting. Serves 8.

The pie can be made early in the day and reheated in a 375° oven for about 40 minutes. Cover loosely with foil to prevent over-browning. After wrapping well, the pie can also be frozen; when ready to serve, allow to thaw at room temperature for 3 hours and reheat it in a 375° oven for 1 hour.

HERBED TOMATOES

6 large ripe tomatoes or 24 small ripe cherry tomatoes
salt
½ cup fine dry bread crumbs
3 tablespoons shallots, minced
¼ cup olive oil
1 clove garlic, crushed
4 tablespoons fresh basil and parsley, or oregano and parsley,
    minced
pinch of thyme
fresh pepper

I.   Preheat oven to 400°. Cut the large tomatoes in half crosswise. Gently squeeze out the juice and seeds. Sprinkle halves with salt and turn upside down. Or, cut the tops off the cherry tomatoes, gently squeeze out the juice and seeds, sprinkle with salt and turn upside down.

II.   Blend bread crumbs with 3 tablespoons minced shallots; add almost all the oil. Crush 1 clove of garlic into the mixture; add the herbs, and mix well. Correct seasoning with salt and pepper. Fill each tomato half or each cherry tomato with a spoonful or two of mixture. Sprinkle tops with a few drops of oil; arrange in a shallow baking dish.

III.   The dish may be prepared ahead to this point. Shortly before serving, place dish in upper third of a preheated oven for about 10 minutes. Place under broiler to brown crumbs for 1 to 2 minutes. Serve hot or cold. Serves 6.

COLD WHITE BEAN SALAD WITH CAVIAR

1 package white beans
1 clove garlic, peeled and slashed

2 shallots, minced
¼ red onion, finely minced
1 tablespoon fresh dill, chopped
1 tablespoon fresh parsley, chopped
French dressing
1 small jar black caviar
chopped chives
chopped parsley

I. Throw the beans into a large pot of boiling water and cook for 45 minutes. This should be done the night before. Allow to cool overnight. Drain the beans.

II. Rub a bowl with garlic; add beans, shallots, and red onion. Add dill and parsley. Toss thoroughly with French dressing till all beans are covered.

III. When mixed, spread caviar lightly over entire top of beans. Decorate with the chopped chives and parsley.

Let Them Eat Cake ... and Pie

Chapter Nine

DENIS VAUGHAN

"Fish and guests turn sour after two days," as my benevolent father used to say. It was a statement not original with him, I discovered later, but aptly apt. Cakes, however, if you treat them nicely and cherish them well, will not turn on you in the same manner.

There was once a woman in my life—Leda Dwelly Foley—who was in a sense a surrogate mother. Often she was better than the real thing, because she listened. In a way, we were both up against the same problem of fighting a losing battle against my mother. Leda was supposedly my mother's best friend.

She had no children, but she did have a very old dog. I think he was old from the day he was born. Bubbles was his name. Bubbles was a Boston bull with a dreadfully misshapen figure, glassy eyes, a catarrhal wheeze that passed for a bark, and a hopelessly splay-footed walk. But how Leda loved that dog. If the world had been hers to give, he could have had it. As it was, he did not do too badly. Only once did I ever see Leda display anything but affection towards him.

It was my eleventh or twelfth birthday, and Leda had baked a chocolate cake with white icing for me, because in all the world it was my favorite cake. Apparently it was Bubbles' too. She had placed the cake on her kitchen table to cool. Next to the table was a chair. Bubbles had never exhibited much athletic prowess during his lifetime, but the aroma of that cake must have been too much for him. He managed to get up on the chair and push the cake to the floor. The thud was what brought Leda and me to the kitchen. There was the culprit, stranded high and dry on the chair, afraid to make the leap and looking forlorn, guilty, and extremely abashed. For what must have been the first and last time in his life—and Leda's too—she spoke sharply to him He jumped from the chair, paws going in all directions. From that day to this, I have never heard a dog cry like a baby.

His crazy little body was wracked with sobs, and, instantly, so was Leda's, followed by mine. The cake was gone beyond repair, but the incident only strengthened in me what has become a lifelong love of animals.

LEDA FOLEY'S CHOCOLATE CAKE

4 ounces chocolate
1 cup milk
1 cup light brown sugar
3 egg yolks
1 cup white sugar
½ cup butter
2 cups cake flour
1 teaspoon baking soda
½ teaspoon salt
¼ cup water
1 teaspoon vanilla
2 egg whites

I.   Preheat oven to 375°. Lightly grease two 9-inch cake pans.

II.   In the top of a double boiler, combine the chocolate, ½ cup milk, 1 cup light brown sugar, and 1 egg yolk. Keep below the boiling point, and cook until thick and smooth. Set aside to cool.

III.   Sift the sugar if necessary, and beat the butter until smooth. Add the sugar and blend until light and creamy. Beat in 2 egg yolks, one at a time.

IV.   Before measuring sift the flour, and then resift with the baking soda and salt. Combine ¼ cup water, ½ cup milk, and the vanilla. Add the flour to the butter in 3 parts alternately with thirds of the liquids. Stir in the chocolate.

V.   Whip 2 egg whites until stiff but not dry. Fold them lightly and carefully into the cake batter.

VI.   Pour the batter into the cake pans, tap lightly on a hard surface. Bake for about 25 minutes. Top with a white icing (my favorite)—or with Bert's chocolate icing.

BOILED WHITE ICING

½ cup water
⅓ cup light corn syrup
2½ cups granulated sugar
⅛ teaspoon salt
2 egg whites, at room temperature
1 teaspoon orange juice
1½ teaspoons vanilla

I.   Boil the water, corn syrup, and sugar until the mixture thickens and forms a firm ball when dropped into cold water, or a thread about 3 inches long when dropped from a spoon.

II.   Add the salt to the egg whites and whip until stiff but not dry. Pour the hot syrup into the eggs in a very fine stream, constantly beating the whites. After the syrup is absorbed, continue beating until it is the right consistency for spreading. Add the orange juice to keep the icing from becoming gritty, and beat in the vanilla.

If the icing is too thin, beat until thick in the top of a double boiler. If too thick or if it thickens while icing, add a few drops of boiling water and more orange juice.

BERT GREENE'S CHOCOLATE ICING

3 squares bitter chocolate
1 can condensed milk
½ stick sweet butter cut in small pieces
1 beaten egg yolk

I.   Melt chocolate in a double boiler. Add condensed milk; stir constantly until the mixture is smooth.

II.   If too bitter, add more condensed milk. When smooth, add the butter and beat in until it has been absorbed.

Then quickly add a beaten egg yolk and continue stirring until the frosting becomes smooth and creamy. The mixture will thicken as it cools. If it becomes too thick, thin with coffee. Makes enough for a 2-layer cake.

I sit at this typewriter and wonder why the hell I am writing about desserts. I don't eat them, don't even like them; all I can do is prepare them. My idea of dessert is a pear, an orange, and maybe a piece of Brie, if I have not had it with my salad. But, there is something I can tolerate, and tolerate well, if done properly—without those damned gelatinous messes that supposedly hold things together—and that is cherry pie. Start it with the best crust imaginable. Here are recipes for both.

PÂTE BRISEE

8-9 INCH SHELL
1½ cups flour
¼ teaspoon salt
pinch of sugar
6 tablespoons chilled butter and 2¼ tablespoons vegetable short-
ening
3¾ to 4½ tablespoons cold water.

10-11 INCH SHELL
2 cups flour
½ teaspoon salt
2 pinches of sugar
¼ pound chilled butter and 3 tablespoons vegetable shortening
5 tablespoons cold water

I.   Place the flour, salt, sugar, butter, and vegetable shortening in a big mixing bowl. Rub the flour and fat together rapidly between your fingers until it is the texture of coarse oatmeal.

II.   Add the cold water; blend quickly with one hand. Press the dough firmly into a roughly shaped ball. Place on a lightly floured pastry board, and with the heel of one hand, rapidly press the pastry by small bits down on the board and away from you in firm quick smears.

III.   Gather the dough back into a mass and knead it briefly into a smooth round ball. Sprinkle lightly with flour and wrap it in waxed paper. Place in your freezer for about 1 hour or until firm.

IV.   To roll the dough, place it on the top of a lightly floured board and knead it briefly. Always roll away from you, starting at the center, lifting and turning it, and then rolling again until it is the size you require.

CHERRY PIE

pâte brisée
4 cups fresh, pitted sour cherries
1¼ cups sugar (varies depending on the fruit)
4 tablespoons flour
2 teaspoons quick-cooking tapioca
1 tablespoon lemon juice
1 drop almond flavoring
1 tablespoon kirsch liqueur
1 tablespoon butter

I.   Preheat oven to 450°. Line a 9-inch pie pan with pastry dough. Reserve half of the dough for the topping.

II.   Place the cherries in a large mixing bowl. In another bowl, combine the sugar, flour, tapioca, lemon juice, almond flavoring, and kirsch. Mix well and sprinkle over the cherries, stirring gently until well blended. Pour into the shell; dot with butter and let sit for 15 minutes.

III.   In the meantime, roll out the rest of the dough and cut into strips or leave whole. Cover with a whole top or cover with a lattice of pastry. If completely whole, poke holes in the top with a fork.

IV.   Bake in a 450° oven for 10 minutes; reduce heat to 350° and continue to bake for about 35 to 40 more minutes.

My partner Bert has a friend who has a mother who lives in Golden, Colorado. (Where is that you say? How the hell would I know? I have never been to Colorado.) Putting all that to one side, Mildred Schulz has left a legacy with her son—she has not left us—that can be yours as well. Do it right, or suffer the penalty.

MILDRED SCHULZ'S RHUBARB PIE

pâte brisée for 10-inch pie
2½ cups fresh rhubarb, cut up in small cubes
½ teaspoon cinnamon
3 tablespoons flour
¼ teaspoon grated lemon rind
pinch of grated orange rind
⅛ teaspoon salt
1¼ cups sugar
3 tablespoons melted butter
3 eggs, lightly beaten

I.   Preheat oven to 400°. Split the dough in half and roll out enough pastry for the bottom of the pie; place in the pie pan. If desired trim the edges in a decorative pattern. Partially bake (10-12 minutes at 450°).

II.   In a large mixing bowl combine the rhubarb, cinnamon, flour, lemon rind, orange rind, salt, sugar, and butter. Mix well and let sit for about 5 minutes. Put into the prebaked shell. Pour the beaten eggs over it.

III.   Roll out the remaining dough and cut into strips about ½ inch wide. Carefully arrange over the pie in crisscross patterns, pressing down the edges. Sprinkle lightly with sugar.

IV.   Bake for 15 minutes in a 400° oven; turn down to 350° and bake 45 minutes more.

The dulcet voice that breathes to me over the phone is so like my mother's that I think, "Oh, God, she's returned from the dead!" Actually, thank God, she hasn't. The voice belongs to Beatrice Grover, a lady so full of elan that it oozes from her fingertips. She is giving a party for Jean Stafford, famed author, also famed for cardiac arrests. And Beatrice wants to know what we can do for a cake of some sort? A Reine de Saba. It is rich, rich, rich, and does not guarantee uncardiac arrest.

REINE DE SABA

4 ounces semi-sweet chocolate
2 tablespoons rum or coffee
¼ pound softened sweet butter (1 stick)
⅔ cup granulated sugar plus 1 tablespoon granulated sugar
3 egg yolks
3 egg whites
pinch of salt
⅓ cup pulverized almonds
¼ teaspoon almond extract
¾ cup sifted cake flour

I. Preheat oven to 350°. Butter and flour an 8-by-1½-inch round cake pan.

II. In the top of a double boiler, melt the chocolate with the rum or coffee. Cool.

III. Cream the butter and sugar together until pale yellow and fluffy. Add the yolks, one at a time, beating well after each addition.

IV. Beat the egg whites and salt until soft peaks form. Sprinkle on 1 tablespoon sugar and beat until stiff.

V. With a rubber spatula, blend the chocolate into the butter. Stir in the almonds and extract. Immediately stir in half the beaten egg whites to lighten the batter. Delicately fold in the remaining whites in thirds alternating with thirds of the flour. Do this very gently.

VI. Pour the batter in the pan, pushing it to the rims with the spatula.

VII. Bake in the middle of the oven for about 25 minutes. Cake is done when it has puffed and when a toothpick plunged 2½ – 3 inches around the circumference comes out clean. The center should be slightly oily. Cake must be thoroughly cooled before icing with the chocolate icing that follows.

CHOCOLATE ICING FOR REINE DE SABA

1 ounce semi-sweet chocolate (1 square or bits)
1 tablespoon rum or coffee
3 tablespoons sweet butter

I.   In a double boiler, stir the chocolate and rum or coffee over not-quite-simmering water until the chocolate has melted into a very smooth cream. Remove the saucepan from the water and beat the butter in, a tablespoon at a time.

II.   Over a bowl of cold water, beat until the mixture is cool and of spreading consistency. Spread at once over cake with a knife or spatula.

I have living with me a Scottish terrier whose manner is slightly dour, whose eyes are liquid brown, and whose glance can be at once soulful or quizzical, depending on the tilt of his head. We have spent fourteen years in each other's company, Comfort and I, and have come somewhat to know each other's tastes. I respect him and he respects me—to a degree. We never trod on each others toes—or paws, as the case may be. Comfort has developed a taste for a cake that we make in The Store, and when he gets a whiff of it, he instantly sits up with right paw pressed against his heart. (I never taught him this whimsical method of wringing one's heart; he picked it up from a mentor, whom I will tell you about.) Given the opportunity, he could devour the entire cake. You might, too.

SOUR CREAM COFFEECAKE

1 cup butter (½ pound)
2 cups plus 4 teaspoons sugar
2 eggs
1 cup sour cream
½ teaspoon vanilla extract
2 cups flour
1 teaspoon baking powder

¼ teaspoon salt
1 cup chopped pecans
1 teaspoon cinnamon

I.   Preheat oven to 350°. Grease and flour a 10−11-inch round cake pan.

II.   Cream the butter and 2 cups sugar together until very light and fluffy. Beat in the eggs, one at a time, very well. Fold in the sour cream and vanilla.

III.   Sift the flour with the baking powder and salt. Fold into the batter.

IV.   Combine the remaining sugar, pecans, and cinnamon.

V.   Place about one-third of the batter in a well-greased and floured pan. Sprinkle with three-quarters of the pecan mixture. Spoon in remaining batter. Sprinkle with remaining pecans and bake about 1 hour or until done. Cool on a rack before removing from pan.

The mentor I spoke of above was anything but an angel. He was a crazy, blond cocker spaniel of decidedly bastard origin. I met him one very grey, overcast day in midwinter on the streets of New York, where he was nestling in the leather jacket of the son of the local grocer. The boy, near tears, had been ordered to dispose of this six-week-old dog because he cried. All the mother in me rushed out; I took him instantly, named him "Folly," and was promptly bitten on the ear. Folly, from that day to his end, which came some fourteen years later, was a true connoisseur of food. No dog food for him—*ever*. No meal was complete for him without a sweetie at the end. He deeply enjoyed angel food cake. I think he gave Comfort, who came into his life when he was about five, a few pointers in style and eating habits as well. (Comfort, however, steadfastly refuses to wear the scarlet "Mad Ludwig of Bavaria" dog coat that Folly affected in his lifetime.) Here is one to an angel in my life—and there have been damned few:

ANGEL FOOD CAKE

1 cup sifted cake flour
1½ cups granulated sugar
1¼ cups egg whites (10-12) at room temperature
1¼ teaspoons cream of tartar
¼ teaspoon salt
1 teaspoon vanilla extract
¼ teaspoon almond extract

I.   Preheat oven to 325°. Sift the flour and ½ cup sugar together four times.

II.   Beat the egg whites until foamy; add the cream of tartar and salt, and beat until moist peaks form when beater is withdrawn.

III.   Add the remaining sugar, about 2 tablespoons at a time, beating in after each addition. Add the vanilla and almond extracts. Sift about ¼ cup of the flour-sugar mixture at a time over the meringue. Cut and fold it in until no flour shows.

IV.   Turn into an ungreased tube pan and bake about one hour. Invert pan and let cake cool in the pan. Either dust with powdered sugar and grated orange rind or ice with white icing.

We will wander down the canine route for only two more recipes, both regarded highly by the subjects in question.

When Comfort came of an age to sire, I thought it would be splendid if I found him a mate. Ho, ho! Well, she's a charmer, full of breeding, background, and full of family tree. A history of awards, prizes, and blue blood flowed through her veins; but she resolutely refused to be deflowered. Ultimately, she was. Artificially.

Her progeny were four. It happened one night when I was watching Joan Crawford and John Garfield in *Humoresque* on the late show. Joy, for that is her name, had been acting the coquette for several days, disregarding the maternity ward I had set up for her in the kitchen, looking at me as if I were out of my mind for escorting her on leash for her physical needs, and generally acting as if business were going on as usual.

Suddenly, as Joan Crawford was about to walk into the sea, Joy emitted a scream that would raise the dead, flashed me an angry look, and fled to the door. I followed with a leash. Believe me, Niagara could not have done as well. We returned to the maternity ward and she delivered herself of the four. Brace yourself for this: the one I kept, until his father became an alpha figure, I named Tidings. Tidings of Comfort and Joy—doesn't it make you sick?

Tidings, who is now in the loving and capable hands of Myra Greene, loves:

BLUEBERRY MUFFIN CAKE

2 cups blueberries
2⅓ cups flour
1 teaspoon cinnamon
1¼ cups sugar
½ cup butter
2 teaspoons baking powder
½ teaspoon salt
1 teaspoon vanilla
1 egg
½ cup milk
rind of one lemon, finely grated
dry bread crumbs (for dusting pan)
½ cup finely chopped walnuts

I.   Preheat oven to 375°. Pick over and wash the berries. Drain in a sieve and turn them onto a towel in a single layer. Pat dry with a second towel and set aside to dry thoroughly.

II.   In a small bowl, combine ⅓ cup flour, cinnamon, and ½ cup sugar. Cut in ¼ of the butter until the mixture resembles coarse crumbs. Set aside.

III.   Sift together the remaining flour, baking powder, and salt. Place blueberries in a bowl and sprinkle with 1½ tablespoons of the dry ingredients. Toss gently. Set aside.

IV.   Cream the remaining butter with the remaining sugar. Beat in the vanilla and the egg very well, until the mixture is light and fluffy.

V.   Stir in remaining dry ingredients alternately with the milk, starting and ending with the dry ingredients. Stir in the rind.

VI.   Spoon the stiff batter over the blueberries and with a rubber spatula fold until just mixed. Turn into a buttered pan that has been dusted with dry bread crumbs. Spread evenly.

VII.   Sprinkle with the nuts and then the cinnamon topping. Bake 50 minutes or until done. Allow to cool on a rack in the pan for 30 minutes. Loosen around the sides with a knife; place a large sheet of foil over the cake and invert it onto a rack. Place plate over bottom and invert again so that the crumb side is up.

And his mother, Joy, stylish lady that she is, can be tempted with either version of this soft, old-fashioned sponge cake.

SPONGE CAKE I

4 eggs
1 cup sugar
grated rind of ½ lemon
¾ cup cake flour

I.   Preheat oven to 325°. Separate the eggs. Beat the yolks until lemony and gradually add the sugar. Add the lemon rind and continue beating until the mixture is foamy and very pale. Stir in the flour.

II.   Whip the egg whites until stiff, and fold into the batter.

III.   Butter a 9-inch tube pan and sprinkle with sugar. Place in the oven a moment before filling with batter. Remove and pour in the batter. It should fill only half the pan. Bake 1 hour in the oven. It will double in size. It is done when golden brown and firm to the touch. Remove and let cool before removing from the pan. Dust with powdered sugar or a dribbling of white icing.

SPONGE CAKE II

5 egg yolks
1¼ cups sugar
grated rind of ½ lemon
1 teaspoon vanilla
1 cup cake flour, sifted twice
5 egg whites, beaten stiff

I.   Preheat oven to 325°. Rinse a mixing bowl with very hot water and wrap a hot towel around the base of the bowl. Beat the egg yolks in the warm bowl, gradually adding the sugar. Add the lemon rind and vanilla; continue beating until the mixture has doubled in volume.

II.   Fold in the cake flour, lifting the batter with a mixing spoon to introduce as much air as possible. Fold in the beaten egg whites, gently but thoroughly.

III.   Butter the cake pan and sprinkle with sugar. Pour the batter into the pan (should be ½ full), and bake for 1 hour in the oven. The cake is done when golden and firm to the touch.

In the early days of The Store we had a partner, Jaquelinne Allison, who smoked a great deal and was given to endless anecdotes about her past at *Vogue* magazine. She also laughed a great deal, talked about her skirmishes with the rich and famous, and made a fantastic apple pie. If you want to, you can do as well by following her recipe.

APPLE PIE

6 medium-sized green apples (or more)
1 to 1½ tablespoons flour
¾ cup of sugar (more or less, depending on tartness)
pinch of salt
1 tablespoon cinnamon
⅛ teaspoon nutmeg

1 tablespoon lemon juice
grated peel of ½ lemon
½ teaspoon vanilla
1½ tablespoons butter
1 egg, beaten
pâte brisée for 9-inch pie

I.   Preheat oven to 450°. Peel the apples; core, and cut into wedges. Place in a large mixing bowl and combine with the flour (use more if the apples are very juicy), sugar, salt, cinnamon, nutmeg, lemon juice, lemon peel, and vanilla. Mix well.

II.   Roll out the dough so that the bottom crust hangs well over the sides of the pie pan. Place the apples in the pie shell. The idea is to pile the apples in layers, as high as they will go, so use more apples if necessary. Dot with butter.

III.   Roll out more dough and place over the top of the pie. Press or flute the edges together tightly. Brush with beaten egg, prick several times with a fork, and bake at 450° for 15 minutes. Turn the heat down to 350° and continue baking for about 50 minutes more, less if you prefer a crunchy taste to your apples.

I once had a great and good friend to whom at parting I said, "If one could keep one's mouth shut, look aside, pretend there is no one else, be gentle, warm, kind, understanding, and above all, disappear when one is obviously not wanted, all would be paradise." It is a song cue. This recipe can only be prepared if it is snowing, and then, only if you have your wits about you and get the snow before it is polluted.

PARADISE PUDDING

1 can, 8½-ounce size, dark Bing cherries, drained
1 can, 8½-ounce size, crushed pineapple, drained
1 tablespoon Grand Marnier liqueur
1½ cups heavy cream
½ cup confectioners' sugar

1 tablespoon vanilla
3 cups fresh snow
1 tablespoon cognac (optional)

Quickly blend the cherries and pineapple with the Grand Marnier. Refrigerate. Whip the cream adding the sugar and the vanilla. Remove the snow from your local drift and the fruit mixture from the refrigerator. Carefully blend the snow into the whipped cream. Fold in the fruits. Now, if you are feeling sort of kicky, you can add a tablespoon of cognac. It enhances. Put the pudding in a bowl in your freezer for about 15 minutes.

Try it, it's good, even if it does not always guarantee you paradise.

I have come to realize there is a way of getting around everything and everyone in this world—be sweet. This method, I have found, if done properly and with enough naivete, can apply to anything from traffic tickets to income tax returns to tarte l'orange. And here is that sweet—it can do no wrong to anyone, except to add a pound or two.

TARTE L'ORANGE

PASTRY
1¼ cups flour
⅛ teaspoon salt
2 tablespoons sugar
½ cup sweet butter
1 egg yolk
2½ tablespoons water (approximately)

CARAMEL
⅓ cup sugar
2 tablespoons water

CREAM FILLING
3 egg yolks
¼ cup sugar
¼ teaspoon vanilla
1½ tablespoons cornstarch
¾ cup milk, scalded

½ cup heavy cream, whipped

TOPPING
4 large navel oranges
½ cup apricot preserves
1½ tablespoons sugar
1½ tablespoons Grand Marnier liqueur

I.   Preheat oven to 400°. To prepare the pastry, place the flour, salt, sugar, and butter in a bowl. Work the butter into the flour with your fingertips until the mixture is yellow and lumpy. Combine the egg yolk and water; stir into the flour mixture to make a dough. (Add more water if necessary.) Either chill or use immediately.

II.   Place the dough on a lightly floured board and roll out ¼ inch thick. Ease into a flan ring. Trim and decorate the edges. Line the shell with waxed paper and fill with raw rice or dried beans to keep the dough in shape. Bake 20 minutes; remove rice and paper, and bake 10 minutes more or until browned. Cool on a rack.

III. To prepare the caramel, place the sugar and water in a small saucepan. Heat, stirring until the sugar dissolves, and then continue heating without stirring until the mixture turns to a light caramel color. Pour into the shell, coating the entire bottom.

IV.   To prepare the cream filling, combine the yolks, sugar, and vanilla. Beat with a whisk. Mix in the cornstarch and whisk in the milk. Bring the mixture to a boil, stirring constantly. Transfer to a clean bowl; cover tightly with plastic wrap, and chill. When cold, fold in the whipped cream. Set aside.

V.   Section the oranges and set aside. Combine the preserves, sugar, and Grand Marnier in a small saucepan; bring to a boil, and simmer five minutes. Strain through a fine sieve.

VI.   To assemble the tart, place the cream filling in the bottom. Arrange the orange segments in an attractive pattern on the top and brush or spoon over the warm apricot glaze. The tart should not be assembled more than 1½ hours before serving for best results.

I seem to know a lot of tense, jittery ladies, but since I am pretty tense and jittery myself, I cannot afford to cast any stones. Here, however, is a recipe from one of the tense, jittery ladies. She is mostly pretty distrait, but always charming. She is Hattie Strongin, wife of the former music critic of *The New York Times*. They both now live bucolically in Amagansett. One day, when she was in an expansive mood, she offered me this recipe:

CHOCOLATE ANGEL FOOD CAKE

1¼ cups egg whites (10-12) at room temperature
1 teaspoon cream of tartar
1¼ cups granulated sugar
¼ teaspoon salt
¾ cup cake flour
¼ cup of cocoa
1 teaspoon vanilla

I.   Preheat oven to 325°. Beat the egg whites for a few minutes until foamy, then add the cream of tartar. Beat until the egg whites stand in peaks.

II. Sift sugar and salt together and add to the egg whites slowly, about 2 tablespoons at a time. Sift the flour and cocoa together and add to the above mixture, sifting in slowly. Add the vanilla. Turn into a 10-inch tube pan.

III. Bake at 325° for about 1 hour. Turn upside down on a wire rack and let stand until cold.

If you drift through life with no apparent aim or purpose for too long, the ailment becomes chronic and it begins to look as if nothing will ever happen through those lovely, endless days of staring at trees, contemplating a bittersweet blight that might be the hopeless tangle of one's own life, never saying or doing the right thing, but always knowing what the right thing is; communicating with dogs, cats, and birds because they sense the real you. Why, you are as normal as blueberry pie. The going may get rough, the money short, the days endless, the nights lonely, and the weather sometimes foul, but here is a recipe to cheer you:

DEEP-DISH BLUEBERRY PIE

4 cups fresh blueberries
4 tablespoons flour
¾ cup sugar or more, depending on the berries and your taste
pinch of salt
1 tablespoon lemon juice
½ teaspoon cinnamon
peel of ½ lemon
1 tablespoon butter
pâte brisée

I.   Preheat oven to 450°. Wash and pick over the blueberries. Drain in a sieve and turn them onto a towel in a single layer. Pat dry with a second towel. Place in the bottom of a deep 7-inch soufflé dish or ovenproof bowl.

II.   Add the flour, sugar, salt, lemon juice, cinnamon, lemon peel, and stir gently until well mixed. Dot the top with butter.

III.   Roll out enough pastry to cover, and place on top of the pie. (The bowl should be just deep enough for the pastry to rest gently on the top of the berries.) Pat the edges to seal. Lightly prick the top with a fork so that the steam can escape.

IV.   Bake in a 450° oven for 15 minutes; turn the heat down to 350° and continue baking for 45 minutes more.

Did you ever get the feeling that if you simply let go you could slip over into booby-land? I often get the feeling, but the plot always takes another turn, and I know I will not make it. It is frustrating, especially if you would like to be a booby. Really true boobies have, I think, a good time in life

if they do not think about it. If they do think about it, they
get very sad, and that is very bad because they cannot cope
with sadness. I once knew a cat, beautiful, sleek, and aloof,
who managed during his lifetime of nineteen years to look
as if he were wearing a black mink coat. Haughty and removed were his glances, but he was a booby when it came
to the aroma of the following cake. His name was Pyewacket—
and he was a love.

THE STORE NUT TORTE

½ pound sweet butter
1½ cups sugar
12 ounces almonds and hazelnuts, finely ground
½ teaspoon vanilla
6 eggs, separated
⅔ cup cake flour
1½ teaspoons baking powder
¼ cup dark rum
1½ cups rough ground bread crumbs
¼ cup coffee

I.   Preheat oven to 350°. Cream the butter and sugar
      together until light yellow and creamy. Add the ground
      nuts and the vanilla. Mix well.

II.   Beat the egg yolks into the butter-sugar mixture one
      by one, beating well after each addition.

III. Whip the egg whites until stiff but not dry.

IV.   Add the cake flour sifted with baking powder, rum,
      and bread crumbs to the butter-nut mixture. Stir in
      the coffee and quickly fold in the egg whites.

V.   Place in buttered cake tins (round) and bake for 35
      minutes or until a straw comes out clean when in-
      serted in the center of the cake.

I am going to bring down the curtain on my participation
in this work in concert with a recipe that I think I must be
insane to include, since it is sure to rot your teeth or give you
the pip, but many, many people love it. Not I.

PECAN PIE

3 eggs
2 tablespoons melted butter
2 tablespoons flour
½ teaspoon vanilla extract
⅛ teaspoon salt
½ cup sugar
1½ cups dark corn syrup
1½ cups broken pecan halves
½ cup halved pecans
pâte brisée

I.   Preheat oven to 425°. In a mixing bowl, beat the eggs until light. Blend in the melted butter, flour, vanilla extract, salt, sugar, and syrup.

II.   Sprinkle the broken pecans over the bottom of the pastry shell. Gently pour the mixture over. Make a ring of pecan halves and another ring inside it until surface is covered.

III.   Bake at 425° for 10 minutes, reduce heat to 325° and continue baking for about 40 minutes. Garnish with sweetened whipped cream.

The Mousse Trap

Chapter Ten

BERT GREENE

People in The Store. People with a capital P. We take it for granted after awhile that famous names will hit the ochre-colored door like a swarm of flies in July. Does one famous name tell another? They act the same as you and me, of course, all of them. They wait their turns at the counter (because there is always that wait), casing the cookie jars for crumbled freebies, sniffing the redolent kitchen airs just like any ordinary person in a state of summer spree. But that is an effect The Store seems to have on all, the impressive and the unimpressed alike.

The names do have their little idiosyncrasies, though. Barbra Streisand, for example, likes to be recognized. She became frosty, downright glacial, actually, when the girl behind the counter refused to peer beyond the shades and straw and separate the star from her mufti.

"Is this to be a charge? And under what name, please?"

There was no immediate answer, just a penetrating, super-cool stare. A check to make certain that this was not a ploy.

"I beg your pardon, but what is the name, ma'am?"

Funny Girl! Dolly! Pussycat! You take your pick. The irate Miss S. whisked away her packages without a departing word, leaving only her card behind for later identification (and coincidental billing).

The nicer names come back again and again. You even begin to enjoy the fact that they like to call you by your first name—while you are expected to remain a respectful distance from theirs.

Some do become friends and supporters, of course. When Jimmy Coco was slated to be the subject of a cover story in *Life* magazine, he insisted on being photographed in The Store ("Because you know it can't *hurt* business!").

He was duly photographed at our dining table, with me proffering a gorgeously baked ham in one hand and a molded fish mousse in the other. Jimmy mugged; I tried my best to look thin. But *Life* folded before the three hams or the mousse made it to the nation's newstands. Fame is not always the spur, you see.

Gwen Verdon is a Store chicken pie addict. One simply cannot calculate how many of them she has ordered in our short lifetime. Once in dead of winter The Store opened specially to make a batch that was delivered frozen to her in New York. Just to keep that habit flourishing.

Mr. and Mrs. Dick Cavett, from New York or their Montauk aerie, dream of nothing but Store Ham, it seems. We have sometimes rendezvoused with Mrs. Cavett at some snowy halfway point on the road from Amagansett to Montauk, so she could take early possession of that most precious gift of all—her Christmas ham.

On a scorching summer afternoon, her husband, eschewing any disguise, has marched himself into The Store and past a coven of Asparagus-Beach refugees (who suddenly become possessed with autographmania) merely to take a pound of ham and a couple of apricot mousse back to Cavett's Cove, as the inlet where they hole up is affectionately dubbed.

Other name droppings: Princess Lee Radziwill is said to nurture a passion for my lemon mousse. Gael Greene reported this in her book *Bite! A New York Restaurant Strategy*. It was a rumor started by Truman Capote, who passed it to his Bridgehampton neighbor, Eleanor Freide, who passed it to M. F. K. Fisher. That distinguished and lovely lady passed it to me, and I pridefully told Gael.

The Princess has come into The Store many times—and a fine tawny tourist attraction she makes—ordering curry and chutney in a multitude of delectable variations. She has also on occasion requested deep-dish blueberry pie, sour cream coffe cake and lots of brown sugar cookies. She orders in the confidential way of one who has long acknowledged the fact that kitchen collaboration is a necessity of the good life. But a lemon mousse, I have *yet* to see her take away.

Seven centuries or so ago, a noble Persian wrote:

> "If of thy mortal goods thou
>   art bereft,
> And from thy slender store
>   two loaves alone to thee are left,

Sell one, and with the dole
Buy hyacinths to seed thy soul."

The Store's partisans, I fear, would reject the floral fiat and merely make more investments in mousse. It may have been Tammy Grimes who first called the place a "mousse trap," but whoever, that name has stuck. We make mousse in the summer until it hurts just to break another egg.

Our repertoire of these cool concoctions seems endless. We have made chocolate, coffee, mocha and macaroon, lemon and apricot, peach and fresh fig, all whipped into drifts of air as the spirit has moved us. And in season, our strawberry, raspberry, blackberry and plum are pretty classy eating as well.

Our count of the prominent mousse eaters is too large for reportage here, but we even made a cup of the confection for Richard M. Nixon when he was hitting the campaign trail from the Montauk hills. He never came back for more. And we have never been invited to the White House to do our "moussifying."

Tennessee Williams came to The Store with Edward Albee, who is definitely a mousse repeater. Williams shuddered when he was shown the shivering mounds of delight nesting in the dessert case.

"They look dreadfully fattening," he said.

And they are, having added poundage to Bella Abzug, Betty Comden, Adolph Green and his wife, Phyllis Newman. John Wingate, the newscaster, publicly announced he was swearing off them for six months, and poet Sandra Hochman once dashed off a sonnet to one right on the premises.

Actress Dina Merrill came to price a peach mousse for fifty people, and with horror, eschewed the pleasure of presenting it to her company when she was informed that quantity would cost fifty dollars. The price has gone up slightly since.

Paula Prentiss, Richard Benjamin, Tom Paxton, Joan Fontaine, Eleanor and her former husband Frank Perry, Paul Anka, Dustin Hoffman, Rex Reed, and painter-genius de Kooning all are, or were, mousse-eaters. Some have even taken lessons on how to make the stuff themselves.

Chocolate mousse, I have always felt, is precisely the kind of fattening indulgence that a portly Faust might have sold his soul for. I learned a kindergarten version of it (when

I was in my mid-twenties) that has always stuck in my head because it is so absolutely simple to make. It never fails, and it is probably the one recipe I can tell someone off the top of my head without forgetting some key component, because it unequivocally exacts the same number of ingredients as there are guests for dinner. If there are six persons, you use 6 eggs, 6 teaspoons of sugar, 6 squares of chocolate—and you usually receive six compliments later.

BERT GREENE'S UNCOMPLICATED CHOCOLATE MOUSSE

6 teaspoons of superfine sugar
6 teaspoons of coffee or water
6 sections (4-bite-sized pieces make a section) of semi-sweet
    chocolate
6 large eggs, separated
1 teaspoon vanilla

I.   Combine sugar and coffee or water in the top pan of a double boiler. When the sugar dissolves add the chocolate pieces and cook, stirring often over boiling water until the chocolate is melted and smooth. Remove from the heat but leave the top pan in the double boiler.

II.   Beat the egg yolks separately until they are light and lemony in color. Then add the beaten egg yolks to the chocolate mixture and stir well. Remove the top pan from the double boiler and cool. When it is cool enough so that you can stick your finger in it, stir in the vanilla.

III.   Beat the egg whites till they are stiff but not dry. Then fold the egg whites gently into the chocolate mixture, making sure you do not break down the texture of the whites by over-stirring. Pour the mousse into individual cups or a serving bowl. (I always use a white fluted soufflé dish.)

IV.   Cover the bowl well with plastic wrap and keep refrigerated for at least 12 hours; 24 hours is the optimum time to chill this treat, but eager appetites usually prevail over sounder minds. Serves 6.

Chocolate mousse takes to whipped cream like a duck to water. And I prefer it straight (no sugar), as the perfect adjunct to the classic emotional experience.

At The Store, chocolate mousse as a confection, goodness knows, is a much more demanding emotional experience.

Pure coronary collusion. Unless your cholesterol count is sound, pass it by, please. And cooking neophytes: plan your whole day in the kitchen.

After so much caution, permit an addendum: the results are absolutely incredible. Men usually propose after a spoonful, and surrender their precious chauvinism entirely after a more substantial portion.

A warning: in this case, whipped cream is a necessity rather than a garnish, because it palliates the excessive richness.

THE STORE'S RICH, RICH CHOCOLATE MOUSSE

6 ounces or squares of semi-sweet baking chocolate
4 tablespoons strong coffee
1½ sticks softened sweet butter
4 egg yolks
¾ cup superfine sugar
¼ cup Grand Marnier liqueur
4 egg whites
pinch of salt
1 tablespoon granulated sugar
1 cup lightly whipped cream for garnish (If you wish, sweeten with powdered sugar, but remember this is very, very rich mousse.)

I.   Melt the chocolate with coffee over hot water in a double boiler. Remove from the heat and beat in the butter a bit at a time to make a smooth cream. Set aside to cool slightly.

II.   Beat the egg yolks and superfine sugar together until the mixture is thick, pale yellow and forms a ribbon as it falls back on itself. Beat in the liqueur. Then set the bowl in which you mixed it over not-quite-simmering water and continue beating for 3 to 4 minutes until the mixture is foamy and too hot to touch. Then beat over a pan of cold water for 3 to 4 minutes until the mixture is cool and again forms the ribbons.

III.   Beat the chocolate into the egg yolks and sugar.

IV.   Beat the egg whites and salt until soft peaks are formed; sprinkle on the granulated sugar and beat until stiff peaks are formed. Stir ¼ of the egg whites into the chocolate mixture. Fold in the rest.

V.   Turn into individual serving dishes or a bowl. Chill for at least 12 hours or overnight. Serve accompanied by the whipped cream. Serves 6 − 8.

Fruit mousse, the classic combination of flavoring-cum-custard, further enriched with whipped cream and beaten egg whites, is a thing of certain fragility. But it is practically failure proof once you get the hang of folding in the egg whites in soft, fluffy drifts. The air in the whipped egg whites is the architecture for all other ingredients.

The New York Times once printed my recipe for lemon mousse, and I received over twenty frantic calls at my office at *Esquire,* from tentative recipe-users who wanted to double-check whether or not one folded both the cream and the egg froth at the same time rather than stirring one and folding the other later. They had all travelled the mined waters of mousse making at one time or another, and knew just what disaster might imperil their final results.

In this case, the lemon mousse was definitely seaworthy. But then I have been adrift myself too often not to want to throw out a lifeline to others. The art of mousse making does require a few practical tips and perhaps a word or two about beating and beaters as well.

The whipped cream and egg whites, I always do by hand with a wire whip, but that is my own eccentricity and I do not demand it of you.

If one whisks, as I do, a balloon whisk made of open piano wire is absolutely the best tool to use. If you go whisk shopping, buy two, one larger than the other, and preferably with a wooden handle that you can grasp in your palm. Those little ditsy, wire whisks are decorative enough, hanging on your pot rack, and with a little luck can beat the lumps from a negligible béchamel sauce, but they are absolutely out of the question for any serious kitchen wizardry.

The secret of whipping cream is to do it quickly. The way I have found to do precisely that (whipping the cream to the point where it is neither too sloshy nor too dense nor buttery) is to chill both the bowl and whisk in a cold refrigerator or freezer for about 15 minutes before you begin.

Cream that is whipped with a rotary hand beater is never as light as whisked cream, and I avoid the infernal object like the plague.

Braun manufactures an excellent mixer with a wire whisk attachment that does produce a satisfactory and not too solid cream, but it must be watched lest the cream over-churn. It is a good idea to start the machine on low speed and then gradually increase the speed as the cream thickens. No matter how you whip it, the cream is à point (or is ready) when a soft swirl sets firmly on the tip of your finger. When using a mixer, I always put the bowl and whisk attachment in the freezer first as a precaution.

I have some marginalia here on the art of whipping (anything):

If you are beating cream by hand, always use a larger bowl than you think you need (one that you can comfortably press against your stomach muscles as you whip).

After you have combined the chilled cream, flavoring, and confectioners' sugar, hold the bowl toward you with a firm hand and rhythmically brush the whisk through the mixture with your other hand. A good whisk plus a little manpower should whip a pint of chilled cream in less than five minutes flat. I am generally a non-aggressive type, but I find that whipping cream by hand in this way rids me of a good bit of latent hostility.

The correct sound of a wire whisk beating cream should remind you of Gene Krupa brushing his cymbals through some vintage Benny Goodman. But here is a word of warning to music lovers: don't become overly infatuated with the sound. Well-whipped cream is just barely firm. It stands up on the end of the whisk, but it is never solid or yellowy. Think of soft clouds, and you have it.

When you whip egg whites, think of soft snow peaks.

And when you are whipping egg whites, for goodness' sake, forget everything you just learned about whipping cream. For perfect results in the egg white department, both the eggs and the bowl must be at room temperature. If you have neglected to leave your eggs out of the refrigerator, however, do not dismay; an egg bath in warm (not hot) water and a quick dry afterward insures a heaven-high froth. For whipping egg whites, any large earthenware or glass vessel will do; aluminum will not. It turns the mixture grey. On the other hand, a copper bowl is an absolute largesse. For some miraculous reason that I have never properly understood, the chemical reaction of copper to albumen produces double the quantity of egg whites when whipped. It is a fact of life that I accept without question. Just as adding a pinch of salt or a dab of cream of tartar hastens the whipping process early on, or sprinkling a bit of granulated sugar on the soft peaks of beaten whites to produce a firmer, more resilient meringue later.

Egg whites must never be over-whipped, because they dry out and the froth turns into the kind of scuddy foam one finds on an Amagansett beach after a seventh wave has come and gone. Nice enough for a surfer perhaps, but disaster in a mousse.

When there is the problem of whipping both cream and egg whites, I always whip the cream first and chill it while I do the eggs, secure in the knowledge that while even a perfectly beaten egg white will not last indefinitely, chilled cream can sit for hours, properly covered. The following random fruit mousse recipes are all composed of fairly equal amounts of both these ineluctable ingredients, and their success depends solely on their swift alliance. At its best, a lemon mousse is a blizzard of citrusy cream. At its worst, it can be leaky, which always means that the egg whites were zealously over-whipped, or slightly bitter to the tongue, a pitfall that can be attributed to grating some of the acrid, white inner skin of the lemon along with its aromatic yellow peel.

THE STORE LEMON MOUSSE

3 lemons
4 eggs, separated
1½ cups sugar

1 package unflavored gelatin
1 teaspoon cornstarch
¼ cup Grand Marnier liqueur
1½ cups heavy cream
3 tablespoons confectioners' sugar
toasted slivered almonds

I.   Grate the rind from the lemons and set aside. Squeeze the juice and set aside.

II.   Beat the egg yolks with the sugar until the mixture is light colored and forms a ribbon when spooned back on itself.

III. Soften the gelatin in ¼ cup cold water. Place over hot water and stir until gelatin is dissolved.

IV.   In a large bowl combine the cornstarch with ⅓ of the lemon juice and stir until smooth. Add remaining juice, lemon rind, and gelatin to the mixture. Stir well. Add to the beaten egg mixture. Turn mixture into a double boiler and cook over hot water until it thickens, stirring constantly. Add ½ the Grand Marnier and cook 1 minute longer. Do not allow to boil. Chill until it sets.

V.   Whip the cream with the remaining Grand Marnier and confectioners' sugar until stiff. Beat the egg whites until stiff but not dry.

VI.   Fold the cream and egg whites into the lemon mixture and spoon into a soufflé dish, bowl, or individual cups. Garnish with almonds. Serves 8 – 10. This recipe can be easily doubled if desired.

Lemon and apricot mousse do not appear to have much in common at first glance, but both are dependent upon the subtlety of rue. In the recipe for apricot mousse it is the decided persuasion of orange (the rind and juice partnered in the purée) and the infinitesimal shading of Grand Marnier to the whipped cream that gives this dessert its essential distinction.

This version of créme pastissiere has an added thickening agent: cornstarch. It is the basis of almost every fruit mousse recipe in this book and can also be used as a filling for a classic French fruit tart with the simple addition of a cup of whipped cream (added after the pastry cream has sufficiently chilled).

Crème patissière is fragile stuff. It stores in a well-covered glass jar in your refrigerator for about a week or 10 days only. With the whipped cream enrichment it can raise any simple stewed fruit to the heights of a great dessert compote.

CREME PATISSIERE

1 cup heavy cream combined with 1 cup milk (both brought
  to the boiling point)
1 cup granulated sugar
5 egg yolks
½ cup cornstarch
1-inch piece vanilla bean
1 tablespoon sweet butter (optional)

I. Combine 1 cup of heavy cream with 1 cup milk and bring almost to a boil.

II. Slowly beat the granulated sugar into the egg yolks, whisking well for 2 or 3 minutes after all the sugar is added. The mixture should be a pale lemony color and quite smooth in texture. The test is to lift up a spoonful. It should form a ribbony spiral as it falls back on itself into the mixture. (Never beat eggs beyond this spiral stage because overbeaten egg yolks can become granular and lose their velvetiness.)

III. Pour the hot cream and milk mixture over the corn-starch and whisk it well, until it is frothy and free of lumps. Combine the beaten egg yolks with the hot mixture in the top of a double boiler. Add the vanilla bean and stir gently (over moderate heat) until the mixture thickens and coats a wooden spoon. (This will take about 20 minutes.)

IV. When cool, discard the vanilla bean. The mixture will be quite thick. To prevent an unpleasant skin from forming on the surface of the custard, cut 1 tablespoon of sweet butter into bits and float on top of the crème. But be sure you beat the melted butter into the cooled custard before you chill it. Crème patissière may be made in advance—and stored in a cold place until you are ready to use it. Makes 2½–3 cups.

If you wish to reduce the amount of crème patissière by half follow the same instructions, but use:

½ cup heavy cream
½ cup milk
½ cup granulated sugar
3 egg yolks
¼ cup cornstarch
1-inch piece vanilla bean
1 tablespoon sweet butter

APRICOT MOUSSE

½ package dried apricots (Those organic kind from a health
*   food store are absolutely the best—but are twice as*
*   expensive as Del Monte. So —you decide.)*
1 long curl of orange peel
juice of an orange (about ½ cup)
1 cup granulated sugar
slice of lemon
water to cover the fruit (if needed)
2 tablespoons cognac
3 tablespoons Grand Marnier liqueur
1 cup of crème patissière (see preceding recipe)
1 cup heavy whipping cream
3 tablespoons confectioners' sugar
4 egg whites whipped with a pinch of salt and 1 tablespoon
*   granulated sugar*
4 candied apricots and ¼ cup toasted pignolia nuts, for garnish

I.   Place the dried apricots in a saucepan, add the orange peel, orange juice, granulated sugar, and a slice of lemon. Barely cover the fruit with water, and bring to a boil. Simmer about 30 minutes until the syrup is quite thick and glazed. Place the apricot mixture in the jar of your blender. Add 2 tablespoons of cognac and blend at high speed until the mixture is completely homogenized. It should be a thick purée. Then add

2 tablespoons of the Grand Marnier and allow to cool. (May be made in advance to this point.)

II.   In a large bowl, combine the apricot purée with 1 cup of crème patissière. The mixture will be a nice light pumpkin color. Set aside.

III. Whip 1 cup of heavy cream in a chilled bowl, with 3 tablespoons of confectioners' sugar and the remaining 2 tablespoons of Grand Marnier. It should be very thick and airy. Chill until the egg whites are whipped.

IV.   Beat the egg whites with a pinch of salt until soft peaks form. Then sprinkle with granulated sugar and continue to whip until the mixture is stiff but not dry. Egg whites are whipped if the mixture clings to the spoon—in defiance of gravity.

V.   Blend the flavored whipped cream into the apricot-custard base with a large spoon and gently mix it together. Add the beaten egg whites and quickly fold into the mixture. The result should be pale gold clouds—like an Amagansett sunset in August.

VI.   Place the mousse in a large bowl or individual cups and refrigerate until well chilled, about 4—5 hours. Before serving, cut candied apricots into half moon strips and encircle the mousse with them. A sprinkling of toasted pignolia nuts adds a nice toothsome note— to an incredibly smooth confection.

Fresh berries in season do for the dedicated dessert maker what a comparable range of dazzling pigment does for a painter's palette, exploding their gorgeous fragrance and viable flavor until the entire canvas or kitchen is stained an optimistic rosy hue.

I must admit to a compulsion where fresh berries are concerned. I go blindfolded past a farmer's market in July lest I madly scoop up quarts and quarts of strawberries and raspberries just to satisfy my eye.

STRAWBERRY MOUSSE

1 pint of hulled fresh strawberries
¾ cup granulated sugar
¼ cup orange juice
⅓ cup Framboise liqueur plus 1 tablespoon of the same
1½ tablespoons gelatin
1 cup confectioners' sugar
¾ cup crème patissière
1⅓ cup grated macaroon crumbs (use stale macaroons and blend
   until a fine powder)
1 cup heavy cream for whipping
4 egg whites
*crystalized mint leaves**

I.   Wash the strawberries and divide into 2 portions, reserving 8 of the plumpest berries for garnish.

II.   Cut up one portion of the berries and combine with a cup of granulated sugar, half the orange juice, and the liqueur. Place in a saucepan and stew over medium heat until the berries become sticky and the base thickens. Cool and reserve.

III. In a small bowl, combine the gelatin with the remaining orange juice and place it over a pan of not-quite-simmering water and stir the mixture well until the gelatin completely dissolves. When the liquid is quite syrupy and no longer grainy, pour it into the jar of a blender and add the remaining portion of strawberries and 1 cup of confectioners' sugar. Blend at high speed for about 2 – 3 minutes, until the mixture is a bright pink purée.

IV.   Combine the strawberry purée with ¾ cup of the crème patissière in a large mixing bowl. Add the cooked strawberry base and quickly fold in the powdered macaroons. Mixture will be quite dense at this point.

V.   In a chilled bowl whip the cup of heavy cream with an extra tablespoon of Framboise until the cream thickens and holds a soft peak at the tip of the beater.

VI. Whip the egg whites, using the pinch of salt on the unbeaten mixture and sprinkling a tablespoon of granulated sugar as soft peaks form. Beat as before, until stiff but not dry.

VII. Add the whipped cream to the strawberry mixture, folding it in with a large rubber bowl scraper or a shallow wooden spoon. Fold in the egg whites quickly and lightly as soon as it is mixed.

VIII. Place the strawberry mousse in a bowl or soufflé dish and chill it well, about 5 or 6 hours, so the gelatin will set. I have, in times of stress, placed this mousse in my freezer for about 4 hours and served it semi-soft (like a French bombe). Before serving, ring the bowl's edge with cut strawberry halves and crystalized mint leaves.

*Crystalized mint leaves are available by mail from Aphrodesia Products Inc., 28 Carmine Street, New York, N.Y. 10014.

Note: half a teaspoon of red food coloring (a trick borrowed from a great French chef) brings the color back to a fading fruit mousse base after it has been enveloped in a crème patissière. For goodness' sake, do not be indiscriminate in the use of food coloring; a little is more than enough.

RED RASPBERRY MOUSSE

1 cup granulated sugar
¼ cup orange juice
1 tablespoon grated lemon rind
¼ cup water
1½ pints fresh red raspberries or 2 10-ounce packages frozen raspberries, thawed
1 tablespoon gelatin mixed with ¼ cup of water
1½ cups crème patissière
1 cup heavy cream
1 tablespoon of kirsch liqueur
4 egg whites (plus a pinch of salt and 1 tablespoon granulated sugar)
12 ripe raspberries for garnish
*a few candied violets**

I.   Boil the sugar, orange juice, lemon rind, and water for a few minutes to make a thin syrup. Add 1 pint of raspberries and boil for 3 minutes only. Remove from the heat. (If using frozen berries, strain the juice into a saucepan, reduce the sugar to ¼ cup, add the orange juice and lemon rind, and omit the water. Place over high heat and rapidly boil down to slightly less than half a cup. Add the berries, remove from heat and proceed as indicated.)

II.   Soften the gelatin in water in a small bowl over not-quite-simmering water. When it is melted and quite syrupy, add it to the raspberry mixture.

III.   Pour the cooked raspberries and all the liquid into a blender jar and run at high speed until a smooth purée is formed. Cool thoroughly.

IV.   Add the raspberry-gelatin purée to 1½ cups of crème patissière; mix well.

V.   Whip the cream in a chilled bowl with a tablespoon of kirsch until the cream becomes thick and holds a whipped swirl at the end of the whisk.

VI.   Working quickly, beat the egg whites, adding salt and then the sugar to stiffen the soft peaks. Whip until they are stiff and hold their own shape.

VII.   Add the whipped cream to the raspberry custard, then the egg whites, folding both in gently with a bowl scraper or a shallow wooden spoon. At this point, fold in the remaining raspberries, making sure that the rosy fruit is well scattered through the mousse. (This is impossible when using frozen berries.)

VIII.   Gently pour into a serving bowl and chill for 4−5 hours in a cold refrigerator.

IX.   Before serving, garnish the bowl's edge with a ring of plump red raspberries—and place a few candied violets* in the center. Serves 8−10.

*Candied violets and rose petals are available by mail from Aphrodisia Products Inc., 28 Carmine St., New York,

N.Y. 10014, or Trinacria Importing Co., 415 3rd Ave., New York, N.Y. 10016, or at most fine gourmet departments across the country.

When I first came to Amagansett in the late fifties, wild blackberries grew in bogs just beyond the high beach grass. Now their territory is usurped by an architectural playland of cantilevered glass and an army of A-frames. Blackberries still arrive in August; but now they are in plastic see-through containers.

FRESH BLACKBERRY MOUSSE

1½ tablespoons gelatin
¼ cup cold water
½ cup fresh orange juice
1 tablespoon cornstarch
grated peel of 1 orange
1½ pints of washed blackberries
4 egg yolks
1 cup of sugar
¼ cup Grand Marnier liqueur
½ teaspoon powdered cinnamon
1½ cups of heavy cream
4 egg whites
½ cup confectioners' sugar
fresh mint leaves
ripe blackberries for garnish

I.   In an enamel saucepan, soften 1½ tablespoons of gelatin in ¼ cup of cold water. When the gelatin loses its graininess and becomes syrupy, after about 5-6 minutes, add the orange juice, 1 tablespoon cornstarch, orange peel, and ¾ of the blackberries. Heat gently, stirring constantly, until the cornstarch dissolves and the mixture thickens slightly, about 10 minutes. Remove from the heat—and cool to room temperature.

II.   In a bowl, beat the egg yolks and sugar until they are a light lemony color. Add the Grand Marnier and cinnamon and place in the top of a double boiler. Whisk over simmering water, until the mixture becomes too hot to stick your finger into it. (It should have the quality of a dense zabaglione.) Combine the blackberry mixture with the custard and cool to room temperature.

III. Whip the cream in a chilled bowl until it is quite airy and has doubled in quantity. Beat the egg whites until they are stiff but not dry (having first added a pinch of salt and sprinkled the soft drifts with a tablespoon of sugar).

IV. Fold the cream into the blackberry syrup. It may lose a little of its rich color.

V. Now, blend the remaining blackberries and ½ cup of confectioners' sugar over high speed until it purées. Streak the purée through the mousse cream in a marble pattern, and gently fold in the beaten egg whites.

VI. Pour into a bowl and refrigerate, covered, for at least 6 hours. Garnish with fresh mint leaves and a few ripe blackberries. Serves 8 – 10.

PLUM MOUSSE

6 ripe purple plums
1½ cups granulated sugar (or more, depending on tartness of the fruit)
half the rind of an orange, finely grated
half the rind of a small lemon, finely grated
¾ cup orange juice
2 tablespoons cornstarch
1½ tablespoons water
2 tablespoons Grand Marnier liqueur
1½ tablespoons unflavored gelatin
1½ cups crème patissière
1 cup whipping cream
1 teaspoon vanilla
4 teaspoons confectioners' sugar
4 egg whites (plus a pinch of salt, and 1 tablespoon granulated sugar)
4 candied oranges for garnish

I.   Remove the pits from the plums, but do not peel. Cut the fruit into small chunks. In an enamel saucepan, combine with the plums, 1½ cups granulated sugar, the grated orange rind, lemon rind, ½ cup of orange juice, 2 tablespoons cornstarch, 1½ tablespoons water, and 2 tablespoons Grand Marnier. Wrap the plum pits in a packet of doubled cheese-cloth tied up with string, and tuck into the saucepan as well. (The pits contain natural pectin.)

II.   Cook the plum mixture over fairly high heat so the fruit steams up quickly, then lower the heat and stew it gently, stirring from time to time, mashing the plums as they cook—until the mixture takes on a thick, purplish jam-like consistency. Discard the bag of pits; cook the mixture.

III.   In a small bowl, combine the gelatin with ¼ cup orange juice. Place the bowl in a pan of not-quite-simmering water and stir until the gelatin dissolves and the liquid is not grainy. Add to the cooled plum mixture and chill for another 15 minutes or until the mixture becomes quite thick.

IV.   In a large mixing bowl, combine the cooked fruit with the crème patissière. Keep in a cold place.

V.   Whip the cup of cold cream in a bowl with 1 teaspoon vanilla and 4 teaspoons of confectioners' sugar. It should be quite thick and form a peak on your tasting finger.

VI.   After anointing the egg whites with a dash of salt, whip them until they become cloud soft. Sprinkle on the bit of granulated sugar and finish them off to a nice silken stiffness.

VII.   Combine the plum mixture with the whipped cream, gently working the cream into the soft custardy mass. With a large rubber bowl scraper, fold in the whipped egg whites.

VIII.   Place in a bowl or serving cups and refrigerate, covered, for about 5 or 6 hours. Garnish with candied orange slices cut into thin strips. Serves 8 – 10.

LEMON POSSET

Technically not a mousse at all, this updating of a moyen-age conceit was thrust (like a problem child) upon The Store by an East Hampton beldame, who had sampled a version at Robert Carrier's restaurant in Islington and wished to have the dessert duplicated for a dinner party.

Not to be put off, she made the request so frequently that we felt impelled at last to attempt the reproduction. Mr. Carrier's illustrious cookbook includes the recipe for such a posset— but it is one that proved quite unremedial in our kitchen. The posset sank like a yellow submarine.

The following recipe goes back to an earlier-on source, Mrs. Beeton; she adds gelatin for staying power, and makes a winey respite from all that plush mousse you have probably been imbibing.

2 bright skinned lemons
1 cup of granulated sugar
4 tablespoons Grand Marnier liqueur
1½ tablespoons gelatin
1½ cups good white wine
2 cups heavy cream
4 egg whites

I. Grate the rind of two bright-skinned lemons. Squeeze the juice and add it to the grated rind. Beat in a cup of granulated sugar slowly and add 2 tablespoons of Grand Marnier liqueur. Set the mixture in a saucepan over low heat and let simmer until the sugar melts and the liquid becomes quite syrupy.

II. In a small bowl, mix 1½ tablespoons of unflavored gelatin with ¼ cup cold water. Set the bowl in a small pan of boiling water and stir constantly until the mixture dissolves and the liquid is no longer grainy.

III. Add the melted gelatin to the lemon mixture (still on the stove) and beat in 1½ cups white wine. Stir well and raise the heat so that the mixture comes to a boil. Immediately reduce the heat and simmer for about 2 minutes longer.

IV. Remove from the heat. The mixture should be a smooth,

translucent sauce. Let cool and then place in a cold refrigerator for about 30 minutes or until the base begins to jell.

V.   In a chilled bowl, whip the 2 cups of heavy cream with 2 tablespoons of Grand Marnier liqueur. It should be quite airy and thick enough to form a peak on the tip of your whisk. Immediately fold the whipped cream into the lemon-wine base and whip the egg whites. Be sure to add a pinch of salt to them and a sprinkling of granulated sugar once the soft peaks form. The egg whites should be beaten until stiff but not dry.

VI.   Fold the beaten egg whites carefully into the lemon cream, making sure you introduce a lot of air into the posset by scooping it up lightly. Pour it into a dessert bowl. Grate a fresh lemon over the surface. Chill well, about 4−5 hours. Serves 6−8.

Edna St. Vincent Millay once called a collection of her verse, "a few figs from thistles." My collection of mousse would hardly be complete without a dessert concocted of that redoubtable fruit. This fig (use them fresh if you are lucky enough to find them; dried or preserved in syrup, if you are not) ripens into a lyric poem when combined with a snippet of vanilla bean, some cream, and a zest for velvet on the tongue.

FRESH FIG MOUSSE

1½ cups sugar
1 cup of water
1 tablespoon strong vanilla
1 long curl of orange peel
1-inch piece of vanilla bean
6 ripe figs or 2 jars, 4-ounce size, preserved figs or 1 package, 8-
    ounce size, figs
1 tablespoon gelatin
¼ cup orange juice
1½ cups crème patissière
1 cup heavy cream

1 teaspoon vanilla extract
3 egg whites
bright-skinned orange for grating

I.   In a saucepan, place 1½ cups sugar and 1 cup water. Bring to a boil. When mixture is boiling, reduce heat and add 1 tablespoon vanilla, a curl of orange peel, and 1-inch piece of vanilla bean. Cook for about 10 minutes until the mixture becomes syrupy and thick. Add the whole figs and poach them for about 25 minutes or until they are fork tender. Cool.

(If using preserved figs, remove the figs, and place the syrup, orange peel, vanilla bean, and the vanilla in a saucepan with 3—4 tablespoons of water. Bring to a boil for 1—2 minutes. Return the figs to the hot syrup; coat them well with glaze, and cool.)

(If using packaged dried figs, reduce the sugar to 1 cup and the water to ¾ cup. When the mixture in step I becomes syrupy, add the figs and remove from the heat. All other instructions are the same.)

II.   In a small bowl, combine the gelatin with the orange juice and place it over a pan of not-quite-simmering water and stir the mixture well until the gelatin completely dissolves. When the liquid is quite syrupy and no longer grainy, add to the cooled fig mixture.

III.   Remove one fig for a final garnish later and then place the other fruit, orange peel, and syrup into the jar of a blender. Slit the vanilla bean down the center with a sharp knife and scrape the seeds, at random, into the mixture. Blend at high speed for about a minute or until the mixture becomes a thick honey-colored purée.

IV.   In a large mixing bowl, combine the cooled fig purée with 1½ cups crème patissière.

V.   In a chilled bowl, beat 1 cup heavy cream with 1 teaspoon strong vanilla extract. Whip the cream until it holds its shape well, but do not overbeat.

VI.   Dust the egg whites with a pinch of salt and whip them to a fine froth. When soft peaks form, sprinkle on a tablespoon of granulated sugar and then beat them hard until they hold their shape.

VII.　Combine the fig mixture with the whipped cream, gently working the cream into the custard with a large rubber bowl scraper. Immediately fold in the drifts of egg whites.

VIII.　Place in a bowl and refrigerate for about 4-5 hours. Just before serving, grate the rind of the bright-skinned orange over the entire surface. Snip the reserved fig into thin strips and ring the sides of the mousse with them. Serves 8 – 10.

In contrast, here are two orange mousse. One is actually a thawed frozen soufflé, slivered with candied fruit strips, and the other, a tangerine mousseline of such delicate persuasion that the mouth remembers it with a golden glow long after the last spoonful is downed.

FROSTED ORANGE SOUFFLE

2 egg yolks
1¼ cups sugar
3 tablespoons flour
dash of salt
1 cup milk, scalded
¼ teaspoon vanilla
2 tablespoons grated orange rind
½ cup fresh orange juice
¼ cup Grand Marnier liqueur
7 egg whites, at room temperature
⅛ teaspoon cream of tartar
2 cups heavy cream, whipped
2 oranges
¾ cup sugar
¼ cup water

I.　Beat the egg yolks with ¼ cup of sugar until thick and pale lemony in color. Beat in the flour and a dash of salt. Gradually add in the hot milk, beating so that the mixture remains smooth. Heat the mixture, stirring constantly, until it thickens. Cook, stirring, on a very low flame until all taste of raw flour has disappeared. Stir in the vanilla. Cool, cover, and chill. This is the pastry cream.

II. Combine the grated rind, juice, and Grand Marnier, then beat it into the chilled pastry cream.

III. Beat the egg whites until frothy; add the cream of tartar and a dash of salt, and continue to beat while adding the remaining cup of sugar very gradually. Beat until you have a shiny, stiff meringue.

IV. Fold the flavored pastry cream into the meringue. Fold in the whipped cream and pour into a 6-cup soufflé mold fitted with a 3-inch-high, buttered, double-foil collar. I usually affix this collar with white masking tape to the soufflé dish, because it comes off easily later. Put in the freezer for at least 4 hours.

V.   Cut the colored peel from two oranges with a potato peeler. Cut into 1½-inch lengths and into 1/16-inch slivers. Place in a small saucepan and cover with cold water. Bring to a boil and simmer 8 minutes. Drain.

VI. Meanwhile, place the ¾ cup sugar and water in another small, heavy pan; heat, stirring, until sugar dissolves. Boil the syrup without stirring until it registers 238° on a candy thermometer, about 20 minutes. Remove from the heat.

VII. Add the drained peel to the syrup and let stand at room temperature 30 minutes or longer.

VIII. To serve, remove the collar and allow the soufflé to stand at room temperature for an hour. Drain the candied rind from the syrup and use to garnish the center. Ring the top of the soufflé with thinly sliced, seeded orange sections. Serves 8–10.

MOUSSE A TANGIERS

4 large bright-skinned tangerines
4 large sugar lumps
¼ cup orange juice

1½ tablespoons of gelatin
7 egg yolks
1 cup granulated sugar
1 cup heavy cream plus ½ cup milk
2 teaspoons cornstarch mixed with 2 tablespoons lemon juice
1½ cups chilled cream for whipping
2 tablespoons Galliano liqueur
7 egg whites
pinch of salt and 1 tablespoon of granulated sugar
peeled section of 2 tangerines, coated with Galliano and
*   sprinkled with sugar*

I.   Rub the tangerine skins with the sugar lumps until all sides of the sugar are imbued with tangerine oil. They should turn an orange color. Mash the lumps in a mixing bowl. With a grater shred the skin of two tangerines into the bowl.

II.   After carefully removing the pits and the fibrous membranes with a sharp knife, place the tangerine sections in a blender jar with ¼ cup orange juice. Blend well for 2-3 minutes and strain. (This should make about ½-¾ cup of liquid.) Sprinkle the gelatin over the juice and reserve.

III. Add the 7 egg yolks to the tangerine sugar and grated rind in the mixing bowl. Beat until it becomes a light yellow color. Gradually beat in the cup of granulated sugar and continue the beating for 3 or 4 minutes or until the mixture forms a ribbon effect when it falls back on itself.

IV.   Bring the cream-milk mixture to a boil, and beat in the cornstarch and lemon juice. Beat well for a minute or two and then mix into the beaten egg yolks. Pour at once into a saucepan and set over medium heat. Stir often with a wooden spoon until a custard forms. The mixture should thicken enough to lightly coat the spoon. Be careful not to overcook or the eggs will curdle.

V.   Remove from the heat and add the tangerine juice-gelatin mixture, beating well to make sure the gelatin is completely dissolved.

VI.   Pour the custard into a large bowl and allow it to cool. Do not chill or the gelatin will start to set. Meanwhile, whip the cream with the Galliano (in a chilled bowl) until it doubles in volume and is quite thick and dense. Refrigerate it while you do the egg whites.

VII.   Beat the egg whites and salt until soft peaks form. Sprinkle with granulated sugar, then beat a bit longer until the egg whites are stiff but not dry.

VIII.   Fold the chilled whipped cream into the cool custard using a rubber spatula making sure the mixture is well blended and quite fluffy. At this point, immediately stir in ⅓ of the egg whites and then gently fold in the rest. Using a sweeping gesture, fold from right to left, scooping up the unmixed portion from the bottom of the bowl and gently flipping it over on top of the already blended portion.

IX.   When the egg white is no longer visible in the pale golden mixture, ladle it into a large soufflé dish or chilled bowl. Cover with waxed paper and chill well for about 4-5 hours, or overnight, until the gelatin sets the mousse into a high chiffonade.

X.   Just before serving, decorate the top of the mousse with unsweetened whipped cream and a nest of tangerine sections that have been sprinkled with Galliano and then dipped in sugar. Place the garnish in a ring around the edges. Serves 10 − 12.

This recipe makes a fine finish to a party because it is concocted for 10 − 12 hearty mousse-loving appetites. Ambitious cooks with smaller families can easily halve the recipe by using 4 egg yolks and 4 egg whites. This makes enough for about 6 people.

Peaches and cream alone is a wonderful dessert. This peach mousse retains the same simplicity of taste and adds a variable dimension in its schaum-torte garnish. Coincidentally, this is the dessert Dina Merrill did *not* have for dinner.

PEACH MOUSSE

4 large ripe peaches
¾ cup granulated sugar
3 tablespoons grated orange rind
½ cup orange juice
1½ tablespoons cornstarch
1½ tablespoons cognac
1½ tablespoons water
½ cup confectioners' sugar, sifted
½ teaspoon almond extract
2 teaspoons Grand Marnier liqueur
1½ tablespoons gelatin (The unsweetened variety; I always
  use Knox.)
1 cup whipping cream
1 teaspoon vanilla
4 egg whites
pinch of salt and 1 tablespoon of granulated sugar
1 cup crème patissière
4 almond macaroons for garnish

I. Peel the peaches in the following manner: plunge them whole into a large saucepan of boiling water for about 2-3 minutes. Then spear them out with a roasting fork and quickly remove the loose skin with a sharp knife.

II. Roughly chop the peeled peaches and divide into two portions. Combine one portion in a saucepan with ¾ cup of sugar and the grated orange rind. Add ¼ cup of orange juice that has been mixed with the cornstarch, cognac, and water. Cook over medium heat, stirring all the while until the mixture takes on the consistency of a thick fruit soup. Cool.

III. Combine the second portion of chopped peaches with ½ cup confectioners' sugar and toss well. Add ½ teaspoon almond extract and 2 teaspoons Grand Marnier. Cool. Even though the cut fruit becomes quite wet and juicy, do not drain.

IV. In a small bowl, combine the gelatin with the rest of the orange juice. Place the bowl in a pan of not-quite-simmering water, and stir the mixture well until the gelatin dissolves and the liquid is not grainy. If you require more liquid, add a few spoonfuls of water as you need it.

V.   Add the gelatin to the uncooked peach mixture and chill for about 15 minutes, or until the mixture becomes thick and syrupy.

VI.   In a chilled bowl, whip the cream with a teaspoon of vanilla until the cream is quite thick and holds a soft peak on the top of the whisk.

VII.   Sprinkle the egg whites with a pinch of salt and beat until soft peaks form. Then sprinkle a tablespoon of granulated sugar over them and continue to whip until stiff but not dry.

VIII. In a blender, purée the cooked peach mixture at high speed for a few minutes and place in a large mixing bowl. Add 1 cup of crème patissière and mix well. Add the chilled whipped cream to the peach custard base and gently fold the two together. Quickly fold the egg whites into the cream and custard—taking care not to break down the consistency of the egg whites as you do.

IX.   Place in a large bowl or in individual soufflé cups. Refrigerate for at least 4-5 hours. When well chilled, decorate the top with a ring of crumbled macaroons. Serves 8 – 10.

One of my favorite mousse desserts is not a mousse at all, but a bavarois. I learned this recipe from an ex-opera singer, the generous mother of a French girl, whom I misspent a good part of my life courting. Though I was clearly the lady's favorite choice for a son-in-law, no successful alliance was ever achieved with her daughter—either in or out of the pre-nuptial sheets. But I came away from that long and painful relationship with a wonderful recipe. Which is a good deal more than I can say for a lot of others I have had since.

HEDVIG WOOLF'S PINEAPPLE BAVAROIS

1½—2 cups crème patissière
1 small can of crushed pineapple
1 small can of pineapple chunks
3 tablespoons Grand Marnier liqueur
1½ cups heavy whipping cream
3 tablespoons confectioners' sugar
1-inch piece vanilla bean
grated orange rind

I. Drain the pineapple (both varieties) in a colander until it is absolutely free of liquid. Put it in a bowl and cover with Grand Marnier. Let it macerate for at least one hour; longer, if possible.

II. Put the confectioners' sugar and vanilla bean in a chilled bowl; add the heavy cream and whip. The cream is properly whipped when it forms peaks on the tip of the beater. Remove the bean. Chill the cream slightly to allow it to settle.

III. Drain the fruit a second time. Combine the liqueur-flavored fruit with the crème patissière. The mixture should be fairly thick and custardlike.

III. By spoonfuls, fold in the cold whipped cream until the mixture is a pale white-gold color. Chill for an hour or so. Serve with a grating of bright orange rind over the surface. Serves 8—10.

The reserved pineapple juice combined with Grand Marnier makes an excellent spike for a fresh fruit compote, and an interesting variation to a blended daiquiri.

Afterthought

BERT GREENE

When our store was new, and we were somewhat younger and eager to please, a certain reporter for *The East Hampton Star* became an early rooter. Rooter is an embellishment of her mild approbation. But she was, we knew, a particularly spare lady.

One of the first to discover the pleasures of our back door, she would pass through it several times a day, making small excuses to make small purchases. No great spender or lavish party giver, she just liked to hang out in our kitchen, and though we were never entirely comfortable under her watchful eye, we became used to the fact of her. The way you become used to all kinds of weather.

Perhaps she drank a little.

Who cared? She was one local customer who appreciated us genuinely. She always wore a French duffel coat, rope-tied, and let her hair hang loosely in what, twenty years earlier, we had called a glamour bob. A transplanted New Englander with another life and a story she had never any intention of divulging, she was obviously as much an outsider in the tight-fisted community as we were—and that makes a link.

"You people," she would say, "are crazy, you know."

She had pure Connecticut brass in her speech, but the voice would fade from time to time like a radio in need of a new antenna.

"Crazy cats! Cooking this way in this day and age! Certifiable looneys is what you are, my dears, because you can't keep it up. Time and tide are agin you. It's just too good for them."

We would, as I remember, become slightly embarrassed at this laudation, and bustle about the kitchen making excessive clatter to cover up her praise, but she was not a lady to be put off.

"You enjoy yourselves too much for one thing. No, it can't last. It would be wonderful if you could pull it off, and really make it pay, but how? You've got too much against you—computerization for one thing, Colonel Sanders for another. Time's running out for quality. No, um, it can't possibly last. This, um, place is just like Camelot! And Camelot simply cannot last."

How we laughed at that conceit after she had gone, poor lady. Camelot? When we were up to our forearms in scorched pots? When we had seasoned all the Thanksgiving pies with salt instead of sugar, and had to send retrievers all over the South Fork to replace them before dessert was served? When we made meringues for the first time and the entire kitchen floor became covered with a fine sugary snow that no known detergent would remove? Camelot, we twitted as we scrubbed. Some Camelot this is!

She never lived to see her prophecy out. The lady was killed one wintry night in a car crash on the road to Amagansett. The funeral was spare, too. But her curious vision somehow survived. In our heads and in our hearts, we began to believe that she was right—that our store, somehow, was a little bit like Camelot.

That is what gives The Store its raffish dignity. In a rather policed state it is a store where stray dogs are still fed—and where a customer, short on cash, is still given the merchandise and trusted. A place where the only serious business disagreement partner Denis and I have had was his absolute defiance of the credit card as currency. "Because," as he said, "it cheapens us so!"

It has been a wonderful place to run. And when it goes, it will go with a good bang and no whimpers. (How long we can hold out against the rising cost of everything with our energies sinking at the same rate of exchange is still anyone's guess.)

The Store may not last forever. But it was once here and that is something worth writing about. So let's have another drink. To Camelot and to Miss Nancy Brown, visionary, wherever you are.

Index